Developing Inquiry-Based
Science Materials

Developing Inquiry-Based Science Materials

A GUIDE FOR EDUCATORS

Herbert D. Thier with Bennett Daviss

A Project of the Lawrence Hall of Science
Center for Curriculum Innovation

Teachers College, Columbia University
New York and London

Published by Teachers College Press, 1234 Amsterdam Avenue, New York, NY 10027

The writing of this book was supported in part by the National Science Foundation through Small Grant for Educational Research #ESI 9729256. Ideas and opinions expressed are those of the authors and not necessarily those of the Foundation.

Library of Congress Cataloging-in-Publication Data

Thier, Herbert D.
    Developing inquiry-based science materials : a guide for educators / Herbert D. Thier with Bennett Daviss.
      p. cm.
    "A project of the Lawrence Hall of Science, Center for Curriculum Innovation."
    Includes bibliographical references and index.
    ISBN 0-8077-4124-8 (cloth : alk. paper)—ISBN 0-8077-4123-X (pbk. : alk. paper)
    1. Science—Study and teaching—Activity programs—United States—Handbooks, manuals, etc. 2. Inquiry (Theory of knowledge) I. Daviss, Bennett. II. Title.

  LB1585.3 .T485 2001
  507.1—dc21   2001027310

ISBN 0-8077-4123-X (paper)
ISBN 0-8077-4124-8 (cloth)

Printed on acid-free paper
Manufactured in the United States of America

08 07 06 05 04 03 02 01   8 7 6 5 4 3 2 1

To Marlene:

My colleague, friend, and wife,
truly the love of my life,
whose ideas and support have helped to shape this work

Too often, we hold fast to the clichés of our forebears. We subject all facts to a prefabricated set of interpretations. We enjoy the comfort of opinion without the discomfort of thought. Mythology distracts us everywhere. The great enemy of the truth is very often not the lie—deliberate, contrived, and dishonest—but rather the myth: persistent, persuasive, and unrealistic.

—President John F. Kennedy

Contents

Acknowledgments

THIS BOOK IS A RESULT of more than 40 years of my experience. All of that experience has been informed and enhanced by the people with whom I have been honored to work.

I thank all those teachers and students who, over the years, have welcomed me and my colleagues into their classrooms as observer and teacher. They have provided the "laboratory" that has been essential in the development of new and better ideas and materials.

Also, I am indebted to the many exceptional colleagues who have been part of our development teams. In particular, I thank SEPUP's current and former team members as well as my colleagues at the Lawrence Hall of Science and at our centers nationwide who have reviewed, critiqued, and thus helped to shape (sometimes unknowingly) many of the ideas and approaches outlined in this book.

Throughout my career, I have had the privilege of interacting with outstanding program officers and other staff members of the National Science Foundation, which has supported most of my work. I am especially grateful to Dr. Gerhard Salinger. As the program officer for SEPUP (and for this book), he has become a valued critic and true friend.

Attempting to list all the individuals who have contributed to my understanding of materials development would require a list that easily could be longer than this book. However, I must acknowledge two in particular. Through his wisdom and leadership, the late Robert Karplus helped me refine my respect for the pursuit of understanding. Rebecca Thier Schofield, our 6½-year-old granddaughter, radiates an interest and exuberance that continuously rekindles my interest in ideas and their explanation.

The authors have benefited greatly from the work and wisdom of Constance Barsky, Charles Ericson, Seymour Sarason, and Kenneth Wilson, as well as from the keen editorial instincts and guidance of Jackson Daviss during early drafts of these chapters.

Finally, I want to express my appreciation to Bennett Daviss, my collaborator and friend, who has contributed so much to the quality of this work.

That which readers find insightful and enlightening in the following pages is a product of the contributions of all these people and countless others. However, the responsibility for the ideas expressed in this book, including any that might be bothersome or disagreeable, is mine alone.

Introduction

IN 1999, I RECEIVED my 36th consecutive 1-year appointment to the academic staff of the University of California at Berkeley. Despite appearances, that is not a record-breaking quest for tenure, because tenure was neither my goal nor even a possibility. My real quest has been to design better materials for science education. Specifically, I've sought to create educational materials that can foster greater public knowledge and understanding of science through the design of experience-based, inquiry-oriented learning activities to be used wherever "young people" of all ages come together—primarily in schools.

I present this book as a guide to beginning and experienced developers alike who aspire to join this quest.

Because of the ways in which our education system works, this quest requires the developer to write and submit proposals to design and fund projects. These are different from marriage proposals in that the ending date is known at the beginning, but similar in that they demand the proposer's unconditional commitment if they are to succeed. This book identifies, describes, and analyzes what must take place for a developer to fulfill that commitment—the processes that need to occur between the arrival of the idea that sparks a project proposal and the final report that describes the endeavor's outcomes.

My own quest began in August 1962 when, as a newly minted doctor of education from New York University, I became the assistant superintendent of schools for instruction in Falls Church, Virginia. A few months later, officials at the state's department of education invited me to help them review elementary-grade science materials and make recommendations about which to adopt. Soon after accepting the state's invitation, I was besieged by publisher's representatives and found I no longer had to pay for my own lunches. I also realized that among the more than 20 different series of books being submitted for review, only one was accompanied by any kind of equipment or materials: D. C. Heath's Schneider Series offered (but didn't actively promote) a supplementary kit enabling students to carry out activities suggested in the text.

It was one of the first stirrings of a trend. In its post-Sputnik surge of support for science education reform, the National Science Foundation (NSF) had funded several innovative materials development projects and programs. Although most (if not all) of them were working to create hands-on, materials-centered approaches to science education, none had yet had time to bring its wares to the educational marketplace.

In the years following, I became part of the creative team that developed the NSF-funded Science Curriculum Improvement Study, or SCIS. In 1989, some 25 years after my experience in Virginia, our SCIS group was preparing to distribute a revised version of our materials and I again surveyed the learning materials available in elementary-level science. This time I found that among the more than 20 programs available, only one did *not* make available a kit of materials. Some development programs, primarily those that the NSF had funded, included no textbook at all and used activity-centered materials exclusively. Today, after the publishing industry's flurry of mergers and takeovers, there are far fewer available programs for elementary science, but every one of them offers, and strongly recommends the use of, a related materials kit.

This change from a textbook-centered to a materials- and activity-centered approach has been the lasting success of the NSF's work in science education begun in the late 1950s. Several programs launched during those years, or their descendants, are still widely and effectively used—among them SCIS3+, Science: A Process Approach, Elementary Science Study, PSSC Physics, CHEM Study, and the trio of biology programs from the Biological Sciences Curriculum Study.

However, that busy period in materials development did not originate the idea of, nor the call for, "hands-on science." Practical work in science courses has been expected and required in high school science during most of the 20th century. Since their establishment, all national organizations that accredit secondary schools have required that high school science courses provide laboratory facilities. Most colleges and universities that require science credits for admission specify that the credits must be earned in laboratory science courses. Even elementary-level science textbook series written in the early and middle 20th century by Brandwein, Craig, and the Schneiders highlighted the educational value of direct, personal experiences. Often in years past, teachers have attempted to fulfill this goal by arranging the occasional field trip.

Now, science educators at all grade levels have come to understand that students' direct experiences are not an adjunct to a school science program but are its heart and soul. They are working to expand students' opportunities for learning science in a real-world, inquiry-oriented, and activity-based context. In short, schools and educators are realizing that science education can no longer be centered on lectures and textbooks.

As the 1996 National Science Education Standards mandate, "Inquiry into authentic questions generated from student experiences is the central strategy for teaching science. Teachers focus inquiry predominately on real phenomena, in classrooms, outdoors, or in laboratory settings, where students are given investigations or guided towards fashioning investigations that are demanding but within their capabilities" (National Academy of Sciences, 1996, p. 31).

However, the structures and mechanisms of education have not yet caught up to educators' new understandings. Much of what takes place today in our science classrooms still contradicts our newfound goals for, and understandings about, how science is best learned. This assertion seems to be proven by the continuing strong sales of fact-oriented textbooks and the national acceptance of fact-dominated standardized tests as the measure of student success in science.

Textbooks teach *about* science and do so in a way that leads students to believe that science is something that happened in the past and that their task is to learn what happened, when, and who did it—and then to memorize related terminology. (Studies by Hurd [1994, p. 102] and others show that in many textbook-driven high school biology courses, students are expected to learn more new words than they are in the first year of a foreign-language course.) The purpose of traditional instruction is, of course, not to deepen students' mastery of the processes of scientific analysis but to enable students to demonstrate science knowledge by doing well on fact-oriented standardized tests.

The situation is even worse in elementary schools, where the most commonly used science program today is nothing at all. Even in districts or schools where a particular science program is adopted, it is not unusual to find books or materials kits lying unopened. All too often, teachers either cannot find time to teach science or else do so sporadically, after they have complied with mounting pressures to teach the "basic" subjects of reading, writing, and mathematics on a daily basis to prepare students for standardized tests.

Those teachers who do have kits and want to conduct materials-centered investigations in their classes often cannot: Their kits are not maintained or resupplied because funds are allotted to other priorities seen as more urgent.

Clearly, if *experiencing* science instead of reading *about* or hearing *about* science (or memorizing more new words than in the first year of a foreign-language course) is to become the norm in American science education, a fundamental change in attitude and approach—among policy makers, regulators, parents, and education's other constituents—is as essential as it is absent today.

This bleak view of science education at the dawn of the 21st century may upset some readers. It might especially pain those educators who are already working so hard under difficult conditions, and without adequate funds, to nurture an environment in which students can learn to genuinely appreciate, understand, and use scientific knowledge and processes in their daily lives.

But now they have reason to believe that their work is not in vain. There is positive evidence of change wrought by dedicated teachers who are creating environments that encourage students' mastery of science. One of the best indicators of that change is that the demand for inquiry-oriented, activity-based learning materials is outstripping their supply.

My goal in writing this book has been to equip developers with tools and techniques that can help them meet that growing demand.

I have three major objectives within that goal.

The first is to guide developers who need external funding to make their work possible.

The second is to help those working with materials developers—classroom teachers, administrators, community leaders, funders, and, of course, learners—to understand the complex process of bringing new learning materials from idea to classroom. By understanding the process, those constituents can support developers' work while also analyzing their own relationships to development projects to ensure that their own needs and goals are being met. A detailed understanding should lead to the kind of synergistic relationship among all involved that is crucial if development is to benefit all stakeholders, especially learners.

Third, I have highlighted the human issues and interactions that make the materials development process work. I also suggest approaches to those issues that meet the need for professional growth and development of the individuals involved.

Grants and projects end and each edition of materials soon reaches the end of its shelf life; the people involved are the only truly lasting and growing resource in materials development. Indeed, one of the most enduring products of any project is the enriched professional capacities and self-confidence that project team members have gained by participating. From developers themselves, who hone their skills in the course of a project, to the involved classroom teachers who strengthen their analytical, planning, and assessment skills, the process of creating classroom materials in a collaborative way can be the finest kind of staff development.

To accomplish these objectives, a new understanding of the complexities of interactions between teachers and students in the science classroom is needed. These interactions form the basis for a redefinition of the term *curriculum*. In this book, I define *curriculum* as the human interaction that takes place between teacher and students in the context of educational materials that have been chosen by a school system with (we hope) the advice of its teachers.

The purpose of the curriculum is to foster students' engagement, which is essential if genuine learning is to take place. To achieve that goal, I propose an approach called "guided inquiry" as the conceptual organizer that effective teachers and schools can use to transform learning materials into curriculum. The challenge to materials developers is the creation, field testing, evaluation, and revision of engaging, standards-based, academically rigorous learning materials. Schools and teachers should select from among such materials to construct the course or program that is the basis for the curriculum in that discipline.

The purpose of this book is to provide developers with a greater understanding of the process of materials development for guided inquiry while helping them to organize and carry out a development project.

Those and the other approaches and ideas presented in this book are based on my more than 35 years of full-time effort in materials development. I have spent the last 17 of those years directing a program that has evolved into what is now known as the Science Education for Public Understanding Program (SEPUP). The principles, recommendations, and examples offered in the book are drawn from my own experiences in materials development, the privilege of being part of the team that is SEPUP, and ideas suggested by colleagues in other development efforts.

The insights expressed are based primarily on experiences in science education because that is the field in which I work. However, many (and perhaps most) may apply to any area of education in which materials developers are attempting to create innovative, experience-based materials for use in classroom or community group learning. I invite and encourage materials developers in other fields to consider the value of these ideas in their work.

NOTE TO READERS

All projects referred to or cited as examples in the text are listed with their contact information in the List of Science Projects.

1

The Teacher's Stradivarius

The point is to develop the childlike inclination for play and the childlike desire for recognition and to guide the child over to important fields for society . . . a school demands from the teacher that he be a kind of artist in his province.

—Albert Einstein, *Out of My Later Years*

IT IS OFTEN SAID that a course is only as good as its teacher. That is undeniably true. But it also may be said that teachers—given the demands on their time, energy, and creativity—cannot far outperform the classroom materials they use.

GUIDED INQUIRY IN SCIENCE TEACHING

If science educators are to meet society's new demand for mastery learning on the part of all students, they first must engage students. If teachers are to engage students without draining their own creativity in the process, teachers themselves must first find the materials engaging while also maintaining academic rigor. Such materials define, and approach, learning in a way that is starkly different from what conventional textbooks and worksheets do: This new kind of material is organized around issues and principles that touch students' lives directly. The conceptual organizer for materials embodying this new approach can be called "guided inquiry."

Materials for guided inquiry not only present science content in a new way, but they also necessarily must be created in a new way. Traditional textbooks can be written by content experts alone, but materials that engage students in guided inquiry can be effective only to the extent that they are designed and refined by a team of diverse specialists—content experts, veteran classroom teachers, editors, illustrators, assessment specialists, and others—pooling their individual expertise to ensure that materials are as imaginatively stimulating as possible while remaining academically challenging.

That combination poses a new challenge to the designers of instructional materials. Helping materials designers meet that challenge—how to do it, why, and what it can mean to teachers, parents, students, and their communities—is the subject of this book.

MAKING GYPSUM: GUIDED INQUIRY IN ACTION

Eileen Smith's eighth-grade science students are manufacturing gypsum. Working in pairs, the students collect a few pieces of plastic lab equipment and small vials of calcium carbonate, sodium sulfate, diluted hydrochloric acid, and water. The students measure calcium carbonate powder into a small cup and record details of the powder's appearance. Next, following the procedure outlined in their lab guide sheets, they add 75 drops of hydrochloric acid to the powder, stir the mixture, wait for it to stop bubbling, then filter it through moistened paper cones.

The students look through their magnifying lenses to examine the liquid more closely. They debate, observe more carefully, then record in their lab notes what they agree and disagree about regarding what they have seen.

Smith prods the students with a series of questions about the liquid that dripped slowly through the cone, leaving a small chunk of white solid behind. Why filter the mixture? What's the solid left behind? What's in the liquid that goes through the filter? The classroom hums with the buzz of debate, questions, discussions, and the occasional exclamation that punctuates disagreement and discovery.

"Is the white stuff calcium chloride?" a student asks.

"What could you do to find out?" Smith asks him.

Another student says, "Didn't we test for that in the last lab?"

"Check your notes and decide," Smith replies.

After checking and discussing their previous lab notes, the students conclude that the white residue is calcium carbonate that did not react with the acid. They also decide that the liquid in the bottom of the cup is a calcium chloride solution. Only after the investigation is complete and students have drawn their conclusions does Smith show them the chemical equation that describes the reaction.

MAKING TRADE-OFFS

The previous day, Smith had introduced an investigation into factories and their by-products by raising a dilemma. She asked the students to write down the first word that came into their minds when they heard the word *industry*. The responses were mostly positive, including words such as *stuff, jobs*, and *money*. But their reactions to the word *factory* were markedly negative—dotted with pejoratives ranging from *smoke* and *traffic* to *pollution* and *sweatshop*. Smith then asked them, "How would you characterize the general difference between your response to *industry* and *factory*?"

In talking about the differences, the students realized that to have what they want—products and jobs—they must also deal with things that they do not want, such as pollution and heavy traffic. They began to articulate the trade-offs between the positive and negative results of industry. By making gypsum, the students gather the scientific evidence they need to weigh and confront the social, economic, and environmental consequences if a factory moves to their idyllic New Hampshire village.

BLENDING THE FACTS AND PROCESSES OF SCIENCE

In the next step, the students add 50 drops of sodium sulfate to the calcium chloride solution and stir again. "Why is this turning cloudy?" a girl asks.

"Does anyone have an explanation?" Smith asks the group.

After a few moments of silence, a boy says, "Because you're forming a precipitate."

Smith turns to the girl. "What's a precipitate? We talked about it yesterday."

"That's when you add two things together and a new thing comes out of it."

Other students agree, and Smith adds that the formation of a precipitate is evidence that a chemical reaction has occurred.

Filtering the mixture a final time, they collect a small amount of white powder in the bottom of the filter cone and clear liquid under it in the cups. The students pool their final bits of clear liquid in one cup, which Smith holds up. "We're saving what's in the cones because that's gypsum—that's our product," Smith says. "But you've also made this. It looks like water, but is it?" The students ponder. "Can we just flush it down the sewer?" she prods.

"OK," says one boy, joking.

Smith smiles. "That's what some people think, and maybe it would be OK to just throw it away. But what if there's something besides water in it?"

"Maybe there's something in it that would pollute the ground or the water," a girl says.

"Right," Smith says, "and that's important. Remember, nothing ever just goes away; it always stays around in one form or another. But also remember that you're running a gypsum factory. Why else would you want to find out what's in this liquid?"

Hands go up. "Maybe there's something else in there you could use," a boy volunteers. "Maybe you could sell it," another says.

"And how could you find out what's in here?"

"Heat it," says one girl.

"Boil it," a boy adds.

"Why?" Smith demands.

"Because when you boil it, the water goes away and you can see what's left."

To prove the point, the pairs of students boil a sample of the leftover liquid on a hot plate. A white residue collects on the sides of the dish as the liquid evaporates.

Smith then reviews the two simple chemical equations that express the reactions that the students have observed. The students note the elements and compounds that recombined or were used up in the reactions and conclude that the white residue left in the dishes after evaporating the water must be sodium chloride—simple table salt. The students talk about economic uses for this by-product of their gypsum factory.

In the following days, each student team decides where in the village it would locate its gypsum factory. After preparing a list of raw materials and the factory's other needs, the teams devise ways to meet each need while respecting community concerns about smoke, pollution, and other drawbacks the students had listed for factories in general several days earlier at the beginning of the activity. Finally, each team writes an environmental impact statement, detailing the ways in which its factory would benefit the village economically without despoiling its natural setting.

CONFIRMING FACTS: ACTIVITY WITHOUT INQUIRY

In an eighth-grade classroom in a town not far away, students are having a different kind of science experience. In the darkened classroom, the recorded narrator of a filmstrip is talking about seeds. "Birds eat berries," the narrator says, "and deposit the seeds elsewhere as waste. New plants begin to grow from the seeds."

Students murmur and giggle. "Jeremy!" snaps teacher Alice Jones. But Jeremy, like most of his classmates, ignores the filmstrip and its droning soundtrack. Jones stops the filmstrip and poses a few questions to her students to focus their attention on the lesson. When the filmstrip starts again, the room falls momentarily silent, but then the whispers resume. Some students doodle or write notes to each other. Jones orders one to a different table to separate him from the friend he keeps talking to.

During the filmstrip, Jones poses more questions in a futile attempt to keep her students engaged. "Jamie, name one way in which seeds are transported."

"The wind blows them," says Jamie in a bored voice.

"Allison, name another way."

"Birds drop them," mutters Allison, not looking up from her doodles.

The filmstrip ends; the classroom lights go on. "Today, we're going to dissect seeds," Jones announces. "A lima bean is a seed. A seed carries out one of the five functions of a plant that we've talked about. Which function is that?"

"Reproduction," two or three students mumble, still intent on their notes and drawings.

The teacher hands out a blank sheet of paper and two lima beans to each student, explaining the parts of the beans the students will see when they split open the beans. She explains the function of each part and instructs the students to open the beans and draw what they see on the sheet of paper. Each student works alone while the teacher moves around the room to answer questions and to keep students on task. At the end of the period, Jones collects the papers and checks to see that the students drew the parts as she had instructed them to. She is not satisfied with the lesson but had no time or budget to find or create materials that would be more interesting and effective for her students—and, with another class starting in five minutes, she has no choice but to repeat the same lesson for the next group. Besides, her science background is limited, and she feels unsure about deviating from the textbook's teacher guide or skipping the filmstrip provided by the school district.

THE BOND BETWEEN LEARNING AND INVESTIGATION

In both classes, the students would say that they're learning science. But in only one classroom would that assertion be accurate.

In the second classroom, students read and hear *about* science—and that is all they do. They do not *do* science. They replicate experiments and observations, having been told in advance what results to expect. These students are performing rote tasks, a euphemistic way of saying that they are going through motions. They experience none of the hesitation, analysis, decision making, responsibility, engagement, or personal empowerment—and, usually, none of the nagging curiosity or uncertainty—that mark the actual scientific process. They are outside the experience looking in, like passersby who glance in a bakery shop's window at the breads and pastries but cannot feel their textures, smell their aromas, or taste their delicate, complex flavors. The people inside are having a banquet; those looking in see lumps of dough and wonder what all the fuss is about.

But in Smith's class, the students *are* doing science. They wrestle with questions, not knowing the answers they are expected to produce. They experience the process of discovery and its necessary corollary, uncertainty. Only after they have conducted an investigation and experienced its outcomes do they learn the equations, abstractions, and terminology that define what they have done. To Smith's students, science is not a chapter in a textbook or problems on a worksheet; it is a human process that leads from questions and hunches to possible answers—and always to new questions.

Jones and her students are mired in a curriculum shaped by traditional assumptions about learning and an extensive arsenal of one-way instructional materials that defend and enforce those assumptions. But Smith and her students are part of an educational revolution—a new approach to learning through guided investigations and experience, an approach rooted in new discoveries about the way students internalize skills and knowledge. Obviously, that process demands more than just "reading about" science in a textbook or "covering" the textbook's chapters in a calendar-driven forced march. For those and other reasons, these new approaches and discoveries call for a new approach to the design and development of instructional materials.

THE TEACHER'S STRADIVARIUS

A Harvard professor once developed an interest in the acoustics of the violin. As an experiment, he collected a range of instruments from a cheap beginner's model to the finest Stradivarius. He assembled a small audience in a concert hall and hung a screen between them and the stage. Then he had virtuoso Yehudi Menuhin stand behind the screen and play each violin for the group. He asked the audience to choose the best-sounding violin of the collection.

The professor was stunned by the result: Each violin received about the same number of votes. He expressed his surprise to Menuhin, who compounded his shock by agreeing with the outcome. "Yes, they sounded about the same," the great musician said. "The difference was that the Strad played itself, while I had to work like hell to make the cheap violin sound like anything at all."

Teachers know the feeling: A dedicated teacher willing to commit enough energy, skill, and imagination can make a dusty chemistry textbook seem like a passport to a magic land—but has to work like hell to do it. Besides, it is at best a short-term strategy. Even gifted teachers have neither the energy nor the stamina to work that hard every day, year after year, with every student in every class. Instead, to make it possible for all students to learn effectively and consistently, teachers have to rely to a significant degree on the quality of the materials they use and the learning experiences for students that those materials structure. A dusty science book can too easily alienate students and render them apathetic or even hostile to a subject, regardless of what a teacher does (or does not do). But an effectively designed student learning experience, structured through the use of the right materials, grabs students' attention, brings ideas to life, and fills a classroom—including the teacher—with new energy as effectively as a great piece of music.

THE NEW CHALLENGE TO MATERIALS DEVELOPERS

Teachers and students together make that music, but the developer of educational materials makes their instruments. The developer's challenge is to create for every teacher the educational equivalent of a Stradivarius: materials that embody academic concepts and principles in a rigorous way and also empower teachers to use their full range of skills, imagination, and creativity. This combination of carefully designed materials and skilled teaching can help each student weave those concepts and principles, rich with meaning, into his or her practical understanding of the world.

In education as in art, society's needs evolve and become more complex. Older forms are respected and preserved for the value they offer. In music, the harpsichord was replaced as the dominant instrument by the more versatile piano; parlor music gave way to ragtime and jazz. In education, lectures and textbooks no longer are assumed to meet the needs of all students. New definitions are emerging of what it means to educate and be educated. These definitions measure learning not by what students are able to recite or the books they have been assigned, but by what students are able to do. That means that "learning" can no longer be defined as taking courses and passing tests, but only as mastery of a subject or skill demonstrated by the ability to apply concepts and processes flexibly and accurately outside the classroom. New definitions of learning, in turn, call for a new understanding of what a "curriculum" is. Driven in large measure by our society's changing economic needs, these new educational standards and definitions demand new kinds of learning materials—and a new approach to creating them.

MOVING FROM INQUIRY TO "GUIDED INQUIRY"

Emerging from the tumult of educational change and "reform" of the 1980s, the National Science Education Standards embody that call (National Academy of Sciences [NAS], 1996). Indeed, they do nothing less than mandate a completely new approach to science education and, therefore, science learning materials (see Figure 1.1).

THE NEW DEFINITION OF *QUALITY* IN SCIENCE MATERIALS

These new benchmarks of educational quality are only a few of dozens of similar ones set forth in the standards. They reflect the view of the science professions (as well as of business and industry) that a curriculum built around textbooks, lectures, and drills is starkly inadequate to meet the need for scientific and technical skills, knowledge, and literacy shared by a 21st-century workplace and a technological society. Instead, a course of learning that emphasizes knowledge within a framework of process skills—and that places both in the context of life beyond schools and classrooms—is needed to fulfill these new demands.

But this is not news. The struggle to articulate these new definitions of teaching and learning began in the 1960s (Piaget, Gruber, & Vonèche,

Figure 1.1. The National Science Education Standards content guidelines. *Source:* National Academy of Sciences (1996), p. 113.

Less emphasis on:	More emphasis on:
Knowing scientific facts and information	Understanding scientific concepts and developing abilities of inquiry
Studying subject-matter disciplines for their own sake	Learning subject-matter disciplines in the context of inquiry, of technology and science, of personal and social perspectives, and of the history and nature of science
Separating science knowledge and science processes	Integrating all aspects of science content
Implementing inquiry as a set of processes	Implementing inquiry as instructional strategies, abilities, and ideas to be learned

1977). The movement began in earnest in the early 1970s with a push for hands-on science study and activity-based learning (Stohr-Hunt, 1996). Although an important idea, it too often has failed to yield the results its champions had hoped for. The reason: Frequently there has been little or no structure linking an activity solidly to the scientific ideas the activity is intended to present.

Richard Duquin, a middle school science teacher in Kenmore, New York, cites an example. In a classroom activity popular in the 1970s, students used rings and fasteners to mimic the bonding of atoms and molecules. "It was a great hands-on activity," Duquin recalls. "The problem was, they forgot to put in the content. There was no material moving students from rings and fasteners to the scientific vocabulary, concepts, and content that should have been part of it." The hands-on movement was a crucial step in moving science education forward. But many of its materials lacked consistently effective instructional frameworks guiding students' attention from what they were doing to the scientific principles they were modeling. As a result, the hands-on movement made a contribution but failed to expand students' usable knowledge of the physical world to the extent desired.

BEYOND HANDS-ON SCIENCE EDUCATION

Seeking to forge the missing link, educators in the 1980s began to unite content with activities to foster "inquiry education" (see, e.g., Olson & Loucks-Horsley, 2000; Welch, 1981). Students still conducted activities, but those activities were wedded to academic content—another crucial step forward. But, again, inquiry education has its weaknesses. Specifically, individual inquiries often lack a comprehensive direction or framework: They sometimes are left to stand by themselves, discrete from others or from a larger network of interrelated ideas, or they lead students to the abstract concepts presented in textbooks without leading students beyond understanding to meaning. Also, surprisingly often students have been left to look into whatever topics happen to interest them, an approach that destroys the foundations of the sequenced curriculum on which mastery learning rests.

GUIDING STUDENT INQUIRIES

If students are to find personal meaning—another word for relevance—in science as the new standards mandate, science education must move beyond the old definitions of inquiry learning. As educators have discovered, mere inquiry does not automatically lead to learning, much less to the mastery of skills and information or the ability to apply them (which the new standards also call for). There must be a plan that guides students as they move from activity (or at least a reading that motivates them to ask questions) to information, then through the synthesis that leads to understanding, and, finally, relevance—meaning in the students' own lives (Linn & Hsi, 2000).

To chart that path, educators and materials developers need to expand the idea of inquiry to a larger one that can be described as "guided inquiry" (Tafoya, Senal, & Knecht, 1980). We would define guided inquiry as the sequencing and integration of appropriate processes and information (or of activities and rigorous academic content, to use education's preferred terms), chosen through research, to fashion experiences for students. These experiences should lead students to:

- Confront scientific concepts and principles in the context of real-world problems or situations
- Use data and evidence to reason their way through a particular problem or issue
- Reach independent conclusions or decisions justified by the data and evidence

The concept of "guided inquiry" gives equal weight to knowledge and skills, retaining a hands-on or activity-based focus that relies on strong content. Sequencing activities in a larger curricular plan or design enable educators to reach their curricular and instructional goals. Placing scientific ideas and processes in the context of actual issues—balancing the risks and benefits of industrial production, for example—can suddenly give formerly abstract concepts meaning within students' own lives, a key element in helping them master knowledge.

The task of teachers and materials developers in guided inquiry is twofold. First, they must define and structure those experiences to achieve specific, substantive educational goals that include the development of the higher-order skills the new standards call for. Second, they also must frame and structure those experiences in the most engaging and effective ways—to build an educational Stradivarius, so to speak. The teacher's challenge is to "play" that instrument in a way that coaxes out all of its possibilities: Teachers use their full range of professional skills and instincts to orchestrate the performance of the materials and their processes (the teachers' own performances as well as those of students) in a way that brings the ideas embodied in the materials to life in the mind of each

student (Sarason, 1999). The materials best able to achieve that goal result from the intimate collaboration of materials developer and teacher—
craftsperson and performing artist, if you will—each translating and
enhancing the skills of the other.

CURRICULUM AND THE TEACHER'S ROLE IN CREATING IT

It might not seem obvious at first, but this collaboration between materials developer and classroom teacher is, in fact, a different way of defining
the term *curriculum*.

Many educators, consciously or not, define curriculum as the textbooks
or other materials that are delivered by publishers and other materials
producers. This view relegates the teacher to the role of a repeater station
between the content specialist, who is broadcasting, and students, who
become the equivalent of radio receivers. Instead, we would argue that
materials are not a curriculum any more than a blueprint is a building or a
violin is a tune.

Materials are a detailed plan that becomes curriculum only when a
competent teacher uses them to shape and guide interactions with and
among students. The curriculum itself is the opportunities (spontaneous
as well as planned) for learning that arise from the meeting of minds between teacher and student through materials.

Materials developers can create, design, and produce research-proven
learning materials. But no matter how well conceived the materials are,
their effectiveness depends on the human interactions between teacher
and student as the two interpret together the materials' meanings and
implications. This interaction, sparked by the materials, sets the stage for
a guided inquiry into the materials' content that fosters a complex and
essential engagement between student and teacher. That engagement,
which can (and should) reflect all of the complex dimensions of human
interactions, is the basis for what we mean in the following pages by
curriculum.

THE TEACHER'S ROLE IN GUIDED INQUIRY

In that very practical sense, teachers are the true creators and leaders of a
curriculum—especially in an activity-based classroom using guided inquiry, where engagement gives life, meaning, and immediacy to questions
and ideas. The teacher's task in guided inquiry is to integrate each student's
needs, motivations, and strengths with the design and execution of the

experiences that comprise the curriculum—all of which is directed toward accomplishing the educational program's overall goals.

Thanks to the National Science Education Standards, those goals now emphasize students' abilities to carry scientific principles and processes beyond the classroom and use them in making decisions in their own lives. If students are to achieve that goal, educators must create a context in which the student can experience and practice the questioning, evidence-based approach that characterizes science. Fashioning classroom materials that create this context of engagement requires the guidance and expertise of the curriculum leader and manager known as the teacher. With that guidance, developers then can unite informed, enabled teachers with effective instructional materials. That union makes possible the engagement of teacher, student, and materials that we define as the curriculum.

This new definition of curriculum necessarily redefines the mission and role of the teacher. If the old view cast the teacher as an information transfer station, the new one casts him or her more in the mold of a performance artist and facilitator of learning.

The teacher is the acknowledged expert on using available materials effectively in different settings and for different students. Despite their overwhelming class loads, teachers are aware of students' difficult situations at home, their anxieties, and their joys. A skilled and informed teacher takes care to integrate students' needs, strengths, and motivations as he or she uses materials to design learning experiences that will help each student accomplish the instructional goals of the program. It is this concerned, enabling, facilitative interaction among teachers and students that accomplishes the academic goals of an instructional program and determines what we define as the curriculum.

While the old definition of curriculum views the teacher as a worker who follows instructions from administrators and textbook authors, the new definition views the teacher as an entrepreneur—using the academic and human capital at hand to create and then seize the teachable moment.

Through guided inquiry—a structured course of experiences and investigations—students internalize a lasting, practical understanding of the principles and processes of a discipline, along with enough of its facts and history, to be able to collect, analyze, interpret, and apply ideas and information, especially in their lives beyond school. In science, that means that students will learn to use evidence to make reasoned, fact-based decisions about issues of science and technology in their own lives and in taking on the responsibilities of citizens in an increasingly complex democratic society.

This new definition of the teacher's role—including the idea that the teacher is the key to promoting lasting change—has guided developers such as SEPUP in two areas: creating materials that can become a foundation for instructional reform and creating professional leadership and development programs to help teachers implement those materials.

In a typical secondary school, science teachers usually are the only professionals with a formal background in science. As real education budgets shrink nationwide, many U.S. school districts can turn to no other local sources of expertise in science content, not to mention the ability to combine content with effective educational strategies. Therefore, many projects, including SEPUP, have come to believe that it is essential to put the science teacher in the leadership of any planned change.

Developers are adopting this policy because they believe science teachers are an essential resource that schools and the community need to work with if they are to attain scientific and technological literacy. The students are society's most important resource, and the science teacher is the key to improving the scientific and technological literacy of students and hence of the community. Policy makers who really want to bring about meaningful long-term improvements in the educational system need to take the risk of investing their limited resources in teachers, the only group with the capacity to reach the learner. I use the term *risk* because, as a society, our attitude and treatment of teachers has done little to encourage them to take leadership. In all too many school systems, teachers are considered little more than hourly employees, with administrative concern focused on when they come and go rather than on what they do when they are there.

Teachers are actually the "academic executives." The school is responsible for using available resources as effectively as possible to accomplish the educational and social goals that the community has set for its students. Teachers should not only be part of but also lead and guide initiatives to improve local science education programs. Instead of depending on a top-down management style in which the principal is the "boss," educators can make change smoother by adapting a suitable version fo the "continuous quality improvement" approach that has become so popular in industry (see Chapter 7 for more information on this). Only then will schools begin to reflect the contribution of their greatest potential academic and instructional resource—teachers.

Reorienting schools to recognize teachers as their chief resource, and to use them accordingly, would be the most effective way to maximize limited resources and begin to accomplish the increasingly ambitious educational goals our society has set for its schools. Accomplishing those goals fully would require a significant new allocation of resources in addition to the structural reforms called for in this book. Because our youth are our only truly renewable societal resource, we—as a concerned, caring, democratic society—can do no less.

ENHANCING THE ROLE OF TEACHERS OF SCIENCE

In a materials-centered, inquiry-oriented classroom, teachers guide, focus, challenge, and encourage students. This is markedly different from the traditional approach to science education—the approach that too many students still experience.

The conventional science classroom is a place where students are expected to be passive and quiet, taking in information, which is to be returned to its source on the test. It is a place where "teaching" means talking and learning is equated with the appearance of listening, even though four decades of cognitive research indicate the opposite. If one watches young children play school, one still will see that the designated "teacher" typically stands while others sit, talks louder, calls for order, and in all ways (including body language) demonstrates an understanding that school is a place where teachers talk and students listen. This is the "fill-the-vessel" theory of learning: The student is an empty vessel to be filled with facts known by the teacher.

This child's conception of the teacher-student relationship is all too accurate in many cases and can be confirmed by checking the dominant assessment method used in a school: if the assessment is based primarily on a fact-laden, short-answer, machine-scored test, teaching in the school is probably based on the "empty vessel" theory of learning.

The National Science Education Standards tell us that, as science educators, our goal must be to develop individuals able to use scientific principles and processes when making decisions about their own lives. The only way that educators can achieve that goal effectively is to create a context in which students can experience and participate in the questioning, evidence-based approach that characterizes science. Providing this kind of learning experience requires the academic leadership of the teacher. The first responsibility of everyone else in the school system is to make this possible.

SEPUP efforts over the last 10 years have yielded evidence from urban, suburban, and rural districts across the United States that when local teachers are given the tools and capacity to lead change, there is a multiplier effect that spreads lasting innovation far beyond the classrooms of the teacher-leaders who worked directly with the project. We are convinced that the positive effect results from the decision to deal with a school as a complex social system, which, like all social systems, resists change until leaders it respects (preferably internal leadership) identifies with and adopts the change (see Rogers, 1995). When teacher leaders lead change within their own schools and districts, the potential for deep, lasting change increases dramatically.

If materials become effective curriculum only in the hands of a skilled and engaged teacher, then materials developers cannot succeed without teachers as full partners in creating interactive materials for guided inquiry. It is teachers whom the materials must first engage if a successful curriculum is to grow from them. The teacher knows what is likely to work with students and other teachers, what likely will not, and why. Without the practical wisdom of working teachers, developers will not be able to create interactive materials that engage teachers and students while still accomplishing the new, skills-based educational goals of a 21st-century society.

ENGAGEMENT: THE LINK BETWEEN MATERIALS AND LEARNING

Uniting the informed, enabled teacher with effective learning materials makes possible the three aspects of engagement among teacher, student, and materials that lay the basis for a successful curriculum. It is this necessary and complex relationship that frames the approach to materials development detailed in the chapters that follow.

The first aspect of engagement must be between the teacher and the learning materials used in class. The materials must capture the teacher's interest and imagination and also provide a clear, effective way for the teacher to use those materials to accomplish classroom goals. The second aspect is the engagement of teachers with students—the interest and care a teacher takes with each, the rapport established with them, and the forum for open communication with and among students fashioned through the creation of a classroom culture. Building on those aspects, the teacher then fosters an engagement between the students and materials. This form of engagement thrives in classrooms that are materials-centered and that employ guided inquiry—with teachers using the materials creatively to guide, focus, challenge, and encourage students' engagement with the concepts, processes, and skills to be mastered.

WHAT DEVELOPMENT FOR GUIDED INQUIRY IS NOT

Finally, this new definition of curriculum in guided inquiry also implies what materials development for guided inquiry is not.

First, it is not grafting pieces of different programs together in short summer workshops—the "cut-up" sessions with which so many teachers are familiar. In these workshops, teachers "cut up" programs, choose the isolated parts they like from different ones, and combine them. That approach is a risky one. One program has a great lab that uses a specialized piece of equipment, another requires a video that a program has created, and a third relies on a unique cooperative learning method. All three are presented in different styles and speak in different voices. Stitching together the uniquely good features of the three will not necessarily produce a top-quality course of science education even if master teachers do the stitching. (There also are questions of copyright involved in such efforts.)

Second, materials development is not what has recently become known as *instructional design*, a term applied most commonly to the creation of educational software. Computers have their place in classrooms and, with more and more schools gaining Internet access, that place is growing. But despite the steady flow of predictions to the contrary, computers at home will not replace schools and computers in any form will not replace teachers. Genuine learning will remain the result of interactions between human beings—communicating not only with words and numbers but also with facial expressions, voice inflections, gestures, and the other qualities that enable educators to seize a teachable moment and use it to transform a student's understanding.

Third, materials development is not a process that one educator, one school district, or one university department can do alone and still do well. Consistently effective materials development for guided inquiry results from collaborations of subject specialists and classroom teachers drawing on the expertise of education researchers, graphic designers, and others. When attempted by an individual or a narrowly specialized group isolated from the unique and necessary resources that other specialists can offer, any development venture risks frustration or outright failure in a variety of ways.

A NEW APPROACH TO MATERIALS DEVELOPMENT

Clearly, guided inquiry's new definitions of education, curriculum, and the teacher's role in learning call for a new approach to materials development. If every teacher is to have the equivalent of a Stradivarius to create curriculum, teachers and materials designers must form a much more intimate partnership than has been common in the past.

When classes are defined by lectures, drills, and textbooks, materials can be fashioned by one or a few content specialists with the minimal involvement of teachers. When curriculum is seen merely as factual content, improving the curriculum is simply a matter of finding content specialists—usually university professors—to write more comprehensive textbooks and delivering this curriculum to teachers, who use it to give more comprehensive lectures and tests. But that process cannot yield materials that enable teachers to help students achieve the new education standards.

To create materials that both engage and educate, a range of specialists must pool their special expertise in a series of steps, many occurring at the same time. Working closely with teachers, materials developers (most of whom, ideally, are or have been teachers themselves) and content specialists fashion activities and materials shaped by current research into how people learn most effectively. Those materials are tested and retested in working classrooms to discover which aspects of them do and do not foster engagement and learning, among teachers and students alike. Assessment specialists collaborate in creating tools and techniques that will accurately and thoroughly measure learning achieved through doing. After revisions, editors and designers craft versions of the materials for publication that will make the materials as easy as possible to use in their intended ways. Even the governmental and nonprofit organizations that fund development projects and the school districts or universities that host them become partners that can influence the success of this intricately coordinated process. And throughout, as we will see, working classroom teachers play an indispensable part—helping to create and test the materials, and then to disseminate them, and coaching colleagues who adopt them.

A FULCRUM FOR CHANGE

Although a collaborative approach is still scarce in materials development (as well as in most other facets of education), it is an adaptation of the same method that a number of fields have relied on to transform themselves again and again in response to public need and demand.

For example, collaboration transformed the airplane from the Wright brothers' 1903 wood-and-canvas contraption to the Boeing 747 in little more than 60 years. Along the way, the process also created the specialties of aeronautical science and engineering to support it. In less than the span of a human lifetime, the same process took the computer from a room-size maze of wires and 10,000 vacuum tubes to notebook-size marvels working at literally millions of times the speed and computing power of the 1945 original.

Although the process of continuous improvement has been used in industry, it does not inhere or work only in machinery, factories, or science and engineering labs. It is instead a deeply human process that orchestrates a diversity of skills, energy, and knowledge toward a common goal of excellence—even as society redefines what excellence is. That point has been demonstrated by a few materials development projects in science and other disciplines that have used versions of the process with notable success.

Indeed, savvy enterprises within education no longer see teachers as isolated specialists, much less as interchangeable information repeaters whose most important job is to carry out rote tasks according to instructions. Instead, schools now find that the greatest value lies in breaking down the walls (or at least opening classroom doors) to bring together teams able to work in cross-disciplinary groups to identify possibilities and solve problems as part of a continuous process of change and improvement.

CONCLUSION

There is a bond between learning and the processes and attitudes underlying investigation. Those processes are open-ended and interactive, yet guided by well-defined steps, objectives, and standards. But the purpose of investigations is not just to keep students busy or to entertain them by allowing them to investigate whatever captures their interest.

The challenge to materials developers is to create materials that foster what we have dubbed "guided inquiry": sequenced investigations that engage students by posing problems that have meaning for them and that also develop students' knowledge and skills in an academically sound and rigorous way.

Using guided inquiry as an organizing principle for materials development enables education to accomplish two goals that are fundamental in the national movement for educational improvement defined by new standards.

First, guided inquiry more effectively structures (and therefore strengthens) educationally meaningful interactions between teacher and students and among students themselves. These interactions—not physical objects such as textbooks and worksheets—are the true curriculum, the real stuff of learning. Therefore, the materials that structure the interactions that form the curriculum play a determining role in the quality of students' learning.

Second, using materials for guided inquiry will enable teachers and students to more effectively implement and achieve new national standards, such as the National Science Education Standards. These standards call for students to *experience* subjects such as science instead of merely reading or hearing *about* them.

Because materials for guided inquiry embody a new approach to teaching and learning, they are best created through a different process than has typically been used to create traditional materials such as textbooks. That process is the subject of the chapters that follow.

2

How Guided Inquiry Fulfills Society's New Definition of Education

It is nothing short of a miracle that the modern methods of instruction have not yet entirely strangled the holy curiosity of enquiry.
— Albert Einstein, *Ideas and Opinions*

THE MOVEMENT TOWARD TEACHING and learning based on guided inquiry— and, therefore, the need for a fundamentally new approach to materials development—is being propelled by three forces: structural shifts in our economy and society, new understandings about how humans learn, and students' increasing demands for meaning and relevance in their learning experiences in school. Our emerging 21st-century economy and society require that *all* students master the higher-order intellectual skills that we previously have expected only of the gifted. At the same time, cognitive research is showing that people learn most effectively not by hearing lectures or reading textbooks but through meaningful experience (see, e.g., Olson & Loucks-Horsley, 2000; Welch, 1981).

These groundshifts rippling through our classrooms demand, and validate, an experiential, inquiry-based approach to learning. At the same time, these structural changes give educators a twofold opportunity.

First, the new shapes of our economy and society are showing us the kind of learning experiences that can be consistently more effective, efficient, and rewarding for all students than conventional curricular approaches have been.

Second, by following that approach, we will be better able to unite students, educators, parents, business leaders, and community members in support of what happens in our classrooms—and end the circular, fractious debates that plague national efforts to revitalize education.

NEEDS OF A 21ST-CENTURY ECONOMY AND SOCIETY

Our dwindling manufacturing economy was peopled by masses of manual workers and run by a small managerial elite. That pyramid has crumbled. The new personal-services economy emerging in its place is rooted in technology, not materials, and fueled by information, not muscle. It values mind over brawn and demands intellectual skills in the volume that the old economy demanded manual labor. (According to the U.S. Bureau of Labor Statistics, in 1912 the fastest-growing work field was factory labor; in 1998, it was computer-related engineering [U.S. Bureau of Labor Statistics, personal communication, 1999].) The new service economy flattens organizations and redistributes management respon-sibilities for problem solving and decision making among rank-and-file workers. All students must now master the intellectual skills that until now we have expected only the gifted to display. This is nothing less than a mandate for revolution in our schools.

During the century-long industrial age, most work was manual and repetitive. Only a small managerial and professional elite needed to be able to think and make decisions. But by the 1960s things had begun to change. The needs of the growing middle class and the increasing complexity of organizations spawned by a powerhouse manufacturing economy were creating demands for broad new classes of workers able to use their minds instead of their hands. In the early 1970s, U.S. demand for sophisticated services—financial management and counseling, business administration, medical treatment, and so on—began to grow faster than the demand for additional mass-produced goods. It was then that schools and our economy began to uncouple.

More and more of us, as workers and as citizens, are called upon to identify, analyze, and solve problems for ourselves. That means that every person must now be able to apply "skills [that] in the past [were] ordinarily only associated with management," noted the congressional board of the federal Office of Technology Assessment (OTA) in its study *Worker Training: Competing in the New International Economy* (OTA, 1990, pp. 14–15). In 1992, the U.S. Department of Education's *Measurement of Workforce Readiness Competencies* survey culled the conclusions of an array of government and industry studies and found that all of them "identi-fied the need for higher-order thinking skills. . . . This development means that much more is expected of even entry-level members of the Ameri-can workforce" (p. 2).

WHY SCHOOLS MUST CHANGE

For more than a decade, evidence has been piling up that an education centered on textbooks and the other traditional materials that still shape so many of our school programs is not enabling most students to develop those necessary new skills. According to the OTA's 1992 *Annual Report to the Congress*, at least half of all young adults aged 21 to 25 "cannot handle even moderately complex quantitative literacy problems" (p. 41). It also noted that a fifth of those young adults could read only as well as an average eighth-grade student, "yet most job-related reading materials require a tenth or eleventh grade reading level" (p. 44).

At the same time, the demands—and opportunities—for the exercise of intellectual skills in our personal lives are becoming increasingly complex. Consider the deceptively simple question, "Is the lake polluted?" Technically, the question asks whether the water contains harmful substances. But which substances? How harmful are they? According to what studies? Do the levels in the water exceed government-set maximum levels for those substances? Many adults do not know how to think about such questions. But by addressing precisely these kinds of issues in science courses, students begin to explore the nature, uses, and constraints of the factual evidence on which so many intellectual decisions depend. Only after the processes of science have provided answers to those questions can informed citizens (a category that also includes students) draw conclusions about the other issues that remain. If substance levels in the water do not exceed government maximums, do we agree with the evidence the government used to decide that these specific levels are safe? And exactly what does "safe" mean? Science tells us what is in the lake's water. Whether the lake is polluted is a public policy issue. By using data gleaned from scientific evidence to confront such issues, students begin to grasp the difference between science, as a process and body of evidence, and public policy—what we as a society decide to do based on that evidence.

Our frameworks of science education are not yet helping most students to develop their abilities to reason from evidence as quickly as our economy and society need to put those skills to work. Fortunately, we can identify an ingredient that will speed the transformation of our curriculum. The missing link between our society's and economy's needs for higher-order intellectual skills and what happens in our classrooms is engagement.

ENGAGEMENT AS THE KEY TO LEARNING

Surveys show that students crave the engagement that is an integral part of inquiry-based learning as badly as companies crave engaged, intellectually skilled workers. Evidence from teachers, schools, and studies (some of which is summarized below) shows that when students are given assignments relevant to their own lives, they thrive intellectually. When Cheryl Dodes, a middle school teacher in Maspeth (an area of Queens in

New York City), implemented an inquiry-oriented, activity-based course that challenged students to investigate and solve real-world problems, "Kids came to class every day asking what we were going to do next," she reports. "They would do extra work or go home and repeat for their parents the investigations done in class. More than one told me, 'I never knew science could be so much fun.'" Dodes showed other faculty members a lab report that one of her students had written and asked them to describe the student who wrote it. The consensus: The report was the work of a high-achieving student. In reality, the student had scored in the third percentile for his grade in writing skills.

Richard Duquin, a science teacher at Benjamin Franklin Middle School in Kenmore, New York, investigated the properties of materials in sports during his use of the course "Issues, Evidence, and You." "Instead of me having to call on people and drag out a response, almost everyone's hand was raised" to talk about racquets, sneakers, safety equipment, and baseballs and bats, Duquin says. "If the assignment is about something directly related to the students, the class discussion the next day is always more alive."

In the past, the challenge of making the important ideas entombed in textbooks and worksheets dance to life in students' minds has been yet another assignment handed to teachers. Dedicated teachers strive to do this and succeed more often than one would think possible. But to routinely expect every teacher to perform to that standard of creativity and success every day with every student in every lesson is as unrealistic as expecting every athlete to perform flawlessly and break records every time he or she goes onto the field.

Placing the obligation to engage students squarely on teachers is fundamentally mistaken. Instead, it is the responsibility of the learning materials that teachers select—and of the teams that develop those materials—to engage both students and teachers in a way that makes learning compelling. It is the educators' responsibility to seek out and use materials for guided inquiry that engage students regardless of their intellectual or socioeconomic class—and also to help design and test those materials whenever they can.

Anyone who has spent an hour in a middle school classroom understands that finding materials that engage students in learning is no small task. Today's students have grown up in a society where authority is routinely distrusted and often scorned. They are not willing to sit through lectures or repetitive exercises simply because a teacher or parent tells them to. The only way to lure students at any grade level into a learning experience and entice them to complete it is to hook them emotionally—to *engage* them—by showing them a personal meaning in both the content and process of the experience.

As part of SEPUP's year-long "Science and Sustainability" high school course, teacher Lori Gillam at the Steller Secondary Alternative School in Anchorage, Alaska, played a game called "Fish Banks Ltd." The class divided into teams, each managing a fleet of fishing vessels in Alaska's northern Pacific. A computer in the classroom assigned fish catches to areas of the imaginary waters, then randomly divided catches among different ships. The object: to maximize catches and income while sustainably managing fish stocks. After nine rounds, or "years," of the game, students had fished out the sea and most of the students' companies were bankrupt. The experience not only challenged them but also let them experience the difficult trade-offs that exist in balancing the needs of humans and their environment.

STRUCTURING ENGAGEMENT FOR LEARNING

It remains the responsibility of teachers and materials developers to struc-ture and sequence challenges that engage students as well as foster their growth in skills and knowledge through systematic, inquiry-based expe-riences. But even bounded by those strictures, educators are left with a universe of opportunity to seize students' attention. Students themselves are telling us how.

First, from student surveys and educators' own stories, we know that students define *engaging* as "real." Instead of reading about science, stu-dents want to do genuine science; instead of doing exercises in algebra or calculus, students want to solve math problems in the course of tackling real-world situations, such as designing bridges or calculating investment returns. Colorado geography teacher Candace Allen found that student engagement and performance soared when she asked them to design a peace plan for warring factions in the Balkans (Wilson & Daviss, 1996). Arizona chemistry teacher Susan Skolnik recalls hearing two students talk-ing about how much they enjoyed a lab. "In their words, this was the first time they had ever gotten to actually do science," Skolnik says, "as opposed to listening to the teacher talk" (Skolnik, 1995, p. 34).

Second, work must also be open-ended. Students are curious; they become caught up in the thrill of decision and discovery as easily as they are turned off by the dull certitude of replicating answers or outcomes that teachers or textbooks announce in advance. Writing in *Educational Leader-ship*, consultants Richard Strong, Harvey Silver, and Amy Robinson (1995) reported on their multiyear research project to determine what engages students in coursework. Among their conclusions: A curriculum "arouses intense curiosity" in students when they must organize and interpret in-formation to use as evidence in exploring subjects that relate to their personal lives. It is this absence of a pat or predetermined resolution "that compels them to understand [the data] further" (p. 8).

Third, that element of discovery is made more intense by work that connects students to the world outside the classroom. Candace Allen's students took their work so seriously that she found them still "doing geography" on the last day of school. At Waldo Middle School in Salem, Oregon, student groups used print and electronic resources to research the plight of particular endangered species. Each group then wrote a recovery plan for an animal, consulting with experts, using spreadsheets to calculate costs, even designing fund-raising campaigns. Finally, each group presented its plan to a "board of directors"—including not only teachers but also regional zoo officials—to persuade them that the plan was well-crafted enough to deserve funding. Teachers found that the immediacy of the project led students to apply the processes and information they were learning to other environmental issues beyond the classroom (U.S. Department of Education, 1992).

Fourth, engaging work is challenging and demanding, but not so far beyond students' grasp that they become discouraged. Educators at the Campus Middle School in Englewood, Colorado, surveyed students as part of a design for a plan to use student portfolios in assessment. The survey results indicated that the projects students remembered most fondly were often the hardest ones—*if* the students completed them successfully. "Again and again, students equated hard work with success and satisfaction," according to district consultant Paulette Wasserstein. "It is not the instant success but the challenge and victory that give students a sense of power. Self-esteem is enhanced when we accomplish something that we thought . . . beyond us" (Wasserstein, 1995, p. 41).

Strong and colleagues (1995) summarize these findings as the "SCORE" approach to student engagement:

> Success, which rewards persistence, results from mastery, and imparts confidence in attempting new challenges
>
> Curiosity, which grows out of open-ended questions and motivates students to engage
>
> Originality, which helps students develop confidence as well as creativity and higher-order intellectual skills
>
> Relationships, which enable individuals to communicate effectively, negotiate, and work together toward common goals
>
> Energy, sparked by the other four elements, to tackle new endeavors

"Students of different abilities and backgrounds crave doing important work," Wasserstein (1995) learned from the Campus Middle School survey. "Passive learning is not engaging. For students to sense that their work is important, they need to tinker with real-world problems, and they need opportunities to [create] knowledge. Hard work does not turn students away, but busywork destroys them" (1995, p. 41).

Clearly, there is a theme linking students' need for meaning to the needs of our society and economy for intellectually skilled workers. That theme is personal empowerment and responsibility. We are learning that workers and citizens must have the intellectual skills that let them analyze, decide, act, and create on their own. These are the same abilities that students want to exercise and strengthen in their coursework. Those abilities, the same ones that bring meaning to work and that make intellectual autonomy possible, are cultivated through engagement. For educators, Wasserstein (1995) says, the concept of engagement "is like striking gold in understanding the relationship of teacher to student, student to learning" (p. 98).

THE CONSTRUCTIVIST LINK

By meeting students' need for personal engagement in their studies, educators will give our society the citizens and workers it needs to flourish in an age dominated by technology, information, and demands for intellectual services. Recent discoveries in cognitive science explain how.

More than six decades of research in cognitive development, from John Dewey (1915) to Jean Piaget (Piaget et al., 1977) to Anton Lawson (1995), has yielded the "constructivist" view of learning. Stated simply, findings have shown that genuine learning—what we call mastery—is deeply subjective and intensely active. Beginning in infancy, each of us constructs a personal understanding of the world, weaving every new experience or fact into our widening fabric of integrated concepts. In that way, every person fashions, out of personal experience, a uniquely structured, personal web of knowledge about how things work. We all might agree that 1 + 3 = 4, but each of us comes to understand why only through an interior process that no one else can conduct for us.

Anthony Lorsbach and Kenneth Tobin (1992) explain what that means to teachers and materials developers:

> Experience involves . . . a personal construction which fits some of the external realities but does not provide a match. The senses are not conduits to the external world through which truths are conducted into the body. Objectivity is not possible for thinking beings. Accordingly, knowledge is a construction of how the world works, one that is viable in the sense that it allows an

individual to pursue particular goals. Thus, from a constructivist perspective . . . teaching science becomes more like the science that scientists do—it is an active, social process of making sense of experiences, as opposed to what we now call "school science." . . . By using constructivist epistemology as a referent, teachers can become more sensitive to children's prior knowledge and the processes by which they make sense of phenomena.

THE LIMITS OF BEHAVIORISM

In contrast, the "factory school" that runs on lectures, textbooks, and batch processing was built out of the theories of behaviorism that dominated psychology during the first half of the 20th century. Behaviorists believed that learning was a matter of conditioning: that students should be shown the problem "$1 + 3 = x$" and corrected in their responses until they consistently produce the answer "4." Behaviorism reinforced the assumption that the teacher's job was to fill a student's mind with pieces of knowledge the way a clerk stocks a supermarket's shelves with boxes of cereal. The growing and persuasive body of evidence coming from constructivist research finally toppled that theory and recognized the notion of passive learning (on which so much of schooling and so many classroom materials have been based) to be an oxymoron. Facts can be learned through brute-force methods such as memorization and drill, but not the skills of application and performance—the skills our economy and society now need so desperately. Guided, graduated, inquiry-based experience and practice internalize skills and make them part of a student's structure of knowledge. The approach also gives meaning and context to facts, helping students to build them into their personal structures of knowledge instead of forgetting them after taking a test. Experience, not repetition or memorization, is the key to retention and, therefore, to genuine learning.

The implications for education are fundamental and far-reaching. If changing a student's internal structures of knowledge is the goal of learning, as constructivism holds, then lectures and textbooks are inefficient mechanisms for stimulating those changes. A variety of studies indicate that students retain less than 20 percent of the information they hear in lectures and read in textbooks, compared to as much as 90 percent of what they learn by doing. These findings corroborate students' definitions of engagement. According to Wasserstein (1995), "Students need opportunities to apply knowledge, to generate and construct meaning, the kind of cognition that combines declarative and procedural knowledge . . . the what . . . [and] the how" (p. 41).

In a very basic sense, then, learning and engagement are two inseparable parts of the same whole. In other words, inquiry-based learning—the kind that engages students—works. Rote approaches that rely solely on lectures, drills, and worksheets do not. Challenging experiences spark engagement and lead to genuine learning; textbooks used alone merely alienate. If educators can take one broad lesson from constructivism, it is that by satisfying students' demands for engagement, our schools finally can foster in students the new intellectual skills our economy and society must have.

GUIDED INQUIRY AS AN ORGANIZING PRINCIPLE

The new social and economic demands for universal higher-order intellectual skills, coupled with our new understandings about the mechanisms of genuine learning, chart a new approach to teaching and learning. That new approach moves beyond attempts to improve the traditional lectures, textbooks, and worksheets and embraces the concepts of guided inquiry.

This will not be easy. The challenge—and the opportunity—that the new social and economic mandate poses to materials developers is to think in fundamentally different ways when creating learning experiences for students. It calls on them to surrender the notions of "instruction" and "lessons" and to think instead in terms of "questions" and "investigations." In that sense, materials developers and the teachers who collaborate with them are "learning engineers": They apply the latest research to create practical methods of helping students achieve not just good grades but also the intellectual benchmarks that new national standards are establishing. To accomplish that, developers and teachers must begin acting less like lone inventors and more like applications teams—working collaboratively in a clearly organized multistep process, sharing ideas, critiquing each other's efforts, and aiming for a steady flow of incremental improvements. Making these fundamental changes of attitude at a visceral level usually requires dismantling the intellectual infrastructure acquired over a lifetime. But we know from experience that the change is worth making—not only to benefit students but also to help developers and teachers continue to find engagement and meaning in their own work.

We emphasize that guided inquiry does not ignore or belittle the value of the information that textbooks, databases, and other repositories of facts have to offer. Neither students nor adults can be expected to rebuild the entire structure of science or mathematics for themselves. Handy sources of data, advice, and examples can be as fundamental as bread, but bread alone does not make up a balanced diet on which children will grow. Educational research and a century of experience have shown us that facts must be given a meaning and context that enable students to assimilate the information into their personal structures of knowledge.

By rethinking the traditional concepts that have shaped schooling for more than a century, guided inquiry redefines the roles of students and teachers alike. Students are no longer passive vessels that teachers must labor to fill with knowledge; they are no longer raw material in a process that trains them to look to others not only for information but also for judgments of its value.

As Pamela Wasserman, a science curriculum coordinator for District 24 in Queens, New York, told us, guided inquiry "lets teachers stop being the all-knowing source of information and lets them become more of a facilitator" or learning coach, a person who helps students master the processes of learning for themselves. As a bonus, guided inquiry can fill the need for the new, more engaging pedagogical techniques demanded by the continuing shift to block scheduling and other new learning formats now making their way into more and more schools.

Equally important, through guided inquiry students can develop the skills of lifelong learning: the ability to frame problems, ferret out facts, test and assess the accuracy and relevance of those facts, articulate conclusions, and make reasoned, evidence-based decisions—crucial survival skills in a world awash in unrefereed information, much of it being peddled by groups with partisan agendas to promote.

GUIDED INQUIRY AND THE TEACHER

Using materials based on guided inquiry to engage students and educate them to meet 21st-century demands is a new challenge for education generally and for teachers in particular. Teachers are leaders of the human interactions we define as the curriculum. Their commitment to the new approaches to education called for in mandates such as the National Science Education Standards is essential if our society is to accomplish all the goals we now set for science education, both in and beyond school. The classroom use of materials for guided inquiry is necessary to implement the new approach and achieve those necessary new standards.

As teachers recognize the challenges to their profession that the new century lays down, they also will recognize the opportunities those challenges open to them. By joining with developers to create materials for guided inquiry, teachers can do more to ensure that their students meet those new standards. By working with developers to implement guided inquiry in their classrooms, teachers can find opportunities for professional growth and begin to accomplish the ideals that brought them into the profession in the first place.

CONCLUSION

Learning materials structured around real-life, open-ended challenges engage students emotionally in academic content. That kind of engagement leads them to find meaning in their studies. Materials for guided inquiry lay the foundations of engagement and meaning that lead to the mastery of facts, processes, and higher-order intellectual skills—the kind of learning that our society and economy now demand of every graduate.

New understandings about how humans learn, and students' increasing demands for meaning and relevance in their studies, are the basis of guided inquiry. Using them, educators can foster an approach to education that will enable our citizens, economy, and society to thrive.

3

Designing Materials for Guided Inquiry: Three Principles

> The most important method of education . . . always has consisted of that in which the pupil was urged to actual performance.
> —Albert Einstein, *Ideas and Opinions*

EFFECTIVE MATERIALS FOR GUIDED INQUIRY rely on three principles that challenge the usual approaches to materials development:

- Emphasizing collaboration among specialists
- Making revolution through evolution
- Using operational definitions

This chapter discusses these principles as a foundation for materials development in guided inquiry. It also highlights science education as an area particularly well suited to guided inquiry's approach to learning.

As these three principles suggest, designing effective materials for guided inquiry requires developers to think differently about their work even before they begin to put ideas on paper.

Textbooks and other traditional materials can be created by specialists working in isolation. One or a few content experts write the materials. The experts deliver their work to a publisher that prints it and then sells it to schools. The teachers then "deliver" the materials' content to students. Guided inquiry demands a more collaborative process of development.

In the case of science education, conventional "delivery" involves imparting equations and technical terms, explaining their meaning, and then leading students through lab exercises to confirm facts and replicate results. Guided inquiry reverses the process. It leads students through experiences first, giving them technical terms and equations only *after* they have experienced a concept or process.

Every so often, science education feels the need to strike out in bold new directions, as it did in the post-Sputnik days of the late 1950s. At such fateful times, some projects propose to sweep aside traditional materials and approaches and replace them with techniques and organizing schemes that are as unfamiliar to many teachers as they are to students. Too often, such revolutionary endeavors fail to produce the hoped-for result and disappear from the materials marketplace within a few years. Guided inquiry challenges the revolutionary approach as well as the conventional approach, working for fundamental, long-term change one increment at a time.

COLLABORATION AMONG SPECIALISTS

Creating materials for guided inquiry demands a combination of widely diverse skills on a scale, and of a specificity, almost unknown in conventional materials development. Ensuring the accuracy and currency of the facts, concepts, and methods that the materials will present is a job for content specialists. But education researchers, not content specialists, can best determine the compatibility of materials' structure and approach with what is known about the mind's mechanisms for effective and efficient learning. Writers and graphic designers, not researchers or content specialists, usually are the most skilled at presenting substantive information clearly and easily in ways that hold students' interest. And, as these experts work together, at every stage working classroom teachers must analyze and question: "How would my students respond to this?" "Would this work for me and other teachers in the classroom?"

This degree and diversity of collaboration in development is rare in materials development. Every adult remembers high school science courses organized around textbooks written by university professors and/or leading conventional teachers: endless pages of facts and formulas, the only relief coming from photos of people in white coats using lab equipment. Those experiences made "education" and "engagement" seem as mutually antagonistic as oil and water. Consequently, few students retained what they had studied any longer than it took to take a test and escape from the course.

Now state and local administrative agencies are granting teachers greater freedom—not only to adopt or adapt materials, but even to create their own. The results are far more engaging for students. But teachers are learning that, even working in groups, they lack the full range of skills needed to design, present, and evaluate materials that are consistently effective.

SEPUP'S DEVELOPMENT PROCESS

To understand the challenge that guided inquiry poses to developers, consider SEPUP's process for creating the equipment and materials that Eileen Smith's class used to make gypsum in Chapter 1. The student experience was developed through months of collaboration by materials developers and classroom teachers, all educated in science. As they put together early drafts, they tested the materials' effectiveness in working classrooms, making students a part of the development team as well. A manufacturing company engineered the equipment, trying out different versions to come up with ones that met the academic need while remaining inexpensive enough for most school districts to afford. Editors, designers, and artists shaped the materials and text to present scientific concepts and procedures in an entertaining way while making the academic content as clear as possible.

Teachers around the country collaborated with the development team to try the new materials in urban, rural, rich, and poor classrooms. Their participation was crucial in helping to ensure that the materials would spark effective learning experiences for students of all backgrounds and learning styles. University professors and other experts in the various fields of science reviewed the materials for scientific accuracy before they were produced in quantity. When the materials were released commercially, SEPUP's development team and the manufacturer worked together to create a national network of teachers skilled enough in their use to offer expert help and guidance to nearby colleagues.

Increasingly, developers also find corporations willing to contribute financial support as well as subject expertise to development projects in guided inquiry. In 1995, for example, Robert Hirsch, then vice president of the Chemfix Environmental Services consulting firm, enthusiastically granted permission to SEPUP to adapt the company's patented process for stabilizing hazardous wastes. The process became the basis of a supplementary classroom activity and, more recently, was included in the program's "Science and Sustainability" high school course. Students simulate the stabilizing process, compare the results to those of precipitation and other traditional clean-up methods, and weigh the advantages and drawbacks of each. Such contributions from the private sector are vital if materials are to reflect the realities and choices that citizens face in a technological society.

More recently, SEPUP has joined with educational researchers who specialize in assessment to create a valid way to measure student learning in activity-based inquiry (see Chapter 8).

Clearly, no single scientist, teacher, professor, or developer could possess the entire spectrum of skills, experience, and knowledge required to create these kinds of materials in even a single subject area. Development of materials for guided inquiry must be rooted firmly in interdisciplinary cooperation.

MAKING REVOLUTION THROUGH EVOLUTION

The process of change in education—in the marketplace of materials as well as that of ideas—is too often marked by chaos, anxiety, and the search for quick answers even though education's issues, conflicts, and structures are complex. Supporters of "whole language" battle the phonics establishment; administrators who want mathematical principles taught in early grades argue about materials with teachers who insist on teaching arithmetic facts first.

Educators often assume the mantle of materials developer because they sense an urgent, compelling need for fundamental change in their classroom processes or materials. "After all the things we've tried, our students aren't achieving quickly or consistently enough," we fret, "so we need to revolutionize what we do." But even though the premise may be accurate, the conclusion is not necessarily so.

The revolutionary approach typically assumes a need to scrap the materials and techniques currently used. But in doing so, educators risk rejecting what has proven useful along with concepts or formats that are less reliable.

In contrast, an evolutionary approach (while perhaps less emotionally fulfilling) begins by identifying and preserving what is valuable in current practice while working to replace what needs to be changed. No matter how far-reaching one's vision or how urgent the need, education's lasting revolutions are almost always achieved through incremental, evolutionary steps rather than by instant and sweeping change. In materials development, too, it is a steady pace of incremental improvement that makes lasting revolutions.

A Tale of Two Projects

To illustrate the difference in effectiveness between evolutionary and revolutionary approaches, we can contrast the fates of two different development projects.

The Chemical Education Materials Study, or CHEM Study, was launched in 1962 (CHEM Study, 1965; Merrill & Ridgway, 1969). At the time, chemistry education in high school was marked by a cookbook approach: students were given recipes for chemical processes and then conducted laboratory investigations that illustrated the ideas and processes they had read about. CHEM Study's materials, which emphasized gathering and analyzing evidence, still used the lab but reversed the process: With CHEM Study, students began in the lab. Only after they had conducted their investigations and observed chemical processes did they convene in class to talk about what they had experienced.

CHEM Study's materials used structures and concepts that teachers were familiar with—lab activities and classroom sessions—but orchestrated them in new ways. The project's materials were so popular that, five years after it was published, CHEM Study had returned more money to the federal treasury in royalties than the National Science Foundation (NSF) had invested in the project.

At about the same time, a project called The Chemical Bond Approach set out to reorganize the entire high school study of chemistry around the concept of chemical bonds—an entirely new and quite powerful way of structuring the subject for precollege students (Diederich, 1969). But the approach was so alien to teachers that relatively few bought or adopted the project's materials. Over time, the program did achieve one of its goals: The concept of chemical bonds has become one of the key organizing principles of high school chemistry courses. But, as an alternative to conventional textbooks, the project's materials were simply too different too suddenly—and they failed in the marketplace.

How Revolutions Can Go Wrong

While these new chemistry materials were being designed, so was a novel approach to mathematics education in lower grades. Following the Soviet Union's 1957 launch of the world's first artificial Earth satellite, the United States was gripped by a panic that it was falling behind its archrival in scientific and technological skills. Federal agencies funded some of the best minds in mathematics and math education to determine what students needed to know and the best ways to teach it to them. The result: a fundamentally new course of instruction based in large measure on the concepts of set theory. According to their creators, the new materials were meant to build a strong mathematical understanding among students who would go on to college and study more mathematics there. (Boosting the numbers of these students was one goal of the post-Sputnik efforts.)

Such radical innovations required equally fundamental changes in what teachers needed to know and to do in class. As soon as the materials were written, textbooks were rushed into print, institutionalizing the dramatic new materials before they could be adequately tested in classroom trials and revisions made. Trainers hosted short summer workshops to introduce the materials to math teachers and to help them learn the unfamiliar approaches and skills the new textbooks demanded of them.

But despite the best efforts of the educators who worked to help teachers master the new concepts and techniques, the "new math" failed abysmally in its goal of revolutionizing precollege mathematics education. Although the concepts of set theory are now a cornerstone of mathematics courses, the new math in its revolutionary urgency created a backlash against the very idea that it sought to promote. As a result, the program delayed by years the adoption of concepts that could have been introduced more smoothly and effectively through an evolutionary approach.

How Evolution Makes Revolutionary Changes

SEPUP's history tells a different story. In 1983, with a small amount of money from the private sector, what was then the Chemical Education for Public Understanding Program began to design inquiry-based, issue-oriented activity modules for use in California as supplements to junior high and high school science textbooks (Thier & Hill, 1988). At the time, it was virtually a unique undertaking. However, its developers did not declare that current course materials needed to be replaced immediately to prepare students adequately for a technological world. Instead, they developed materials to supplement, not supplant, those in current use.

Instead of politicizing their work, the development group simply kept designing, making, improving, and demonstrating a growing collection of modules to larger and larger groups of interested teachers. By 1993, the students who had learned science through the modules numbered in the millions. This inquiry-based revolution in science education succeeded not by pitched battle or emergency action but by winning over one teacher at a time.

In 1987, the NSF was persuaded by SEPUP's outcome data to support the program's plan to expand the scope and number of the modules. At the time, few activity-centered science or mathematics materials were in widespread use in U.S. secondary school classrooms. Consequently, the developers could easily have assumed that they had little to learn from other materials available at the time. Instead, the project team spent a good deal of time analyzing the approach, accomplishments, and problems of the California Earthquake Education Project, which offered a small number of issue-oriented science activities to the state's schools.

The group investigated advocacy-oriented environmental materials from the Acid Rain Project created by educators at North Carolina State University (Stubbs, 1983). It also reviewed issue-oriented courses created in Europe, such as England's "Science and Technology in Schools." The developers talked with teachers and administrators about what worked well in their classrooms and what they wanted but could not find. Finally, the group also conferred with industrial scientists and executives, who helped the team identify scientific and public policy issues that companies and their publics thought important.

By conferring with so many different developers and specialists, the group created for itself a mosaic of the ideas and materials important at the time in issue-oriented science education. The purpose of doing so was to produce additional modules on specific topics so that a wider range of teachers could become comfortable using issue-oriented materials and explore their effectiveness without having to abandon their current, familiar programs of instruction.

Rather than plotting a revolution, SEPUP developers designed materials to take advantage of the best that existed, building on the specific strengths that they had discovered in current materials. They then honed their designs in extensive national classroom field tests, asking teachers themselves which portions of the materials were most useful and which portions were less so. The program's gradual approach was successful enough that in 1992 the NSF underwrote SEPUP's development of two year-long, issue-oriented, inquiry-based courses. By 1999, SEPUP's materials had been used by an estimated 6 million students and its year-long, issue-oriented courses based on guided inquiry were in trials or being used in more than 400 schools in more than 20 states.

Design and Redesign

This evolutionary approach embodies the process of redesign that is so unfamiliar in education—a systematic process of identifying the useful and valuable aspects of existing principles, practices, and materials and designing innovations around those useful aspects to enable them to work even more effectively. The redesign process has enabled science and mathematics to standardize experimental processes, systems of measurement, and other common elements of language and investigation that allow technologies to progress. Although this is the process by which science grows and changes, this uniquely successful, and very human, process of change is distinctly absent from most innovations in science and mathematics education—as well as from education reform in general (Wilson & Daviss, 1996).

Taking an incremental, evolutionary approach to change (and to revolution) accomplishes two goals for a development project as well as for the field of materials development generally. First, incremental changes usually do not alienate teachers and their colleagues, the very people whom a development team needs to win over to an innovation if it is to succeed.

Strident declarations about the abject failure of what those same teachers do now earns a developer more enmity than converts.

Second, an evolutionary approach demonstrates professionalism to a public that is more than a little skeptical about education and those who practice it. A disciplined, instead of spasmodic, approach to innovation shows that education is a discipline that, like all professions, values continuity, learns from its experience, and uses the best of its present to create a better future.

USING OPERATIONAL DEFINITIONS

The process of designing materials for guided inquiry is rooted in a somewhat broader definition of an academic subject than educators, including developers, often conceive. By tradition, subjects most often are defined as packages of content: Chemistry is the study of the composition and properties of matter; history is the study of past events and conditions. But guided inquiry is about process as much as it is about facts. Consequently, in developing and using classroom materials for guided inquiry, subjects must be defined by their processes as much as by their facts and concepts: Inquiry itself is a process, and, to be educationally valid, an inquiry in a subject area must embody the processes of that subject.

Because they refer to the operations that shape a discipline, definitions of subjects in terms of their processes are known as *operational* definitions. In operational terms, chemistry is the group of processes by which the composition and properties of matter are discovered and employed; history is the group of processes by which past events and conditions as well as their causes, effects, and relationships are determined.

Why Teach This Subject?

Before a development team attempts to articulate an operational definition of a subject, it needs to ponder the reasons for teaching that subject in the first place. The answers will shape the materials that result.

For example, one teacher might argue that the reason for teaching mathematics is to ensure that students are able to manipulate numbers. Another could argue that the reason is to enable students to communicate ideas about quantities. A third might decide that the purpose is to develop students' abilities to reason using quantitative information in order to make decisions. All three teachers might be right.

Each, based on the reason deemed most relevant, would choose different classroom materials as the basis of his or her courses. The first teacher could decide that a traditional arithmetic textbook would do the job. The second might opt for materials that emphasize writing about mathematical ideas. The third perhaps would use materials that frame mathematical concepts within real-world problems for which students need to puzzle out quantitative solutions. Similarly, a developer's concept of the purposes for teaching a subject will dictate the character of the materials that the developer will create.

The Purpose of Science Education

So, to develop science materials for guided inquiry, one must first articulate the reasons for teaching science. But before we do so, we need to make clear our assumption about the purpose of education in general: that it is to help students develop the skills and understandings that will enable them to live meaningful, satisfying, and productive lives. We believe that most people, educators or not, agree with that assumption. But by accepting that guiding principle, we also are accepting its chief implication: that education's purpose is to enable people to master, retain, and apply what they have learned in school to situations they encounter outside the classroom. In other words, education is about the mastery of principles and processes that will have use and meaning for people long after they have taken their last school exam.

In contrast, consider the view of science education's purpose that can be inferred from the traditional formats of teaching and testing. That purpose might be stated as: to memorize facts and terms so that they can be recalled with precision during an exam.

That definition, like the rote materials that give rise to it, deemphasizes the processes of science—and especially their applicability in real-world situations—in favor of facts. Again, we do not contend that facts, and remembering facts, is unimportant. It is precisely because remembering facts *is* important that science education must move away from rote approaches to learning and couch facts in the context of activity-based inquiry. Without the context of an experience that engages them, students have no way to make facts meaningful and memorable (see, e.g., Gardner et al., 1990).

The new standards do not belittle the value of memorization, but they *do* mean that memorization is just one necessary process among many that must be mastered to make facts useful.

This new, context-centered view of science education's purpose is reflected in the National Science Education Standards, set forth in 1996 by the National Research Council. "The goals for school science," according to the council, are to educate students who are able to experience the richness and excitement of knowing about and understanding the natural world; use appropriate scientific processes and principles in making personal decisions; engage intelligently in public discourse and debate about matters of scientific and technological concern; and increase their economic productivity through the use of the knowledge, understanding, and skills of the scientifically literate person in their careers. (NAS, 1996, p. 13; see also American Association for the Advancement of Science, 1990)

Borrowing, then, from the standards' purposes for teaching science (with which we entirely agree), we would define the operational purpose of science education as being: to enable a person to use effective and appropriate quantitative analytical processes—and the knowledge and skills the person develops as a result—to articulate problems, derive answers, and make informed personal and professional decisions about the physical world. Implicit in our definition is the notion that learning scientific processes, particularly those related to the collection and evaluation of evidence, is every bit as essential as learning scientific facts.

Pairing that concept of purpose with what we know of students' craving for meaning and context, we can create an operational definition of science to shape the educational materials that will fulfill that purpose. Again, we emphasize that an operational definition compatible with the new education standards does not belittle facts. Obviously, science— whether learned from a textbook or experienced through activities—is built on them. But the new operational definition cannot emphasize facts above process—and certainly does not emphasize memorizing facts when they can always be quickly found in reference books or on the Internet.

Instead, materials for guided inquiry in science embody an operational definition of science shaped by the process of proposing and testing ideas that might be facts. For example, Newton's law of motion is not a law but a theory. But that theory was regarded as a fact, one that shaped people's basic understanding of gravitation for almost 300 years because it stood up under test after test. No one was able to prove it false, so people assumed that Newton had described a fact. But then in 1905 Albert Einstein, with his special theory of relativity, showed that Newton's idea was not a law at all—that it only described relationships that pertain under certain conditions.

Einstein used Newton's law and worked from it (following the prudent principle of fomenting revolution through evolution), finding himself driven to formulate his new concept of the physical world only when he confronted what he called "serious and deep contradictions in the old theory from which there seemed no escape" (Einstein & Infeld, 1961).

Einstein's theory drove legions of physicists to reexamine and, ultimately, to rewrite our understandings of physical reality—even though it was not until the 1960s, when spacecraft could be used in making precise measurements of time and motion, that scientists collected direct experimental evidence that Einstein's theory described the physical world accurately. In the best traditions of science, by the 1990s sophisticated experiments had begun to yield evidence that some of Einstein's ideas may be flawed (see, for example, Graneau & Graneau, 1996). Some physicists even have begun to question the constancy of the speed of light—a question that indirectly casts doubt on the foundation of Einstein's theory (Barrow, 1999).

An Operational Definition of Science

It is this willingness to question, to constantly test and reevaluate and revise, that defines the processes of science. Therefore the same questioning attitude should define both the nature of the science experiences that students encounter in schools and the process of creating and improving those experiences for students. By understanding these processes that define our subject in its essence, we can now articulate an operational definition to guide the development of guided inquiry for science students.

In operational terms, we would define science simply as a way of asking questions about the physical world and of gathering and evaluating physical and quantitative evidence—through personal experiences, simulations, and the work of others—that should help to answer those questions. We acknowledge that our operational definition is simple and that some might quibble with it, but we have found none better to guide the development of activity-based science materials.

WHY SCIENCE EDUCATION MUST BE INVESTIGATION-CENTERED

This operational definition also explains why science experiences for students must be investigation-centered rather than textbook-centered: not because labs are required for high school graduation or college admission, but because investigatory experiences *are* science. Investigations and experiments are the means by which scientists collect information, discover its meanings, and weave it into theories.

Also, through investigations scientists test the value of a theory by its ability to predict results. When researchers discover that a theory does not explain or predict accurately, that discovery becomes the spur to additional research. Through lab work, students not only learn facts and their significance but also experience the processes through which science evolves and refines theories over time.

Through an inquiry-based, structured course of experiences and investigations, students internalize a lasting, working understanding of the principles and processes of a discipline, and enough of its facts and history, to be able to collect, analyze, interpret, and apply ideas and information, especially in their lives beyond school. In science, that means that students will learn to use evidence to make reasoned, fact-based decisions about issues and applications of science in their own lives. That skill has become essential in taking on the responsibilities of citizens in an increasingly complex democratic society.

DESIGNING EXPERIENCES FOR STUDENTS

Having clarified both our concept of purpose and the operational definition of our subject—in this case, science—we can begin to see the nature of the materials needed to fulfill both. These understandings show us that the scientific experiences that we design for students should be:

- Conceptually structured
- Evidence-based
- Materials-centered
- Inquiry-oriented

By *conceptually structured*, we mean that the structure of an experience or inquiry is to be designed to be "transparent"—to reveal the knowledge we want students to confront through the activity, not to make the mechanical aspects of the activity themselves the centerpiece. Each activity or investigation must forcefully convey substantive, specific principles, ideas, and facts within the context of scientific processes. Activity for its own sake can be a way to keep students entertained and busy, but it is as educationally pointless as the rote transfer of data.

Guided inquiry in science must be *evidence-based* because science is defined operationally as a process of gathering and evaluating physical evidence in order to answer questions and make decisions. Increasingly, being able to gather and evaluate scientific evidence is a survival skill as essential as reading. As citizens, voters, and consumers, we are being asked to make more and more decisions related to science and technology. Whether about global issues such as environmental protection or about personal questions such as the value of taking vitamin supplements, such decisions must be made on evidence collected and presented to us by others. Therefore, helping all students cultivate skills in judging evidence and the ways in which it has been gathered, as well as incorporating those skills into their personal lives, is key to ensuring that our society can respond to technical issues appropriately and confidently.

Classroom science must be *materials-centered* because science itself is. Scientific investigations gather and interpret quantifiable information about the material world. Measuring physical quantities and observing external events are key skills in any scientific process, particularly in replicating tests and investigations to assess the accuracy of others' results. If students do not develop skills in using materials, they will not experience science.

Finally, our definitions tell us that students' learning experiences in science must be *inquiry-oriented*. Through inquiry, students experience the processes by which evidence is collected, tested, evaluated, and put to use. These elements of guided inquiry are keys to achieving the National Science Education Standards' goal that students experience science and scientific processes so that the students later are able to use them to make personal decisions and increase their economic productivity (NAS, 1996, p. 13).

The U.S. House of Representatives underscored science education's need for guided inquiry in its 1998 policy report, *Unlocking Our Future: Toward a New National Science Policy*. "Curricula for all elementary and secondary years that . . . emphasize the mastery of fundamental scientific . . . concepts as well as the modes of scientific inquiry, and encourage the natural curiosity of children by conveying the excitement of science . . . must be developed and implemented," the report states (Committee on Science, 1998, p. 80).

Through collaboration, and with clear understandings of purpose and the processes that students need to take with them when they leave school, educators and developers can work together to make the steady, incremental improvements that will gradually but inevitably revolutionize schooling—one modest innovation at a time.

THE TEACHER'S ROLE

Teachers—with their unique, front-line classroom experience—play a vital role in designing materials for guided inquiry. They also play the central role in implementing those materials effectively in classrooms. Because the classroom is the developers' laboratory as well as the ultimate destination for the materials that developers create, collaborations between classroom teachers and a development team must lie at the center of any good development project.

Those collaborations reflect the teacher's role in each of three processes that are fundamental in designing effective materials for guided inquiry.

First, collaborations in which teachers provide the vital links are the foundation of the process of materials design and implementation. Teachers serve as representatives of developers' primary clients—classroom-based educators—and can tell developers whether a particular activity or set of materials is likely to engage teachers, which is the first step in the creation of an effective curriculum.

Teachers also are the link between developers and students and, later, between students and the materials. Both links are essential in the living partnership we define as curriculum. To lay the essential foundation of those partnerships, it is teachers who must help developers recognize approaches, activities, and even specific phrasings of text passages that will engage learners.

Second, developers can become swept up in the novel aspects of their work. When that happens, collaborating teachers can provide them with a reality check by letting them know when and why a change is too revolutionary to succeed, then guiding them back to a more evolutionary approach that will have a greater chance of adoption by teachers.

Third, teachers' collaboration with developers can help ease the transition from a content-oriented to an operational definition of a subject. To many science and mathematics teachers, approaching a subject in operational terms instead of as a content outline remains a novel and, consequently, alien and perhaps daunting idea. By working with teachers, developers can find an evolutionary approach to what, for many educators, remains a revolutionary idea. Here again, developers should rely on working teachers as guides to the realities of contemporary classrooms, including what kinds of approaches and materials educators are and are not likely to accept. Without that guidance from teachers who know today's classrooms, any project risks failure.

CONCLUSION

The three elements forming the foundation of materials development for guided inquiry are emphasizing collaboration among specialists, making revolution through evolution, and working from operational definitions. From this chapter's discussion, it should be clear that the common thread stitching together these three elements is experience. Students learn science not by reading about it in textbooks or hearing about it in lectures but by experiencing the facts and principles of science in their own lives. Teachers are more likely to adopt and use classroom materials that capitalize on their own experiences than materials that force them to adopt approaches with which they are unfamiliar.

Therefore, materials developers need to organize their work around the elements of experience. They must design their materials to create meaningful experiences for students. They also must integrate the experience and expertise of a variety of specialists. Finally, as developers innovate, they must be careful to incorporate the best elements of existing approaches—the best of what teachers' experience has shown to work well. With these three principles firmly in mind, developers next can begin to turn their ideas into usable materials.

4

Finding and Managing Funds

The school has always been the most important means of transferring the wealth of tradition from one generation to the next.
—Albert Einstein, quoted in the *New York Times*

WE BEGIN OUR EXPLORATION of the development process with the search for project funding because the sources and kinds of financial support a project finds so often shape the organization and character of the project that results.

The process of applying for grants involves many more steps than writing a proposal. A person with an idea for a development project must first:

- Appoint a project director
- Affiliate with a host institution
- Select key team members
- Identify possible funders
- Articulate the personal goals and ambitions for the project

When a funder offers a grant, the project director (with help from team members and the host institution's staff) will need to negotiate a final budget and other details of the grant. That begins a process in which the project and director must:

- Control the project's ongoing costs
- Safeguard project funds
- Determine how to handle royalty income
- Manage funds and publicity in ways that enhance the project's image

This chapter introduces potential developers to the complexities of organizing and funding a project.

THE SOUL OF A PROJECT

When we say that the sources and kinds of financial support a project finds so often shape the organization and character of the project that results, we mean something other than that statement's most obvious interpretation. We are not suggesting—and, in fact, strenuously counsel against—the notion that developers should fashion their projects expressly to suit funding fads or trends. On the contrary, creating a project for no reason other than to win a grant is one of the quicker routes to professional burnout, personal frustration, and project failure. The reason: The members of an effective development team are driven primarily by a vision and by a sense of mission about fulfilling that vision, not by the promise of external validation or reward.

If a team compromises that vision solely to suit that of a funding agency, the team's members are offering to commit their creativity, energy, and dedication to a project in which they have less than complete interest. They abandon their driving motivation—carrying out the project that embodies their personal vision—and replace it with a different motivation: collecting a check.

In that case, once the grant check arrives, the motivation driving the project's team, and often particularly its leader, fades. All that remains is months of intense work on a project about which the project director (if not the entire team) is less than completely enthusiastic. Besides, trends can change suddenly; a team might find itself yoked to an uninteresting project when funders suddenly become willing to back just the kind of project the group wanted to pursue in the first place. When tempted to compromise, it is useful to remember the proposer's credo: The only projects you need to concern yourself with are the ones that are funded.

THE KEY TO WINNING SUPPORT

For that reason, regardless of the amount or potential sources of the grants that a developer seeks, one principle should guide the search. A developer should identify those funders that share one's personal and professional long-term goals instead of adapting one's own goals to mirror those of someone else.

For similar reasons, a development team constructing a proposal should not try to bend it to match neatly with every criterion the potential funder sets forth. By trying to fashion a project into the funder's ideal, developers risk making the proposal sound like too many competing submissions. Experienced developers trust another approach: simply to explain what the project team wants to accomplish and to show a funder how the project will help the funder achieve its own goals.

Instead of writing a proposal's text to match the funder's guidelines slavishly, a team should first decide just what it wants to accomplish through its work. After identifying those things that motivate team members, express their professional identities, and fuel their desire to undertake a particular project, the group can then identify the funding agencies whose goals most closely match their own. The team then presents those agencies with a proposal that details the project, its energizing vision, and the expertise and credentials of its team. If no funding agency seems to be a perfect match for the project, the developers can turn to those that seem at least closely suited.

For example, in 1994 SEPUP proposed its Issue-Oriented Elementary Science Leadership Project (IOESL) to be funded as part of the National Science Foundation's Teacher Enhancement Program. At the time, the program's funding guidelines offered support to projects that would provide participating teachers with at least 100 hours of in-service education. That stipulation elicited proposals from other applicants to create enhancement activities for teachers that would usually be conducted during the summer. Individual or small groups of teachers would apply on their own to attend the summer sessions. Each summer, a different group of teachers would be selected from the pool of applicants. In most cases, no relationships would be sought or established between one summer's group of attendees and another's, nor would attempts be made to establish relationships between the enhancement projects and the districts in which participating teachers worked.

In contrast, IOESL proposed to work closely with 10 districts for 3 years, offering enhancement activities each summer but also conducting leadership development seminars for summer participants in their districts during the intervening academic years.

SEPUP's proposal did not precisely match the program guidelines of the National Science Foundation (NSF) and was rejected, although with an invitation to refine the idea and submit a different version. Undeterred, the IOESL team opened discussions with NSF program officers to show them that the project's approach still accomplished the Teacher Enhancement Program's goals, although by an unusual approach. Incorporating suggestions from NSF program officers and the proposal's reviewers, SEPUP resubmitted an improved version of the proposal accompanied by letters from 10 school districts committing to participate. The project was then funded, even though it approached the funding program's goals by a route that did not strictly match the words in the program's guidelines.

A tip: Funders' goals and guidelines change, sometimes without much notice. Before beginning to draft a detailed proposal, check with targeted funders to make sure that the program the team is applying to will continue long enough to fund new applicants under the current guidelines.

THE NEED FOR OUTSIDE FUNDING

In one sense, every classroom is a materials development center. Teachers, professors, and other educators constantly conceive and test new ideas and approaches as an inherent part of their work. But as soon as an educator decides to transplant an innovation to classrooms or other research centers beyond the teacher's personal supervision and control, the need for funding becomes immediate and inescapable.

If an innovation's successes are to be replicable by others, the originating educator's insights, style, and approach must be standardized in a form that can be employed by teachers with diverse styles, experiences, and opinions. The process of making an innovation replicable means extensive design work. It entails lengthy field trials to pinpoint materials' strengths and weaknesses. Then the materials must be redesigned to eliminate flaws, enhance strengths, and ensure that the materials work with equal effectiveness in different school settings and cultures. In most cases, assessment schemes must be designed and tested. Teachers adopting the innovations need initial training and ongoing technical support. These steps demand months, and sometimes years, of work by specialists in content, in educational psychology, in graphic design, and, of course, in the realities of the classroom. Therefore, if an innovation is going to move beyond an innovative teacher's immediate circle of contacts, its journey must be fueled by money.

The need for funding is exacerbated by free-market forces that shape the American process of adopting educational materials. In the United States, adopting and purchasing educational materials is a local affair. Even when adoption decisions are made at the state level, state agencies often approve more than one set of materials for a particular subject. It then is up to individual districts and schools to select the ones they want to use in their courses.

To compete in that arena, a set of materials must offer evidence to potential buyers that it can help them achieve their educational goals more effectively and efficiently than another package. Developing that evidence involves detailed design of the materials, classroom trials, detailed evaluations, and then data-based refinements—all before the materials can reach the market. An extensive, and therefore costly, development process becomes a necessity if the materials a project develops are going to be used by more than a handful of educators.

SOURCES AND KINDS OF SUPPORT

Most development projects will be funded through one, or a combination, of three sources: government agencies, private and corporate philanthropies, or colleges and universities.

Government Agencies

Many, if not most, materials development projects will find opportunities for support among federal agencies and their state equivalents. The National Endowment for the Arts and the National Endowment for the Humanities have made funds available for materials development projects for public schools. Developers in science and mathematics can and should make early contact with the National Science Foundation.

However, large agencies do more than respond to individual proposals. During the 1990s, for example, the NSF began to sponsor a series of "systemic initiatives" granting money to state and local education agencies to test and demonstrate novel approaches to restructuring science and mathematics education. Under the projects, educators conduct classroom research to identify key barriers keeping them from implementing or achieving the new national standards being promulgated in science and mathematics education. They then work with developers to create, adopt, or adapt inquiry-based, activities-centered materials designed to dismantle those barriers.

The projects also enable educators to evaluate the new materials, and perhaps help developers to refine and improve them, before their districts make the investment necessary to adopt the materials in a larger number of schools. These collaborations can also yield new ideas for additional development projects in which classroom teachers and school district staff members can play key roles.

In 1998, the NSF expanded its criteria in judging proposals for teacher enhancement and professional development grants. It created a new category of project, called "local systemic change" projects, which has given more power and discretion to the school systems proposing the projects. In the past, most such NSF support went to university-based projects designed to improve teachers' competence. This initiative has underwritten projects to reform and restructure science and mathematics education systemwide that are based in, and led by, school systems. The program promotes local efforts to implement national standards while broadening the market for materials in guided inquiry designed to help educators achieve that goal.

Some federal funding programs supporting materials development are administered by states. Among the largest is the Dwight D. Eisenhower

Professional Development Program, which deputizes state education agencies to give federal money directly to school districts. The funds are apportioned among states according to their numbers of public school students. Then the money is awarded competitively to districts based on their individual proposals outlining the ways in which the funds will be used to improve science and mathematics education.

Although the money typically underwrites teachers' professional development, a district plan to adapt and test innovative materials can be funded as part of a carefully crafted proposal. In the year 2000, federal funds allotted under Title I of the Elementary and Secondary Education Act (1965)—also administered by states—became eligible for use in improving science education, creating opportunities for developers to work more closely with disadvantaged schools and districts.

Private and Corporate Philanthropies

A few private philanthropies, such as the Sloan Foundation and the Pew Charitable Trusts, contribute millions of dollars each year to various development projects for public education. But only a small portion of these grants is earmarked for materials development programs in science and mathematics education. Projects that are funded in those fields tend to concentrate on research in areas of special interest to the donor.

However, individual teachers and their districts have alternatives to competing among the thousands of applicants that besiege the largest foundations and government funders every year. Most states have more than a few private donors that support innovation in public schools. In tiny New Hampshire, for example, the Walker Foundation gives dozens of grants each year, averaging more than $5,000 each, to support initiatives in science, technology, and mathematics in all precollege grades. Directories listing granting agencies can be found in the reference section of any moderate-sized library or by contacting The Foundation Center in New York City. Rosters of small state or regional donors can often be obtained from a state government library or the office of a state's secretary of state.

Many large corporations, as well as industry trade groups and consortia, have established their own philanthropies. Corporate donors usually give money for educational efforts in the communities in which they are located or do a significant amount of business; industry groups tend to focus on projects in content areas of practical importance to them. While most corporate funders do not emphasize materials development in their portfolios of gifts, a few do. GTE's Growth Initiatives for Teachers, or GIFT, grant program underwrites public school science and mathematics teachers working in pairs to create materials and methods to integrate their subjects. The company's nonprofit foundation also sometimes pays teachers' expenses to attend conferences and workshops on innovative materials. The Exxon Chemical Company and the Exxon Education Foundation (both now part of Exxon-Mobil) have provided more than 10 years of steady support for the continuing development and dissemination of SEPUP's "Chemicals, Health, Environment, and Me" materials for elementary grades (SEPUP, 1997). The program's original development was supported by the Chevron Chemical Company.

Only a few of the largest private and corporate donors provide enough support to sustain a major materials development project over its life. However, smaller grants—even just a few thousand dollars—are often enough to develop and demonstrate a concept that can then attract support from a larger funder or a greater number of funders. SEPUP, organized in 1983, operated as a small project within California, supported by industry gifts totaling less than $100,000 a year, before receiving its first NSF grant in 1987. Today, SEPUP works with tens of thousands of teachers on four continents.

Colleges and Universities

Most large-scale materials development projects in science and mathematics education have been funded by the NSF. The NSF, in turn, has given most of those grants to projects based at colleges and universities. (The NSF also regularly funds development at a few private, nonprofit development centers such as the Education Development Center [EDC], TERC, and the Biological Sciences Curriculum Study [BSCS]. However, these organizations usually work extensively with post-secondary institutions and staff their projects with the institutions' faculty members.)

Partly because of the new national emphasis on educational change and professional improvement, colleges and universities are seeing a new value in materials development projects. Some even count faculty members' work on such projects as part of their professional portfolios to be considered in deciding promotion and tenure. Even in institutions that base promotion and tenure primarily on more conventional publications and research studies, work on materials development projects still can provide excellent raw material for professional papers.

Developers based at post-secondary institutions sometimes can find most, if not all, of the backing their projects need to get underway by looking to colleagues and offices within their institutions (including on-staff grant writers). For example, public relations executive Nancy Kreinberg was hired in the 1970s by the Lawrence Hall of Science, a public outreach and education agency of the University of California at Berkeley. Her assigned task was to promote the hall's programs and services to area residents. In the course of her work, Kreinberg and her colleagues noted the small numbers of girls taking part in after-school children's programs at the hall. To help remedy the lack, the group developed a course called "Math for Girls" (Downie, Slesnick, & Stenmark, 1981). This small beginning grew from the sincere desire of a few individuals to do something that mattered to them. Their persistence gradually attracted additional funding from the university as well as from outside sources. With that support, the program evolved into what is now Equals, an internationally recognized awareness and development program dedicated to creating educational materials designed to improve science and mathematics achievement for girls and other less-advantaged groups. This major materials and teacher development project was seeded by encouragement and a small stipend from one office of a single university.

PARTNERSHIPS BETWEEN SCHOOLS AND UNIVERSITIES

Partnership with a post-secondary institution raises a project's stature in the eyes of many potential funders. Consequently, colleges and universities are likely to be a school's or district's best partners in the search for funds to support development projects. (Most of those institutions also have grants and contracts offices ready to assist faculty members in obtaining grants.) Between a university and a public school, a developer will find most of the expertise a project needs to be meaningful. The practical wisdom of teachers regarding the needs and realities of the classroom can be combined with the expertise of subject specialists, educational psychologists, assessment experts, and even university graphics and publications staffers. With increasing frequency, granting agencies are channeling support to development projects that demonstrate just this kind of collaboration because these are the kinds of projects that have shown a greater likelihood of creating materials that are consistently effective.

CONTRACTS VERSUS GRANTS

Applying for grants is not the only way to fund a development project. Developers sometimes enter into contracts to conduct a specific program of work for a donor or a commercial publisher. Under a contract, a developer carries out a project designed by another party, usually the organization funding the work. Upon signing the contract, the developer accepts responsibility for meeting the goals, objectives, and deadlines stated in the contract. But contractual arrangements almost always allow far less freedom, flexibility, and personal expression than a developer would have under a grant.

Some funders will support materials development projects only through contractual agreements. In those cases, a developer needs professional and legal advice to determine what the proposed contract would obligate the developer to do and be responsible for—especially if the project in question is unsuccessful, or at least less successful than the agency commissioning the project had expected. Contractual agreements are best reserved for detailing the arrangement between a developer and publisher or production company to make materials commercially available after they have been developed, not for the necessarily fluid and creative process of materials development itself.

POOLING FUNDS

A tip: All of a project's funding need not come from a single source, as BSCS showed in developing its "Science for Life and Living" course for elementary students. The program secured funding from four Colorado foundations to create a middle school course called "Making Healthy Decisions." Later, IBM's education division underwrote the cost of a BSCS design study to begin to shape an elementary course that would combine science and technology.

While the study was underway, the NSF requested proposals from projects interested in developing new elementary level science materials. Because the BSCS team wanted to combine science and technology with health education, they were able to use part of IBM's funds to design such a curriculum. The group then persuaded the state foundations to pool some of the money earmarked for "Making Healthy Decisions" with an NSF grant to enable them to create a new elementary-grade science and health course. "That way, everyone got more results for their money," says project director Nancy Landes.

As with the four Colorado foundations supporting the BSCS effort, an agency might want to underwrite a project even though the project's total budget exceeds the agency's grant limit. If a donor is able or willing to finance only a portion of a project's work, that commitment can sometimes attract the interest of other potential donors. Indeed, the first agency may work to call the attention of other agencies to the project. There is a psychological advantage at work here as well: Funding agencies, like venture capitalists, often find a project more attractive if another backer has already made a commitment to it.

PROPOSAL GUIDELINES

Developers can easily find dozens of books showing how to draft effective proposals and grant applications (see, e.g., New & Quick, 1998). We will not reprise that good advice here. Instead, we merely offer five practical tips, hard-won through experience, that will give any project proposal an advantage over competitors who fail to heed them.

First, *explain in detail how a project will measure what students have learned as a result of using the materials the project will develop.* For projects creating materials for guided inquiry, assessment methods have become as important to a project's viability (and therefore its prospects for funding) as any other facet of the project. Increasingly, funders expect to see projects addressing and enacting the new, process-based assessment standards and structures that organizations such as the NSF, the National Council of Teachers of Mathematics (1995), and the National Science Teachers Association advocate (Doran, Chan, & Tamir, 1998; Olson & Loucks-Horsley, 2000). Funders also know that standard quick-answer exams and similar assessment methods are limited in their ability to accurately measure the development of process skills. But rubrics, portfolios, and other new forms of assessment designed to gauge such skills have yet to resolve enough of their initial problems to be accepted by the larger educational community as practical and valid.

This state of flux represents an opportunity as well as a caution to developers. The caution: The current national emphasis on (or obsession with) increased scores on standardized tests means that, to be widely adopted, a development project's materials must produce positive results on assessment measures that the developers did not create and cannot control. The opportunity: This state of flux gives developers the chance to investigate new, more useful approaches to gauging students' learning, including those more closely tailored to work with the materials they are designing. However, increased concern about assessment also leaves a project proposal vulnerable to criticism and easier rejection if this suddenly more complex issue of assessment is not deftly and thoroughly addressed. (For details of one promising approach to assessment in guided inquiry, see Chapter 8.)

Second, *enlist support for a proposal from potential team members and others before the proposal is submitted.* Possible partners even can be recruited to help design the project and draft the proposal itself. Involving a spectrum of experts in a project's design improves not only its chances for success but also its prospects for funding.

In negotiating a project's terms, funders often seek reassurance by asking for letters of commitment from potential project team members and others whom the project will call upon for various kinds of support. For example, letters from school systems committing to take part in a development project's initial tests and field trials can help persuade funders that teachers themselves see a compelling need for the project being proposed.

Written offers of help, advice, and participation from well-credentialed experts in various fields add weight to that argument and reassure funders that a proposed project has already laid the foundation of diverse expertise that it will need to succeed. It is far easier to obtain those letters from people who are already part of the project's planning effort than to introduce the project to them and ask them to commit to it on short notice after the project has already been structured.

Third, *remember that every donor has a specific mission*. Some donors might want to see better computer software for classrooms; others may seek to expand professional development opportunities for teachers. It is not enough to match a development project with a funding agency that has supported other development projects in the past. A developer must show the funder specifically how and why a proposed project will help the funder fulfill its own mission and agenda.

However, funders' agendas can sometimes collide with the integrity of a project. Not infrequently, donors—especially those from the private sector—specify that their gifts are to be used to promote a technology, an industry, or a point of view. Those agendas may coincide nicely with that of a project; for example, both Apple and IBM have underwritten software development and computer installations for education, projects that directly enhance the professional goals of many developers and most educators. But the match between the purposes of donor and project are not always so neat.

As the Australian Consumers' Association has wisely warned in a study it completed for the International Association of Consumer Unions:

> Students could stand in jeopardy if a clear separation is not made in curriculum materials . . . between content that adheres to strict pedagogical principles and content that is overtly or covertly ideological or public-relations motivated. . . . Any organization promoting a program would need to . . . be independent from industry, government, and interest/pressure groups and to have academic credibility and respect. The CEPUP (now SEPUP) program was seen as a good model in that it attracted money from both government and industry but maintained its independence through its advisory board and its academic credibility through its sponsoring body, the University of California. (Isles, 1989)

In taking those precautions, a project needs to set internal guidelines for the acceptance of funds before it solicits them. For example, in 1983 SEPUP set out to introduce issue-oriented science activities in schools. Because the project's goal was to foster students' abilities to gather and weigh evidence and then draw their own conclusions from that evidence, the materials the project created were designed carefully to advocate no particular decision or point of view about the issues presented. As a result, SEPUP established a policy to accept only funds that carried no restrictions on the project's resulting materials. The policy not only preserved the project's integrity but also encouraged interest from potential funders that might have turned away from the project had SEPUP let funders decide its content.

Fourth, *the most effective proposals contain an added urgency.* They not only offer a way to improve student achievement or help a funding agency to achieve its own goals. The most compelling proposals place their projects in a larger context: that by funding the proposed project, the donor gives crucial support to a pressing, broader mission as well.

For example, a proposal could say that the eighth-grade science course at the Jones Middle School is based on an outdated textbook and that the teachers would like funds to design and test a new, laboratory-centered curriculum. A better proposal would offer research results (e.g., Ryand, 1996) showing that students retain 5 to 10 percent of what they learn through reading textbooks and listening to lectures, but that they retain 70 percent or more of what they experience directly through activity. The proposal would go on to argue (if convincing evidence is available) that a new lab-centered course would be educationally more effective while also embracing the goals of the National Science Education Standards (NAS, 1996).

A proposal couches itself in just such a larger, more urgent context if it explains how the guided-inquiry materials that it will develop can help students and teachers meet portions of national standards, such as those for science and mathematics education. Highlighting that context can often make the difference between a merely good proposal and one that is too compelling to be refused.

The fifth and final suggestion is purely tactical and can make the difference between a proposal's failure and success: *Give a funder no obvious reason to say no.* In addition to building a positive case for a project, a proposal must contain nothing that will encourage an agency to reject it.

A donor routinely receives proposals that collectively ask for thousands of times the amount the donor can give. As a result, when the time comes for donors to decide which proposals to fund, the people making those decisions always have too many solicitations to read and too little time to consider each one fully. Frequently, overburdened reviewers look for ways to quickly weed out as many proposals as they can.

Reasons for donors to say no to a proposal can be as arbitrary as they are numerous: A proposal does not follow the outline order that the funder's guidelines specify; a proposal asks for more money than the funder customarily gives to a single project; the proposal has more pages than its readers have time to get through, so the readers never quite get around to reading it. The reasons also can lie in details. "The proposer should realize that the proposal will be considered as a model of the materials to be produced," notes Gerhard Salinger, an NSF program officer (personal communication, May 2000). "If the proposal is filled with typographical errors and bad grammar, it is probable that the materials will have similar problems." By eliminating those reasons, a proposal survives the first (and largest) cut and wins a chance to be considered in more depth.

NEGOTIATING THE PROJECT'S BUDGET AND TERMS

The NSF never and other funders rarely approve a project's grant application without subjecting it to close and lengthy review. Most are scrutinized by the funding agency's program officers and by independent peer reviewers who advise the agency. This close examination usually yields a series of questions about the project's design, goals, methods, and budget. In questioning the proposal's details, grantors are not trying to belittle the project or to find a way to reject it; quite the contrary. They are probing a promising idea for possible weaknesses that can be identified and rectified before those weaknesses cost a project time and money in mistakes.

As funders probe, typically they will suggest that a project alter its approaches, structures, or objectives (or all three) to more closely match the goals, policies, and experience of the funding agency. Those questions and suggestions are the opening gambit in a series of conversations that can determine in significant ways the character and accomplishments of the project that results. (For examples of specific questions that NSF program officers posed to one project, see the appendix to this chapter.)

When a suitable match is made and a grant is offered, the grantor and grantee will negotiate a final budget. The odds are great that a funder will not be urging a project to accept more money than the project team asked for. Usually, as a result of peer reviewers' questions and critiques or because of budget constraints, the funding agency will ask the team to pare down the amount of money requested. "The NSF had a specific figure in mind and, as a result, we had to negotiate away the comprehensive evaluation of our project that we'd planned," one project director recalls. "On the other hand, we were able to get lower special prices with airlines and travel agents than we expected. So we were able to add those savings back into other parts of the project's budget." However, it is poor strategy to submit an inflated budget padded with extra dollars to be negotiated away later. Padded budgets are obvious to seasoned program officers and peer reviewers and the stratagem may backfire, blighting the proposal's chances.

Part of the budget discussions will involve determining the share of the grant that a host institution can claim as "indirect costs"—a catchall category that reimburses the institution for office space, lights, clerical and administrative services, and other overhead expenses incurred in providing a home for the project. Universities' indirect-cost rates may be as high as 80 percent of a project's direct costs, while school districts may charge no more than 10 or 20 percent. As a result, a project's choice of a host institution can make a considerable impact on its budget and, therefore, perhaps on its ultimate success.

A federal funding agency negotiates indirect-cost rates with each host institution. (The rate depends on the kind of work the grant recipient will do.) All federal agencies then use the same indirect-cost rate when dealing with that institution. Private grantors may mandate fixed rates of indirect costs, also depending on the nature of the work to be done. However, regardless of the funding source, a project can always attempt to negotiate a more favorable rate for itself with its host institution—in effect, asking the host to make a grant of some overhead costs to the project.

There are ways other than direct negotiations to reduce the bite that indirect costs take out of a budget. A project director might consider naming as co-director a colleague at an institution that qualifies for a lower indirect-cost rate and housing a portion of the project there. Alternatively, a university-based project can often cut its indirect expenses by subcontracting parts of its work to school districts. Indirect-cost rates for subcontracted work are based largely on the rate fixed for institutions doing the work, not on the rate charged by the host; so the more work that a university-based project can subcontract to school districts, the more indirect costs a project may save. The operative word here is *may*: Although school districts usually charge a project less for indirect costs, they will often bill for specific expenses that universities include as part of the general overhead fee they receive from a project.

Decisions to subcontract portions of a project should be made only after detailed negotiations with subcontractors have clarified the full range of the subcontractors' projected fees and charges. Sharing work and responsibilities can benefit a project financially—especially if the project must undertake economies to secure funding—but the project team must give at least equal consideration to the impact such decisions are likely to have on the quality of the project's work.

If the grantor insists on offering less than the development team sought, the shortfall can be addressed in one (or a combination) of three ways. A project can find supplementary funds from other sources, scale back its scope, or argue its case.

If the offer forces essential changes in the project's nature, the project's plan and budget should be revised accordingly and a copy sent to the funding agency so that its officers clearly see the effect of their stipulations. If a funding agency is made to understand the impact the requested budget reductions will have on a project, there is a better chance that the agency will relent and award an amount closer to the budget the project team originally proposed.

A useful approach is to determine the reduction's impact on aspects of the project that the funding agency particularly values. The project can then emphasize the reduction's consequences for that aspect of the project. For example, if the funding agency considers teachers' participation in materials development and field testing of new materials to be a key factor in a project's success, developers could show the agency the ways in which the proposed cuts would slash the number of participating teachers and test sites.

In any case, developers will be obligated to live up to, or within, whatever terms they agree to during this phase of the negotiations.

For that reason, and because no one person can always divine every implication of a suggested budgetary change, it is never prudent to negotiate budget and terms with funders by oneself. A project director must discuss all possible changes, financial and otherwise, with project partners and as required with relevant academic, legal, and financial specialists at the project's host institution. Even if the funder will negotiate only with the project's director (as the NSF insists on doing), the director is still free to solicit advice, opinions, and guidance from anyone whose ideas may be valuable. It is always permissible for a project director to tell a funding agency's representative that he or she is ethically and legally obligated to consult with the host institution and other team members before committing them to the altered terms or conditions.

This often protracted (and sometimes unnerving) process of give-and-take will almost inevitably change in some way the project's structure, aims, or both—changes that will become conditions of the award. A project team might be asked to shift the emphasis of its materials from one aspect of a subject to another, to revise its assessment scheme, or to scale back the range or number of materials it plans to create. Occasionally, a team is asked to make concessions that fundamentally alter the nature of the proposed project. Such requests may threaten to turn the project into something that is not what the team is eager to do. In such cases, the wisest course in the long run is to thank the funding agency and look elsewhere. (Remember the maxim that the only projects that you need to be concerned with are those that are funded.)

ESTABLISHING FINANCIAL DISCIPLINE

A funding agency, as well as a host institution, will expect a project director to take responsibility for maintaining a project's financial discipline. Exercising financial discipline is somewhat different from financial management. Usually a host institution will handle a project's bookkeeping. The director's fiscal task, aside from detailed budgeting, is largely a matter of ensuring various forms of compliance.

Among other tasks, the director must make sure that the money is used in the ways the funder expects it to be as specified in the proposal. The director must also ensure that the funds are allotted in ways that maximize the value of every dollar. In addition, it is up to the project director to make sure that the host institution establishes a separate financial account for project funds and that the money cannot be spent without the project director's written approval. While a director need not be a financial expert, he or she must be firm in these and similar matters of financial oversight.

CONTROLLING COSTS

The director must make sure that the project—particularly through the enthusiasm of its staff—does not commit resources that belong to the host organization for purposes of the project unless the host organization gives explicit permission. That can be a difficult line to draw. For example, a project based in a school district may "borrow" a computer, teachers' time, or some extra space in a building to meet a sudden need that is either unexpected or not provided for in the project budget. Unless these uses are explicitly cleared with the host organization before they are made, the host could later allege a violation of procedure or present a bill for services. In extreme cases, a host could withdraw its sponsorship and literally put a project out in the street. Grantors routinely permit project budgets to include reimbursement to the hosting institution for actual costs, such as renting or leasing special equipment from the institution, but these items and their costs should be specified in the project budget and approved by the granting agency when the project is funded.

However, educators know that sound discipline tempers enforcement with judgment. A host institution might lobby to use a portion of the project's grant for other ventures that it sees as related or "complementary" to the project. Occasionally, project staffers may argue for new initiatives within the project that would divert funds from the programs and goals specified in the funding agreement. It is not the director's duty to refuse all such pressures any more than it is to indulge them.

In these cases, the director's task is to evaluate the merit of new ideas against the project's goals, plan, and budget and to decide whether the suggested changes advance the project's purpose. It is the director's responsibility to make sure that any reallocation of a project's funds is not done for political reasons—to assuage, or curry favor with, the person or group suggesting the alteration. The only justification for financial redirection is that the change advances the project's goals and results. It is the director who is ultimately answerable to funders and the host for a project's financial decisions.

FINANCIAL SAFEGUARDS

For reasons such as these, a project's design must include a system of financial safeguards. Indeed, the director will probably be asked to detail these safeguards as part of the proposal. The first safeguard is a written budget, which also serves as the project's promise to spend grant funds more or less exactly as it has proposed. In addition to a written budget, safeguards should include policies for dealing with costs that might be more difficult to forecast, such as payments to consultants, expenses incurred by field test centers, and unexpected but necessary travel. Inevitably, small expenditures arise, such as the sudden need to buy materials while visiting a field test center in order to modify an activity in trials. It is prudent financial strategy to anticipate the possible need for such expenses and include contingency funds to cover them in the project budget. (They can usually be allocated under budget categories that the granting agency and host institution will accept as legitimate.)

Otherwise, a project might face the later prospect of having to "borrow" money (with little hope of repaying it) from other vital areas of the project or approach the funder to ask for a supplemental allotment or to justify a reconfigured budget. Putting strong, clearly stated policies on handling expenses, including unanticipated costs, in the proposal can protect a director later from having others criticize or second-guess project decisions.

In establishing financial safeguards, a project's host institution can usually help. Most institutions will already have detailed guidelines and policies for dealing with costs, especially if the institution is accustomed to administering grants and contracts. If the host has little or no experience in dealing with grant funds, the project director will need to foster conversations between the granting agency and the host institution's administrators. Such conversations will be necessary to ensure that those handling the funds understand both the letter and the spirit of the granting agency's rules. A less experienced project director can also seek advice from seasoned directors and from executives at the project's host institution.

RESPONSIBILITY AND REPUTATION

Beyond the obvious ones, there is another good reason to manage project funds meticulously: The project's director and staff should project a positive public image of their project and of their own fiscal responsibility. The guiding rule in protecting that image, and one's own professional reputation, is caution in all things.

As a very real example, consider a common circumstance: During an education convention, a development project sponsors a reception at the hotel to introduce itself and its materials to potential purchasers. Because the reception has a commercial motive, the project's materials manufacturer or distributor might pay its costs, but usually the project director negotiates the arrangements and terms with the hotel. As a way to thank the director for the business, the hotel might upgrade the director's accommodation to a deluxe room, or even a suite, at no extra charge. It is not unusual in such cases for project directors to boast of "living in luxury," creating an impression that the director is squandering grant money—and, indirectly, perhaps our tax dollars. It is no more difficult than that to damage one's reputation as a project director or grant manager. People watch everything that a director does, so taking steps to protect one's professional reputation is to protect one's future.

MANAGING PROJECT INCOME

Successful materials development projects earn income primarily through royalties from the sale of the materials the project creates. Strange as it seems, most foundations and private funders, and even the NSF, have no policies controlling what a project does with that income.

Over the years, the NSF has tested a variety of policies governing ownership and disposition of royalty income earned by the development projects it funds. At one time, the NSF ruled that all royalties were to be returned to the U.S. Treasury as income to the government (Merrill & Ridgway, 1969). Later, the NSF allowed projects to use royalties to sustain themselves or expand their impact during the life of the grant. But at the end of the grant period, the materials became part of the public domain and anyone had the right to revise them as they saw fit (Eakin & Karplus, 1976).

Now the NSF has come to believe that the best way to extend and prolong the dissemination and useful life of the materials its grants have helped to create is to leave all decisions about royalty income to projects and their host institutions. As a result, royalty income can be returned to the project to support ongoing development, shared among project staff, or simply pocketed by the people who created the project.

However, a project team cannot mirror funders' laissez-faire attitudes toward earnings. It needs to know exactly what it will do with any income—and preferably will decide while it is still drafting its funding proposal.

Money has powerful legal, as well as symbolic, significance. The question of income distribution touches on issues of intellectual property rights, the value of an individual's work, and how a project is perceived by colleagues, participants, and potential funders. The way a project answers the question of income distribution can affect the project staff's morale and commitment, influence the decision of key people on whether to become associated with the project, and color the atmosphere surrounding a project. Although it may seem odd to plan what to do with royalty income even before a project has been funded, it is essential to resolve these issues as early as possible.

POLICIES GOVERNING ROYALTIES

Ongoing development programs such as the BSCS and EDC have been dealing with the issue of royalty income for years throughout an array of projects and grants. Their experiences, as well as those of other large development centers, have led many developers to create similar policies governing all royalty income that have worked well enough to recommend them to others.

Many continuing development programs deposit all royalty income from materials sales into a common account, segregated from others of the host institution, over which the program has control. The money in the account is dedicated to underwriting the continuation and improvement of all of the program's projects—especially teacher enhancement activities, such as paying the fees and expenses of teachers attending project-sponsored summer conferences not specified in the budgets of individual grants. That kind of stewardship demonstrates a program's unequivocal commitment to its projects and particularly to professional and leadership development among teachers who participate in the program's projects. Such dedicated funds let a program meet a range of expenses that are not specified in proposals or grant budgets but that strengthen its projects.

An explicit policy on the distribution of royalty income not only pleases proposal reviewers but also prevents false expectations or money-centered contention among project participants. For example, as the SEPUP program was creating its year-long "Science and Sustainability" course for high school students, the project team negotiated an agreement with the superintendent's office of Brooklyn, New York's high school district enabling willing science teachers and curriculum administrators to become co-developers of the course. The district supported the costs of selected individuals to come to SEPUP's California headquarters to work with the staff; SEPUP tapped its fund of royalty income to underwrite staff members' travel and work sessions in Brooklyn. SEPUP's stated policy made it clear from the beginning that royalty income would be used to fund future enhancement activities for those teachers and their colleagues under the program and that no individuals would receive cash payments from royalties. Teachers joined the project out of a genuine interest in it, not with the ulterior hope of personal gain.

What happens to royalty income after a grant ends is a more intricate calculation. If the project team disbands when the grant period ends, that does not necessarily mean that the project's work is done. If its materials are to continue to be used, competitive pressures dictate that the materials will need to be revised and updated at least every 5 years—perhaps in fundamental ways if, during the intervening time, major changes have taken place within the subject area. (The 1996 publication of the National Science Education Standards sent many developers back to their figurative drawing boards to redesign activities or entire programs.) If the project team is no longer together, or if royalty income has been divided among members, who is to pay for revisions? What are the obligations of the person or agency holding copyright in the materials?

The safest and most practical forum in which to specify how these issues are to be handled—and funded—is in the project proposal itself. (Also, see Chapters 6 and 10 for more detailed discussions of the contractual obligations between a project and its publisher or materials producer.) Decisions about the distribution of royalties and the management of project income will, in significant part, shape educators' perceptions of the project and the motivation of its developers.

A WORD ABOUT PUBLICITY

Flushed with excitement because its project has been funded, a development team will be tempted to trumpet the project's objectives and expected accomplishments to colleagues and to educators generally. It is wise to resist the temptation. Like declaring at 45 that you will celebrate your 50th birthday by running the Boston Marathon, early announcement makes the team and its project the object of attention. But it also establishes certain expectations for a project that can bring unwelcome pressures over time.

People outside the project will often ask for details and progress reports, offer advice, and otherwise take up the team's time in ways that do not advance the work of the project. Also, if the project evolves or changes as it goes along (or, as is so often the case, encounters unexpected difficulties), the team could face the embarrassing prospect of having to just as publicly announce midcourse corrections.

We do not counsel against all publicity at this early stage. Announcing that the project has been funded, describing what the project hopes to accomplish, and inviting the interest and participation of colleagues and educators can be useful as the project is being organized. In addition, publishing a regular newsletter about the project and establishing and maintaining a project website can help a team to maintain ongoing interest—among potential additional funders as well as educators—in the work as it progresses.

But too often project teams are seduced by the impulse to tout goals as if those goals had already been accomplished simply because a grant has been awarded—even though no materials have yet been created, much less used by students. Although less satisfying, it is more useful and prudent in the long run to postpone extensive publicity until a project has collected data indicating that it has a chance of achieving its objectives.

CONCLUSION

Securing and managing money, as well as coping with the legal obligations it entails, are probably the aspects of a project with which educators and potential developers are the least familiar. The process involves appointing a project director, affiliating with a host institution, selecting key team members, identifying possible funders, preparing an effective proposal, negotiating budgets and terms with funders, controlling the project's ongoing costs, safeguarding project funds, determining how to handle royalty income, and managing funds and publicity in ways that protect and enhance the project's image.

This chapter's discussion is only a brief introduction to the complexities of each of these steps. It is not meant to be a complete set of instructions. Even experienced project directors must work closely with funders, host institution officials, team members, and others involved to check decisions, procedures, and other details.

APPENDIX
SAMPLE LIST OF FUNDER'S QUESTIONS
AND PROJECT'S REPLIES

In 1997, the SEPUP submitted a grant proposal to the NSF to update SEPUP's 13 classroom activity modules to more closely embody the content and assessment criteria of the National Science Education Standards. Before committing to the project, the NSF posed several questions. Selected questions and SEPUP's responses are shown below. Partly as a result of the answers to these questions, SEPUP was awarded the grant.

Q: What opportunities are there for grouping modules to obtain more effective treatment of specific concepts?

A: In consultation with users, we will analyze each module for the concepts and processes introduced, and [also analyze] relationships between these concepts and processes and the National Science Education Standards (NSES) at the appropriate grade levels. We will then suggest various grouping of modules to help accomplish NSES content and other standards.

Q: How will the assessments emphasize concept development?

A: Our plan is to develop an assessment system for the modules that combines easy-to-score content and performance item banks with embedded, authentic assessment tasks that measure growing student knowledge and understanding regarding the identified SEPUP variables and their related coverage in the NSES. Based on, but somewhat different from, the [assessment system for a previously developed SEPUP year-long course], the emphasis here will be on showing what students learn as a result of their experiences with each module and how the use of groupings of modules will lead to further knowledge and understanding of major concepts and processes. We will also design assessment items that measure student ability to apply what they are learning to real societal issues regarding science.

Q: Do you need to revise all 13 modules? What mechanisms will you use to get input from the user community on what's really needed?

A: Discussions with users prior to preparing the proposal, and our own analysis of the current modules, indicates that it will be necessary and valuable to make some changes in all modules. At a minimum, we want to clearly show each module's relationship to the NSES, how the combination of modules can be used to more effectively and completely accomplish instructional objectives, and any necessary updating of examples used of societal issues and applications of the concepts introduced. In addition, user feedback already obtained, and our experience with [previously developed SEPUP courses], indicates more effective and interesting ways of accomplishing some objectives. We expect additional feedback to be gathered during the project to suggest additional modifications. In cooperation with Lab-Aids [SEPUP's commercial partner], we will review and modify as necessary the equipment and materials used in each module to reflect what we have learned from user feedback and our own continuing efforts to improve all materials.

Q: Will the changes make the old modules totally obsolete? Will people need to buy updates? Are there any low-cost solutions to this question?

A: With the possible exception of one or two modules, the changes will not make the current modules totally obsolete. We expect that the revised modules will provide the users with more effective experiences to help accomplish the overall goals of SEPUP and the NSES.

In most cases, users of the existing modules might need to obtain a new teachers guide and order either a limited number of replacement items or a cost-effective upgrade kit. We expect to continue our policy of providing in the teachers guide specific instructions for preparing or obtaining all consumable materials locally. Some users find this highly cost effective, while others (especially major users) find purchasing materials in bulk from [national supply houses] highly cost effective. Individual items are also available for replacement.

In short, it will be possible in almost all cases to purchase the revised teachers guides (including student pages) and then to upgrade the equipment and materials locally.

5

Putting Together the Project Team

The most important motive for work in school and in life is pleasure in work, pleasure in its result, and the knowledge of the value of the result to the community.

—Albert Einstein, *Ideas and Opinions*

A DEVELOPMENT PROJECT, whether in materials or any other field, is an engine fueled by people—their imaginations, their ingenuity, their devotion, and their personal skills. After a project has been funded and financial safeguards set in place, its first priority is to bring together the team of individuals that will transform the proposed project into a living, working reality. This crucial first phase of a project involves:

- Identifying the project director and clarifying the director's roles and tasks
- Determining the scope of work, timeline, and milestones to be achieved during the project's first year
- Selecting the members of the project team
- Clearly articulating the project's vision and goals

Each of these areas is discussed in detail in this chapter.

THE PROJECT DIRECTOR'S IDENTITY AND ROLES

In some large, ongoing development programs such as the Biological Sciences Curriculum Study, one person or group may conceive the ideas for individual projects, others may write the grant proposals, and funded projects may hire yet other people to manage them. This is not the usual case, however. Typically, the same person who conceives the project writes (or at least helps to write) the grant proposal and ultimately serves as the project's director. For simplicity's sake, and because that is so often what happens, we will assume that the person who conceives and develops the project idea is entitled to first consideration as its director.

We use the words *first consideration* because an imaginative scientist or educator is not always the best choice to lead a development project, just as a brilliant inventor may not be the best person to manage the corporation that develops around the product that the inventor created. Indeed, from an administrative viewpoint, effective project management and effective management of a small business require most of the same abilities; a funded project is, in several aspects, a business venture and must be managed as such. But because a project becomes a director's "baby," in addition to intellectual skills a good project director also exhibits several of the personal traits of a good parent: a director gets out of bed every morning thinking about the welfare of the project and stands ready to champion the project to those who threaten or are skeptical of it. The director knows when, and how, to say yes and no to project team members and outsiders (and, at times, to him-herself) who offer help, advice, or new ideas and also has clear, measurable goals in mind by which to gauge the project's progress.

In addition, a good candidate to direct a project will know from experience the realities of the classroom and, ideally, will have held an administrative post as well (although having managed a classroom may well be administrative experience enough). Not all scientists or educators possess the ideal background to become a project director. Fortunately, both usually make excellent learners, and it is possible for most to cultivate the skills needed to nurture a project to success (see, e.g., Gardner & Laskin, 1995; Monk, 1993).

These disparate skills are reflected in the two distinct roles that a project director fills: administrator and development team member. As an administrator, the director is the boss, the person with the personal and institutional authority to direct the work of others and make ultimate decisions on the project's behalf. At the same time, the director is one of many people on the development team. As such, the director needs to be able to accept criticism of his or her own ideas and genuinely believe that ideas from others can be better.

The distinction between those two roles also needs to be made clear to team members: the director is fiscally and professionally responsible to others for the project's outcome and, therefore, holds the authority to make final decisions. But when the group is working together to design materials, the boss disappears. At those times, the director is a colleague and coequal whose ideas carry no more heft than those of any other team member. More importantly than just communicating the nature of the dual role to other team members, the director must live it, switching as necessary between the two roles as tasks change during the course of a workday. This ability requires a generous dose of humility as well as a devotion to the project's success that outweighs considerations of ego.

THE HOST INSTITUTION

The second team member to be chosen is the institution at which the development project will be based—the school, school district, university, or private nonprofit organization that will house the project and provide its administrative infrastructure.

The choice of a host must not be left to chance: A host's administrative policies, its available facilities, its mix of specialists, and even its culture will play key roles in determining how completely a project achieves its goals. A director needs to weigh a potential host's roster of specialists and experts, the probable stature of the host with potential funders, the space and equipment a host is willing to make available to the project, and the portion of the project's funds that a host will claim as indirect costs. One of the director's early priorities must be to choose a congenial host, or to negotiate necessary understandings with the director's home institution, before drafting a project's funding proposal. By doing so, the director can reassure potential funders that the host's policies will encourage rather than impede the project (or, at least, that problematic policies have been identified and discussed with the host).

In weighing the advantages of a particular host, a project director should consider the degree of personal enthusiasm that the host's executives show for the proposed project. That enthusiasm (or lack of it) can bear greatly on the degree to and ease with which the project succeeds. For example, in 1963 the then-new Science Curriculum Improvement Study (SCIS) settled into the physics department at the University of California at Berkeley, largely because project director Robert Karplus was a professor there (Bowyer & Linn, 1978; Karplus & Thier, 1969). But rather than viewing the project as an imposition on the time, talent, and resources of his group, department chair Burton Moyer publicly endorsed the project and spoke eloquently about its importance to the role and future of the university. Professor Moyer's unqualified endorsement opened several doors to the project within the institution, including the physics department shop, which helped the project design and test equipment for use in elementary schools—quite a departure from its usual work at the cutting edge of research.

In reality, identifying a host may involve little choice. By law, the National Science Foundation (NSF) and most other government granting agencies can give money only to organizations or institutions rather than individuals, and few developers work outside of an educational organization of some kind. Thus in most cases the "choice" will be made by default: The host institution will be the one that employs the project director.

Impact of Host Institution Policies

However, even when no real choice is possible, the director must investigate and clearly understand the institution's policies and expectations that will affect and shape the project. For example, a host organization might require employees to return a fixed percentage of royalties earned by publications they have authored to the organization's publication fund—proceeds from which would underwrite release time enabling the host's faculty to write papers reporting their work. The policy could be a boon to the host's staff members, but it presents a potentially formidable obstacle to a project that plans to use all such royalties to disseminate and help educators implement its materials.

Clearly, a director must understand in every detail the specific policies that the host organization expects the project to adhere to. But the director must also be able to identify any policies of the host institution that might hamper the project's overall success. A project director who has questions or concerns about any such conflicting policies or expectations and their consequences must resolve them by talking and negotiating with the institution's administrators *before* a funding proposal is drafted. Fortunately, even in the most tightly structured organizations, exceptions to policies can often be negotiated if the reason to do so is compelling enough.

For example, soon after SCIS took up residence in Berkeley's physics department, the department helped the project persuade the university to alter a key policy. As a result, SCIS was more easily able to spend money outside of the university, something that was essential in conducting national classroom trials of new materials. Any such exceptions need to be worked out in advance if they can be foreseen. When such changes are negotiated, they must be put in writing to protect the project as well as the director in case administrators in the host organization later try to alter or rescind the exception.

Similarly, the director must investigate and resolve possible clashes between the policies of a grantor and a host. A proposal necessarily offers a number of commitments to funders and can bind a project to a practice or a course of action that violates the host institution's policies. Perhaps a funder may want to hold veto power over materials or research results that the project team wishes to publish, a power that might violate the host's policies governing academic freedom. In return for financial support, a donor might claim copyright for the project's materials even though the host's policy is to own such copyrights itself. In most cases, policy conflicts can be negotiated to accommodate the best interests of a project.

Other Possible Hosts

However, in rare circumstances when key disagreements cannot be resolved, a project director may decide that the obvious choice of a host institution is not the best choice. In such cases, there are alternatives. Any good materials development project will involve a collaboration between a school or school district and a college or university. The director can name a colleague at the partnering institution as a co-director, enabling the project to be based there if more favorable terms can be negotiated. If the issue of moving the project to a different home arises, the director's first step should always be to seek a sympathetic ear in his or her home institution's administration and to collect as wide a variety of views as possible before making a final decision. In all aspects of a project, openness rather than subterfuge will best serve the long-term interests not only of the project but also of the director.

Advantages of a Host University

Most materials development projects will find a home in either a school district or in a college or university, rather than in a charitable foundation or business corporation. The benefits are too many to ignore: subject specialists and classroom teachers—the two key groups in any materials development effort—can be brought together in one organization with a mission, administrative framework, and financial management system already in place and compatible with aims and needs of the project.

Because of the need for collaboration among diverse specialists, most projects will gravitate toward colleges or universities rather than school districts. Developers there have the chance to tap the resources of subject experts, educational psychologists, and other faculty and staff, most no farther away than a short walk. By tracking research, courses taught, and faculty members' publications, developers can identify faculty who could aid the project. Similarly, the news that a development project has arrived on campus could attract spontaneous interest from specialists able to offer vital help. The advantages of basing a project at a university range from access to a spectrum of experts with flexible time to work on a project, to ongoing research projects that might bear on a project's area, to easier connections with specialists at other institutions.

However, every university-based project team must have the participation of experienced classroom teachers throughout its work—and that
presents another chance for complication. The relationships between a
college or university and its nearby schools are not always cordial. Too
often, teachers and administrators feel that post-secondary institutions see
them only as fodder for research—that as soon as university researchers
collect their data, the schools neither hear from them again nor gain any
useful information or insights from the exercise. But university researchers and public schools are finding ways to work together, sharing project
leadership and personnel.

CLARIFYING THE DIRECTOR'S ROLES

Once a host institution has been chosen, the director and host need to agree
on the terms and conditions under which the director will work. In an
educational organization, a project director often will already be a tenured
professional. If the project director is not tenured (at the host or elsewhere),
the director will probably be offered an employment contract for a set
period—usually the length of the project. However, contracts usually contain provisions for periodic renewals during the project. For example, a
project director may be hired for the full term of a 3-year project, but the
director's contract may come up for renewal annually. An annual renewal
gives the host institution a regular opportunity to check on the project's
compliance with the host's policies and on the director's effectiveness as
an administrator and intellectual leader.

It should be clear by now that, while a director is a project's chief
executive, the host institution is likely to regard the director in certain
ways as a middle manager—responsible to the host for ensuring that the
project fulfills all of the host's procedures and regulations about collecting and spending money, hiring team members who do not already work
in the host organization, and so on. Within that context, the director must
know the degree of freedom the host institution will permit in making
project decisions.

Ideally (and normally), the host will acknowledge the director's autonomy in making all project decisions as long as those decisions do not violate the host's administrative or ethical policies. This acknowledgment, if not
a general policy of the institution, should be made in writing as a separate
agreement with the project. A laissez-faire administrator at the host might
later be replaced by a micromanager, in which case a project's only defense
against outside interference may be a previous written agreement.

If the director is not tenured in the host organization, it is prudent at this early stage for the host and director to clarify what the director's place in the organization will be after the project ends. If this point is left vague, the director's enthusiasm may flag just as the project nears fruition. Indeed, the director may begin circulating a résumé, interviewing for other jobs, or simply worrying about personal career issues. Often host organizations have proposals and projects continually in development; an assurance that the director will receive full consideration for places in future ventures frequently is enough to keep the director's attention focused on the current project until its conclusion.

SETTING THE PROJECT'S SCOPE AND TIMELINE

The project director's first step in recruiting the team is not to advertise openings or conduct interviews. It is to set down measurable milestones of accomplishment that the project must achieve at set times within its first operational period—the first year, say, of a typical 3-year project.

Drafting the project proposal has required the director to set a general timetable. But when deciding what kinds of expertise to bring to the project and in what sequence, the director sharpens that projection to make it as specific (and therefore as realistic) as possible. Adjusting the projection is often made even more necessary by differences between the amount of funding sought and the amount granted or by any unexpected time constraints that the funder has imposed. Instead of concentrating on what team members with particular assignments will do, the director first specifies the work that must be done, the order in which it must be completed, and the dates by which those steps must be accomplished.

Doing so before the project's staff roster is finalized is necessary for two reasons. First, understanding what specific tasks must be accomplished by which dates will help the project director decide which skills the project needs to acquire first. Second, individuals being considered for, and considering, places on the project team must know exactly what they will be expected to do, and by when, before they accept a position.

Perhaps the easiest way to calculate a project's timeline is to break the work into its component steps. For example, in materials development projects those steps are usually creating the materials, testing them in classrooms, conducting and evaluating field trials (including students' test results), planning the materials' production and dissemination, and implementing their adoption. In calculating a timeline, a project director might begin by determining what specific work needs to be accomplished by which dates (see Figure 5.1) in order to have trial versions of all materials

Figure 5.1. Sample preliminary project timeline.

Year 1	*Initial exploration and development of course*
Apr.–May	Identify staff biology teacher. Allocate staff resources. Invite summer conference participants. Identify and make agreements with local schools for initial local trials.
Summer	Initial development conference with Life Science Review Panel and invited life science teachers. Review and modify course content outlines.
Sept.–March	Ongoing development of topics for trial testing, including local classroom exploration and research of topics. Meeting of Life Science Review Panel.
Year 2	*Local trial test*
Apr.–May	Formalize school relationships. Prepare working drafts of trial materials.
Summer	Continued preparation of trial materials, including assessment tasks. Meet with Life Science Review Panel and invited life science teachers.
Sept.–Apr.	Local trial testing of course materials. Ongoing revision of materials based on trial tests and meetings with Life Science Review Panel.
Year 3	*National field test*
Summer	Complete revision of materials to produce national field test version of course.
Sept.–May	National field test of complete course, including assessment materials. Site visits.
Jan.–June	Analysis of feedback from field test sites.
Year 4	*Publication of course*
Apr.–Feb.	Revision, content review, and commercial publication of course.
March	Presentation of Issue-Oriented Life Science at National NSTA meeting.

drafted by the time school trials are set to begin, and then constructing the fully detailed timeline (see Figure 5.2).

Team members then can regularly measure actual progress against the projected timeline. By doing so, they will be able to continuously reprioritize their work and adjust their calendars to accommodate the inevitable unforeseen delays or other disruptions that every project encounters.

Figure 5.2. Sample detailed project timeline.

Activity	Su '98	F '98	W '99	Sp '99	Su '99	F '99	W '00	Sp '00	Su '00	F '00	W '01	Sp '01	Su '01	F '01	W '02	Sp '02
Module revision & adv. board conferences																
Develop revision plan																
Modules 1–7 revise & enhance																
Modules 1–7 local trials																
Modules 1–7 training of sites																
Modules 1–7 field tests																
Modules 1–7 re-revise and publish																
Modules 8–14 revise & enhance																
Modules 8–14 local trials																
Modules 8–14 training of sites																
Modules 8–14 field tests																
Modules 8–14 re-revise and publish																
"Guide to SEPUP Modules and NSES" draft available																
"Guide to SEPUP Modules and NSES" final publication																
Video preparation: obtain classroom footage																
Video preparation: final version complete																
Module sequence evaluation data collection																
Module sequence evaluation, analysis, and publication																

Season and Year

SELECTING THE PROJECT TEAM

As noted earlier, a project is as good as the relevant skills of its people. In addition to securing funding, assembling the right mix of experience and expertise is the other most important factor in determining a project's ultimate success.

The ideal team member combines three areas of experience and expertise. First, the individual must have a solid academic and intellectual grounding in the subject content. Second, the individual should show an ability to engage and communicate with the project's targeted age group and the teachers who work with that group. Third, and most important, the prospective developer needs to demonstrate a record as an effective teacher—especially one who habitually has probed and dissected lessons and materials looking for ways to improve them. This intellectual restlessness and habit of questioning is more important than having spent a fixed number of years in the classroom.

Ideally, recruitment begins before a project's funding proposal is drafted. A project's leader usually has specific individuals in mind to invite to join the project team. If those individuals can be recruited at the project's conceptual stage, they can be named in the proposal and their credentials detailed. Those individuals can also help to craft the funding proposal, an involvement that strengthens their stake in the project and the likelihood that they will be available to take part in it if the proposal wins funding.

When funds arrive and the project director begins to recruit a team, the director's first task is to review commitments made earlier to those individuals who helped to develop the project's plan and proposal. People with expectations are the first ones the project director is obligated to contact when staffing a project.

That can be a delicate process. A funder might have required an alteration in the project's design, eliminating the need for a specialist who was promised a place on the team. New ideas about the structure of the project, hatched since the proposal was written, might call for using a certain person on a part-time instead of full-time basis—as that person had been given to expect. Conversely, a person who agreed to serve on the team—and, indeed, might be listed in the grant proposal as a team member in charge of a particular specialty—might no longer be available when the project is funded. Funders typically accept these upsets as inevitable, but it remains the project director's obligation to notify funders in writing of all such unexpected major personnel changes.

These past commitments can create legal and administrative, as well as moral, obligations. Some funding agencies, including the NSF, ask for the names and qualifications of team members as part of the grant proposal. Though rarely, funders sometimes make grants conditional on those specific individuals' involvement. If for some reason those people are not able to take part in the project, the entire grant could be withdrawn. If unexpected changes to the project's budget or structure erase the positions those people were to hold, they might press legal claims that they were promised a job. Usually project directors can skirt these dangers by consulting, and closely following, the host institution's hiring and personnel policies.

When a director encounters these difficulties, they are best handled like any other: directly and with as much diplomacy as possible. Perhaps the person whose special expertise is no longer required for a project has other skills that the project can use. Perhaps the key individual named in the proposal but who has withdrawn can work with the funder and project director to choose a mutually acceptable replacement. Although sometimes daunting, these initial staff adjustments are rarely fatal to a project.

Matching Skills to the Project

After settling previous commitments, the director and the project's initial team members should work together to make a candid appraisal of their own energies, skills, and time that are relevant and available to the project. They can then compare that appraisal with their analysis of the skills the team will need to achieve the project's various goals and objectives by the dates set down in the project timeline. That assessment, moderated by a realistic understanding of the time pressures on team members and the project itself, shows the team the nature of the skills and number of people they must still bring aboard.

For example, the project may call for the production of a video or for the creation of a web page where the new learning materials will be posted. Various team members may have some experience in these areas. But do they have enough skill to carry out the tasks as effectively as the project needs them done, and within the project's time limits? It is never prudent to assume that "we'll cross that bridge when we come to it." Team members should always assume from the start that time will become even more pressing as a project continues. Those time constraints, as well as the range of skills needed to ensure the project's results, become key criteria in hiring the remaining team members or deciding to use freelancers or consultants for short-term or one-time assignments.

A tip: Sequester the salary allotted for one position—at least a half-time position but, if possible, a full-time one—for at least 6 to 9 months after the project begins. During that time, the project quite possibly will discover the need for a certain expertise, or perhaps just an extra person, that was not recognized when the project began but that will be necessary to complete it effectively and on time. If that unforeseen need arises, the reserved funds can pay that additional salary.

Leaving those funds unassigned demands an act of willpower. The urgencies of the project, as well as the team's flush of excitement upon beginning, will give every aspect of the project a tinge of urgency and immediacy. For the same reason, in recruiting experts to a team it is tempting to focus closely on the project's early or immediate needs. Obviously, those needs must be met soonest. However, especially because of the difficulty of integrating a new team member after a project is under way, specialists who will be needed in later stages of the project should be part of the team from the beginning. (In certain ways, this suggestion contradicts the idea of sequestering funds to hire new team members later. This contradiction illustrates some of the dilemmas and choices involved in staffing a project.)

For instance, during the first year of a 3-year project a team might be tempted to think relatively little about disseminating the materials being developed or about helping classroom teachers to adopt and implement them. At first, the team's effort and imagination are consumed by the struggle to create the materials themselves. That makes it easy to concentrate on recruiting designers and developers, leaving to later the task of finding those who will work with teachers to implement the new materials.

For two reasons, that approach is dangerously short-sighted. First, as mentioned, integrating new team members into a project in progress can be as disruptive as introducing a new child into a family. Second, implementation will be most effective when the project members responsible for working with teachers are part of the development process from the beginning. Teachers testing or adopting the new materials will frequently question choices the developers made: "Why do your materials tell me to do this activity in this way instead of that other way that I'd like to do it?" In those cases, a team member needs to understand and be able to explain the evidence and experiences that led the developers to make the choices they did. It is important to be able to tell the teachers, "In early classroom trials, we did it like that but some students and teachers had trouble grasping the concepts underlying the activity. We found that by modifying the materials to their present form, they're consistently effective in communicating those underlying concepts. That's why we do it this way." Such an authoritative response (which is possible only from someone intimately involved in the materials' creation) builds teachers' confidence in the materials' effectiveness—and in the soundness of the project itself.

Making Classroom Teachers Part of the Team

To build a multiskilled team, a project director looks first in two places: among university staff or faculty who worked on development projects that recently ended and among classroom teachers in public schools. Most universities routinely host materials development projects; the skills in development or implementation that a new project needs might easily be found within the halls of the science, mathematics, and education buildings. (If those individuals are not available to a new project, they might know of others with the requisite skills who are.) Most seasoned classroom teachers have implemented new materials and understand the process and problems of doing so. They may also have tried their hands at developing materials on their own. Because they have experienced the creative satisfactions of materials development, or because they see participation on a materials development team as a chance to expand their professional skills, or perhaps also from a sense of professional responsibility, many teachers are eager to join development teams.

Many a project takes the direct approach when it finds a teacher it wants to work with: The project buys all or part of the teacher's contract for an academic year—paying the teacher's salary and benefits for the period or else covering a school district's cost of hiring a replacement. That cuts the project's recruiting time and costs. It also protects the teacher's tenure and seniority in the school district. Ideally, the teacher would be close enough to the project office to be able to divide time between the project and the classroom, giving the project a ready-made laboratory to try out materials as they evolve. Under this teacher-sharing arrangement, the school system also gets to know the project and ends up with a teacher who is intimately familiar with the project's products. That gives the district in-house expertise in using the new materials should the district choose to adopt them.

RECRUITMENT ISSUES

The above description might make the process of recruiting team members seem easy, informal, or both. In fact, it is neither. There are bureaucratic processes to navigate and political shoals that can beach a project, at least temporarily.

First, a project can rarely offer its staff security beyond the life of the grant supporting it. Normally, a university will not offer project employees the concurrent appointments as staff or faculty that would create a berth for them when the project ends. Most school districts frown on giving teachers (especially good ones) long leaves of absence from the classroom, in part because it is difficult to recruit a competent replacement who will accept a lengthy temporary assignment instead of investing those years in establishing tenure in another district.

Second, every project must hire in accordance with the rules and procedures of its funders and host institution. (If a project receives federal money, it must fulfill all expectations and regulations regarding affirmative action.) Typically, that involves posting or advertising the project's open positions within, as well as outside of, the institution. This opens the way for the host to urge the project to take on the host's staff members who are without a current assignment or who have been less than successful in their previous posts. (If a host's policies require that hiring be done first— or exclusively—from within, a project can sometimes skirt that rule if its funder mandates that hiring be done more widely.)

The best defense against such pressures is also the most effective way to put together the best project team: to search as widely for team members as one would in hiring senior staffers or tenure-track professionals. Projects normally advertise in professional journals and contact professional societies. In recent years, some of the best recruiting results have come from using national Internet listservs provided by such organizations as the National Association for Research in Science Teaching, the Association for the Education of Teachers of Science, and the National Science Education Leadership Association. Projects that have web pages can list the details of open positions there, effectively extending a recruitment campaign worldwide. A host institution's candidates may indeed be the best choice for a project team, but the team will not know that until it has looked exhaustively elsewhere.

Another tip: With the flush of excitement and sense of urgency that comes with funding, a director will be tempted to hire the people at hand in order to get the project underway at once. Resist that temptation; remember that the project will succeed or fail on the strengths and weaknesses of its people. Take time to search widely and thoroughly for just the right team members and evaluate them completely before deciding. If a project is funded so close to its projected start date that it does not leave time to conduct a thorough personnel search, negotiate a delayed start date with the funder. Better yet, include in the project design and funding proposal a gradual start-up phase that includes plenty of time to assemble the right group.

In recruiting team members, a project director needs to consider candidates' leadership capacities as well as their niches of expertise. While it is the project director's responsibility to supervise the project team, supervising the project itself is done effectively only as a team effort. The team—or, in a large project, its management staff—should meet at least twice a month to review progress toward the project's short- and long-term goals, to identify problems, and to craft solutions to the inevitable unexpected glitches that crop up. A well-chosen staff will be frank in identifying problems and expressing concerns, as well as shrewd and creative in suggesting solutions, alternatives, and new ideas; a wise project director will listen closely and adopt or adapt the best suggestions. Although a director normally has the power to make decisions against the advice of the project's other staffers, it is usually a foolish director who does so.

THE ROLE OF ADVISORY GROUPS

Two other forms of supervision are essential to a project's success. One is a content review panel. The other, necessary for ongoing programs with multiple projects, is a standing advisory board.

While putting together a project team, the director—with the help of other team members, if possible—should assemble a content review panel that will offer independent advice regarding the approach and subject content of the project's materials. Ideally, the advisory group would include scientists working in concert with science educators and classroom teachers who are not part of the project team.

Every project needs a panel of subject experts that can evaluate the team's work objectively and independently. The panel members need not be classroom teachers but must be acknowledged experts in the subject that the materials are being designed to communicate. The panel will often spot nuances in wording or materials' structure that could lead to misconceptions among learners, and panel members will often suggest ways to present ideas more clearly or accurately before those mistakes surface in classroom trials—or, worse, after the materials are published.

For example, SEPUP developers created an activity in which students gather scientific evidence to help them answer the eternal supermarket question: paper or plastic? The developers had concluded that the energy cost of a paper bag over its life span was less than that of a plastic one. But one member of the project's content review panel procured a copy of a newly released study that had been sponsored by the U.S. Environmental Protection Agency. The study showed that when plastic bags are incinerated and the released energy is captured and reused, then the energy cost of plastic falls below that of paper. As a result, the project delayed publication of its new materials long enough to incorporate the study's results.

In addition to a content review panel for each project, ongoing development programs that engage in a series of projects often have a standing advisory board. Rather than consulting on individual projects, an advisory board serves as a permanent brain trust that carries out a variety of functions, including the following:

- Advising programs on trends and issues in content areas as well as in education generally
- Helping programs or projects set internal policies and directions
- Putting programs or projects in touch with a wider range of experts and others who might otherwise be beyond reach
- Lending prestige to a program or project and attracting attention to it from educators as well as from possible funders and team members

The additional time and labor involved in communicating with advisory and review boards and making them an extension of a project team is an investment, not a cost. That investment can easily save even more effort and expense later that would be needed to fix mistakes, cast about for expert advice or particular contacts, and resolve other time-wasting problems that a good board will help a project avoid in the first place.

CORPORATE PARTNERS

In assembling its team, a project should not fail to contact potential corporate partners that might be of value. Corporations are often the best source of up-to-date information and examples of the application of scientific ideas and principles to real-world problems. As SEPUP developed materials for a module called "Plastics in Our Lives," the Dupont Corporation's experiment station in Wilmington, Delaware, reviewed the materials' content for accuracy. Company researchers alerted the team that substances planned for inclusion in the materials kits had recently been identified as possible health hazards. The company then helped the program choose safer alternatives. In another case, the Chemical Waste Management Corporation donated video footage to SEPUP that followed a load of hazardous waste from its arrival at one of the company's processing plants through its preparation and incineration—a difficult process to duplicate in the classroom. Harold Redsun, then a consultant to the National Food Processors Association, also made himself available to SEPUP's team to answer the project's continuing stream of questions large and small about the program's module on food additives.

However, a project must etch a sharp, clear line between academic and corporate interests when using information or material provided by a commercial concern. To ensure that separation, a project should observe these cautions:

- Do not use corporate materials that the project has not explicitly asked for.
- Make sure that business concerns supplying information or material understand that the project will be the sole, final judge of whether or how the materials are to be used and presented.
- Request that team members and the project's advisory board check all materials supplied by business interests for accuracy and lack of bias.

COMMUNICATING THE PROJECT'S VISION AND GOALS

A project also can streamline its efforts if, once the project team has been assembled, the group takes the time to work together to craft a statement of the project's vision, mission, and goals. Of course, every project's grant proposal also defines purposes and goals. But the proposal is a technical document, sometimes as thick as a small city's telephone book, largely devoted to explaining a project's functional details. It cannot replace, serve as, or fulfill the same needs as the sharply articulated vision, mission, and goals statements honed collaboratively by a project team. The time taken early on to write a separate, concise statement can save confusion and trouble later—especially conflicts that might otherwise arise among team members over fundamental notions about the nature and goals of the project itself.

Volumes have been written about the nature and power of these documents (see, e.g., Covey, Merrill, & Merrill, 1994), and we will not add words to that discussion. We merely urge that a project create the document and refer to it constantly as a guide that fixes and articulates the project's objectives and purpose.

In working together to write these concise statements (no longer than one or two short paragraphs or a brief list of numbered items), each member of the team is called upon to articulate his or her understanding of the project's purpose, methods, and products and to react to others' understandings. Through give-and-take, the team ultimately agrees on a shared, common understanding of what the project is for, what it aims to accomplish and to produce, and the methods it will or will not use to reach those goals.

The process is an effective way to uncover conflicting views so that incompatible ideas among team members can be resolved and consensus reached before clashing assumptions or approaches disrupt the project and delay progress. The process also helps the team to sharpen fuzzy ideas that have not been stated sufficiently clearly before and, not infrequently, to hit upon new concepts that improve the project in some way. Once completed, a commonly derived and shared statement of vision and mission becomes the project's standard: Each team member can judge the relevance of his or her ideas and efforts (and others') by comparing them with the intent expressed in the statement.

For example, when SEPUP received its first NSF grant in 1987, the staff crafted a statement of goals that still guides its work today. "The goals of SEPUP," the statement declares, "are

- "to provide educational experiences focusing on science and technology and their interaction with people and the environment;
- "to promote the use of scientific principles, processes, and evidence in public decision making;
- "to contribute to improving the quality of science education in America; and
- "to enhance the role of science teachers as educational leaders."

These simple statements have become the standards by which SEPUP's developers measure their ideas, their work, and the effectiveness of the materials they create.

As SEPUP's materials were more widely adopted and the program became better known, its advisory board urged the project team to draft a concise mission statement as well. Team members were unsure of the value of the exercise but nonetheless worked with an advisory board member from industry to distill the stated goals into a succinct statement: SEPUP's mission is "to design issue-oriented science education materials that promote scientific literacy and the use of evidence in public decision-making."

Once drafted, the statement proved so effective and efficient in communicating the program's essence to educators, funders, and other constituencies that SEPUP now prints the statement on the back of team members' business cards.

Indeed, such elegantly brief descriptions can serve not only as team-building tools but also as platforms from which a project communicates with its publics. The mission statement, as well as a more detailed summary of objectives and the products or services expected to result, should be released (with appropriate restraint) through the project's own newsletter and offered in presentations at professional gatherings. The statements can entice experts who might want to participate in the project as well as school districts who might be eager to adopt resulting materials.

CONCLUSION

The process of assembling a project team includes selecting a project director and clarifying the director's roles, choosing a host institution and negotiating its relationship to the project, selecting individual team members, specifying the project's scope and work schedule, and clarifying the project's goals. As the detailed discussions in this chapter make clear, it is team members' compatibility of purpose, experience, methods, and objectives that forge a group able to create and implement effective and commercially successful materials.

6

Working with Commercial Partners

Thus do we mortals achieve immortality in the permanent things which we create in common.

—Albert Einstein, *Ideas and Opinions*

THE COMMERCIAL ENTITY OR ENTITIES that publish a project's materials, manufacture its activity equipment, and distribute them commercially is no less important a member of the project team than any individual. Therefore, as much care must go into selecting that partner as goes into choosing any other: the relationship between a project and its commercial partner or partners (which, for brevity's sake, we will refer to as a project's producer-distributor) is usually the project's most delicate and, sometimes, most difficult element.

Also, the relationship between a project and its producer-distributor will outlive the project's links to its funder and perhaps even to its host institution. The longer any relationship lasts, the greater the potential for unforeseen difficulties to arise between partners. It can take a good deal of careful communication, especially at first, to lay the groundwork for a smooth working relationship.

For these and other reasons, selecting a commercial partner requires a project team to confront and consider issues that range far beyond those of compatibility. We explore those issues in this chapter.

COMPLEMENTARY MOTIVES

The project and its publisher-distributor operate from different motives. The project exists to break new ground in education; the publisher-distributor exists to turn a profit. Those motives need not clash but often do, disrupting a project or, in extreme cases, increasing the time it takes for materials to reach the intended market or even preventing them from doing so.

A good commercial partner will share the team's ideals and goals, offer wise counsel during design and refinement, and invest its expertise and time as well as cash in helping to design, as well as producing and disseminating, a project's materials. "Yes, we're in business to make a profit," says Morton Frank, chairman and founder of Lab-Aids, Inc., SEPUP's producer-distributor of project materials. "But we make our profit by supporting developers and teachers. That means giving them what they need at prices they can afford, but it also means lending whatever assistance or expertise we can to help them design and create the materials they envision."

CHOOSING A COMMERCIAL PARTNER EARLY

A project's relationship with its producer-distributor should begin early. Ideally, a project will conduct exploratory conversations and even reach tentative agreement with a producer-distributor even before its work has been funded. Grantors often require it. But even when it is not a requirement, a project that has already arranged for commercial production and distribution of its materials can gain a competitive advantage among funders over projects that do not. Agreements with producer-distributors should be made early for three other reasons as well.

First, if a project's materials are to succeed in the education marketplace, the project needs a producer-distributor's advice on the aspects of design and content presentation that can affect the materials' commercial success. That guidance should inform, but never control, the development process or the materials that result. For example, a producer-distributor might be able to tell a team that the scenario developed as a context for an activity would raise cultural red flags in certain parts of the country. A commercial partner might see that an activity as structured depends on a piece of equipment that cannot be manufactured cheaply enough that schools could afford to buy it in the quantities needed. A project can then seek alternatives that eliminate potential problems in the marketplace while being just as sound educationally.

The operational phrase in these cases, however, is *educationally sound*. In the late 1990s, some school districts and even state boards of education began permitting, or even urging, suppression of any teaching of the theory of evolution. No respectable science education program can acquiesce to such demands.

Second, a producer-distributor might have special expertise in the project's content area and be able to offer suggestions or contacts that make resulting materials more effective. In a complementary way, the project team can help the producer-distributor understand exactly the kind and amount of help the team needs and expects from its commercial partner during the creative process.

Third, the National Science Foundation (NSF) and many other funders require that a project demonstrate a plan for commercial production and distribution of its materials before receiving funds to continue beyond its initial stages. This requirement is usually satisfied best by a project's agreement or contract with one or more producer-distributors. Alternative possibilities are discussed below.

POTENTIAL DIFFICULTIES WITH CONVENTIONAL PUBLISHERS

More often than not in materials development for guided inquiry, a project's commercial partner will not be a conventional textbook publisher. Most textbook publishers exist not to innovate but to make money by providing the books that the largest—and therefore the most conventional—groups of purchasers want. As a result, most traditional publishers see their mission as producing textbooks. They tend to shun unconventional projects that do not yield a hardbound textbook as their primary product. During the 1990s, the problem was aggravated by the flurry of mergers and acquisitions in the publishing industry. These combinations have reduced the number of large educational publishers and left most of those that remain in the control of publicly owned conglomerates that emphasize earning predictable profits from known markets. Relentless pressure from shareholders and financial markets to produce increasing profits every quarter leaves executives leery of making the multiyear investments necessary to commercially establish any innovative materials—such as those so often funded by the NSF and similar agencies—before they begin to pay their own way. Consequently, many innovative projects have encountered enormous obstacles in arranging commercial production and distribution of their materials when the task is given to traditional publishers.

During the 1990s, an array of "niche" publishers entered the field. Many have shown greater interest in innovative materials, and some even an eagerness to publish and market them. But whether these small, young firms have the skills and stamina to succeed commercially is an open question.

Projects react to these commercial realities in different ways. Some projects have succumbed to pressure from publishers and modified the content and appearance of their materials in order to secure distribution. (One major publisher refuses to publish anything other than hardback textbooks, and more than one project that had planned a more innovative format has relented in order to gain this publisher's access to markets.) Others have allied with minor publishers or small printers willing to invest the time and funds to make and market new kinds of materials. The Integrated Mathematics, Science, and Technology (IMaST) project, based at Illinois State University, had contracted with a major textbook publisher that had agreed to invest more than $1.5 million to publish and market its six activity modules. The publisher released two of the modules but dawdled over the remaining four. IMaST's project team finally engaged a lawyer, who found a clause in the project's contract with the publisher requiring the publisher to fulfill its promise within 24 months or lose the project. The publisher, though unenthusiastic, made good on its promise. But that was not the end of the project's troubles. "As that was happening, all of the people we had dealt with at the publishing company had retired, been promoted, or moved on to other companies," says IMaST project director Dr. Franzie Loepp. "The new people did not see our project as 'theirs'; in fact, they saw our project as competing with ones they had already done. So our materials were not being marketed actively." As a result, IMaST canceled its contract with a major publisher and chose a smaller firm. The new partner had published little in mathematics, science, or technology for primary and secondary grades but saw a partnership with IMaST as a way to establish itself in a new field. As an investment in its own growth, the publisher made a contractual promise to share with IMaST the cost of educating teachers to use the new materials. The company also agreed to make its sales staff available to the project for a full week of training—two concessions the project's original publisher never made.

"Our original publisher didn't understand that our deliverable was not a textbook, so the company didn't know how to sell our materials," Loepp notes. "Our philosophies were at odds. Our new publisher is not well known but it's willing to commit to us the support we need to have a good chance in the marketplace."

EVALUATING POSSIBLE COMMERCIAL PARTNERS

A prudent project team screens potential commercial partners at least as carefully, and often more so, than it does other team members. That process begins, logically enough, in identifying potentially compatible candidates. A producer-distributor handling materials by projects similar in approach may seem like a logical choice. Often, developers will know of likely commercial partners by reputation or from presentations that commercial firms have made at educational meetings and conferences.

Once a project has identified possible partners, the team can begin informal discussions with the candidates. Team members will seek to gauge a producer-distributor's enthusiasm for the project's goals and plans, its estimate of the materials' commercial potential, and the amount of money, time, and other resources the potential partner is willing to invest to aid the team's creative work as well as to make and market the materials. The more candidates a project team talks with, the better able it will be to recognize what it does and does not want in a commercial partner.

Some projects have enlisted the services of an author's agent to find and screen potential producer-distributors. A good agent will know the industry and often can quickly point a project to a suitable partner. However, it can require as much effort to find an agent competent in this small, specialized field as it takes to find the right producer-distributor. If a project team does not have a ready connection to a well-recommended agent, the best investment of time might be to search for a partner directly (also saving the 10 to 15 percent of the project's future income that an agent will usually claim as a finder's fee).

TIPS FOR CHOOSING A COMMERCIAL PARTNER

Establishing a good relationship with a publisher or producer-distributor may be the most complex and, for many developers, daunting challenge that a project presents. Developers are often less confident of their business acumen than of their creative ability. When that is the case, developers—like authors of other kinds of creative work—tend to approach the search for a commercial venue emotionally. They may assume the role of supplicant, hoping they can find a publisher willing to "take a chance" on their materials. When a commercial producer does show interest, the developer may be so overwhelmed with gratitude and relief that the developer neglects to negotiate a contract that states and protects the project's interests clearly and firmly.

Alternatively, developers sometimes hold out for the perfect publisher, the one that "feels right" after a few conversations. But the result may be the same because the developer, having made a visceral decision to trust the publisher, may fail to ensure that basic details are spelled out in the resulting contract.

"You have to respect what you have to offer," counsels Linda Chaput, president of Cogito Learning Media, an educational publishing house in San Francisco. "It's part of your responsibility to your project. If you look at it that way, the process becomes not so very personal—and that makes for better decisions."

The alternative can be horrific, she notes: "I have seen developers sign contracts that do not obligate the publisher to either publish the materials within a specified period or return the rights to the developer. I have seen developers sign contracts that do not limit the revisions of the materials that a publisher can demand, sending developers into endless spirals of revisions that never result in publication. I have seen deals in which the publisher had the right to stop promoting and marketing the materials, stop revising them, sell fewer than 10 copies a year, and never be obligated to return the rights to the developer. Bad publishing deals will snuff the life out of materials."

To avoid those kinds of nightmares, Chaput and other veteran project directors and concerned publishers offer these tips to developers venturing into the commercial arena:

1. Apply the same creative, analytical skills to finding a commercial partner that apply to designing a project and creating and testing new materials. Investigate, compare, ask partners to help in the search, and do not assume anything that is not laid out in writing.
2. Review other materials and books similar to those your project is producing. Talk to other developers. Then assemble a list of 10 or 12 possible producer-distributors for your project.
3. Assemble a brief but thorough prospectus outlining the materials, their purpose, their importance, and the kinds of educators who would be likely to adopt them. Chaput suggests enlisting help from experienced businesspeople whom the developer trusts—perhaps a seasoned project director or a person in a local university's business school—to help create the prospectus, or at least critique it, before it is sent to potential commercial partners.
4. When a producer-distributor expresses interest, vet the company as thoroughly as you would any other applicant for a position on the project team. Does the company have experience with projects similar to yours? What similar projects has it marketed? Were those projects' materials marketed successfully? Will those projects' directors vouch for the company?
5. Do not search for the one right producer-distributor. Chaput advises looking for two. "Otherwise, you'll become way too emotionally invested in your one object of interest," she warns. "Finding the perfect partner is for marriage, not a business relationship."
6. Do not begin negotiating a contract until you are certain that the company representative you are talking with has the authority to negotiate and make decisions that will become part of a contract.
7. Assume that nothing will happen unless it is stipulated in the contract. If milestone dates and other obligations are not spelled out in writing, there is no reason to assume they will be met. "Developers who are otherwise very meticulous will rely on someone having said, 'Yes, I'll

do that,'" Chaput says. "Then that person quits the company or is promoted to another department or dies and what that person promised doesn't happen. In business, you do not want an agreement that depends on personalities."

Finding a commercial partner can be time-consuming, especially for the first-time developer. But investing the additional time and trouble to forge a sound partnership early can prevent all the rest of the time, funds, and caring that developers invest in their creative work being wasted.

CONTRACTING WITH A COMMERCIAL PARTNER

Once a project selects its producer-distributor, the two will negotiate and sign a contract. This written agreement will specify their financial relationship and the responsibilities of each in the project.

A good contract will acknowledge the mutual interest of both parties: creating effective, commercially successful materials. That mutual interest creates mutual obligations, which the contract exists largely to spell out. Because the producer-distributor is investing in the project's work in order to have a good product to take to market, it has a right to expect the project team to support its work in producing and disseminating marketable materials. At the same time, the producer-distributor must recognize the development team as the primary experts and authorities on the materials' structure and content. The impact a project's materials make on teachers and students will be determined no less by the personal working relationships between project team and producer-distributor than by the contract that binds them.

Among other details, the terms of the contract will specify the kinds and amounts of time, advice, and expertise (such as editorial or design work) that the producer-distributor will invest in helping the project to create its materials. It also should spell out the rights and responsibilities of both parties as well as the share of revenues that the producer-distributor will return to the project and when.

As a host institution's lawyer once put it, the contract is a snapshot at a single point in time of the parties' complete agreement. It defines every aspect of the relationship between a project and its producer-distributor at the moment they formally agree to partner. Therefore, everything that the two parties have agreed to in discussion must be captured in clear language in the contract: The written agreement will become the entirety of the understandings and obligations between a project and its commercial partner.

The negotiations may be prickly. For example, some publishers expect projects to pay all costs of creating camera-ready art or else charge such costs against the royalties the materials earn for the project. Many producer-distributors do not volunteer to pay royalties on materials and equipment, which may be 80 percent of the salable products that a project creates. In such cases, a project's potential income is slashed to a fraction of what it otherwise would be. A producer-distributor might insist on owning copyright of the materials—a demand to which a project should never accede, because surrendering copyright means surrendering control of the materials' content and design. (A long-term contract giving the producer-distributor ample time to market products and recoup its investment usually solves any impasse over copyright ownership.) Hard bargaining now over such issues not only will weed out unsuitable partners but also will likely prevent confusion, bitterness, and perhaps outright disaster later on.

In most cases, the host institution will shoulder the technical legal work involved in drafting and reviewing contracts to make sure that a project gets as much as it can of what it wants in the agreement and also to help it avoid unpleasant surprises. At the least, a project's host (and, if necessary, perhaps the project's funder) can provide legal expertise to help a project team translate its needs and goals into contractual language to present to potential commercial partners. Similarly, the host or funder can also advise a project in interpreting contractual elements proposed by those partners.

If the relationship between project and producer-distributor is grounded in trust, individuals may make and keep verbal commitments not spelled out in the contract. But a project's verbal agreement with even the most principled individual within a commercial firm can become worthless if the individual leaves for a new job or the company is sold. For these reasons, any alterations to the terms of an already-signed contract must also be made in writing, preferably as formal amendments to the original agreement. Because the contract will bind the project's team members and can shape their work, team members should not only be familiar with the contract's details but also have as great a voice as possible in helping to shape those terms to suit the project.

MANAGING RELATIONSHIPS WITH PRODUCER-DISTRIBUTORS

A project and its producer-distributor must understand above all that, despite their differing motives, they share a single interest: the wide adoption of the project's materials. This is not to say that a project team and a producer-distributor should always see eye to eye in every respect. The same rule governing the relationship among team members should govern that between a team and its commercial partners: Disagreements about strategies or approaches to implementation are not only permissible but welcomed because such disagreements can often lead to better ideas and more effective materials.

But it is crucial to materials' successful dissemination that a project and its producer-distributor work toward their shared goals cooperatively rather than through conflict and antagonism—especially in public. Nothing will damage educators' perception of a project and its materials as effectively as open disagreement or acrimony between the project team and its commercial partner. Educators tend to shy away from adopting materials created by projects that are known to have battled with their publishers. In one extreme case, a development team publicly disowned the version of its materials that its publisher marketed, effectively scuttling its own commercial viability.

Educators need not be made to think that the project and its producer-distributor are always in complete agreement. But the two should behave publicly in a way that reassures potential users of the materials that all members of the extended project team are working earnestly together to resolve disagreements in ways that best benefit the materials and the students and teachers who use them.

ALTERNATIVES TO CONVENTIONAL PUBLISHERS

Fortunately, there are alternatives to working with conventional publishers. One—used by projects such as the Full Option Science System, Science and Technology for Children, and SEPUP—is to contract with a materials manufacturer to also publish a project's printed materials. (This is becoming more common among elementary-level projects but is still unusual in those developing materials for older learners.)

For example, in its early days SEPUP followed a conventional path and contracted with a major commercial book publisher to produce the printed materials for the program's activity modules. At the same time, SEPUP engaged Lab-Aids, Inc. to manufacture, package, and distribute the modules' equipment kits (including the printed pages produced by the publishing firm). The arrangement worked well. But when SEPUP began planning full-year secondary school science courses, the publisher refused to invest in the venture. Among its reasons, the publisher was worried that the resulting suite of materials would compete with textbooks it was already publishing. Instead of trying to persuade another publisher to back the project, SEPUP decided to turn over to Lab-Aids the publication of its printed materials as well as the manufacture of its equipment kits. Equipment kits, printed materials, and even the student hardback guidebook for the program's year-long "Issues, Evidence and You" middle school course were all produced by a single commercial partner.

Such atypical arrangements are made possible in no small way by the advent of desktop publishing. A single desktop computer can replace the old drawing tables, layout and paste-up shops, and proofing runs that conventional printing needed. Because its student books and teachers' guides can be printed directly from computer files, a project's editors and designers can prepare the final pages as computer files ready to print. (As part of its ongoing agreement with SEPUP, Lab-Aids funds the portion of the project designer's and editors' time devoted to the preparation of the printed materials' commercial versions.)

This project-led, computer-based approach to publishing and materials production avoids several potential problems lurking in the conventional developer–publisher relationship. It skirts the conflict of aims that so often crops up between projects developing materials for inquiry-oriented programs and textbook publishers, whose interest and attention remains devoted to the textbooks they sell. Also, this kind of arrangement best enables a project's flexible, cooperative relationships with individual districts. (For an example, see the story in Chapter 11 of SEPUP's relationship with the Brooklyn High School District.)

Some development projects have found successful alternatives to commercial publication and distribution. Great Explorations in Math and Science (GEMS), for example, has published its own print materials for more than a decade and marketed them itself through the Lawrence Hall of Science at the University of California at Berkeley (the project's headquarters) and a variety of wholesale distributors.

Other projects have established their own foundations or nonprofit companies to produce and distribute their materials. In most such cases, the nonprofit entities—organized under the direction of the project or its host institution—carry out the same work usually done by a commercial producer-distributor, delivering the same kinds of printed products ready to be shipped.

The growth and ready availability of the Internet and the World Wide Web has given developers another alternative to traditional publishers and distributors. A project now can make its materials available through its own or related web pages. Individual teachers, schools, and districts then can download printed and software-based materials and replicate the materials they choose for the number of students they have. (In those cases, the quality of the materials' accompanying artwork will be determined by the quality of the computers, printers, and software to which the materials are downloaded.) Of course, distributing materials over the Internet does not alter a project's mandate to base its materials firmly on research, refine them through classroom trials, and conduct comprehensive professional development for teachers and administrators adopting the materials.

Web-based distribution raises an array of issues that currently are unresolved. If a project posts its materials on the Internet, how does the project protect its intellectual property, enforce copyright, or ensure that it can make a financial return on its materials (assuming it wishes to do so)? For example, SEPUP and many other projects use royalties from the sale of materials to fund editorial revisions, teacher development, and other necessary, ongoing professional activities to improve materials and implementation after the grant supporting the materials' development has ended. Without royalty income, such efforts would have to be paid for in some other way. Licensing and sale of educational materials over the Internet can and does take place. However, at this writing, materials developers and distributors have little experience in doing so, or in dealing with the legal and financial questions that result. The opportunities for innovation are clear, but so are the dangers.

CONCLUSION

Finding a commercial partner whose vision and goals are compatible with those of a project team can often be more complex and time-consuming than recruiting any other team member. It requires research, resolve, and a willingness to wait until a producer-distributor is found that fits well with the project's personality and long-term goals.

Even once a suitable match has been found, the legal and financial details of the relationship need to be negotiated and spelled out explicitly by contract. The project's host institution usually can provide qualified attorneys to oversee the bargaining. No project director or team, no matter how experienced, should negotiate and sign a contract without working closely with a qualified attorney throughout the process.

The advice given in this chapter on all of these points can help a project team find and cultivate a relationship with a suitable commercial partner. However, we would remind developers that they should not settle for a commercial partner willing merely to meet the terms of a negotiated agreement. The world's best contract cannot rival or replace a working relationship based on trust, respect, good faith, and shared interests between a project and its producer-distributor.

7

Working Together: Collaborations for Success

We can't solve problems by using the same kind of thinking we used when we created them.

—Albert Einstein, *Ideas and Opinions*

THE EFFECTIVENESS OF MATERIALS for guided inquiry depends on specialists working together. Therefore, it is essential that a development project's team members create a collaborative culture among themselves. A successful project must incorporate not only the different skills but also the different approaches and points of view—sometimes conflicting—of the team's diverse specialists.

Creating a collaborative culture encompasses several steps:

- Identifying an effective management approach
- Cultivating a climate in which team members can give and receive criticism of one another's ideas and still feel secure and supported
- Identifying the most useful project structure

In addition, although a project begins with a plan that funders (and, presumably, team members) endorse, the team must remain open to the possibility that the plan may be "hijacked" by good new ideas—unexpected inspirations that suddenly enable the project to achieve it goals in better ways. In both cases, team members must be flexible enough to welcome changes in the plan even when it challenges their own senses of comfort and security.

That flexibility derives in part from team members' willingness to put the project's goals and success ahead of their own egos. But it also derives from the management style that a project embodies. Openness and flexibility in the face of sudden, and sometimes difficult, change thrive only in an organization that:

- Aligns team members' personal and professional goals with those of the project
- Is structured to recognize and reward flexibility and collaboration over competition or slavish adherence to fixed procedures

This chapter examines the processes involved in creating and balancing a collaborative culture and an effective management structure.

MANAGEMENT BY OBJECTIVES

Unfortunately, the organizational culture that a creative development project needs to thrive is not yet widespread in education. For that reason, a materials development project shaped by teamwork and an evolutionary approach to change can become a demonstration model for a new kind of collaborative guidance and leadership in educational institutions.

Typically, educational organizations operate under some form of management by objectives, or MBO, a common approach to business management since the 1950s. Under MBO, senior management (in education, that usually includes school boards, superintendents, or curriculum directors) defines a series of objectives that workers (such as curriculum directors, principals, and teachers) are expected to achieve. In business, workers who achieve the specified objectives are rewarded with pay raises or promotion; those who do not may face a shaky future in the organization. In education, teachers rarely have the chance to win pay increases through performance, and their only opportunity for advancement is to leave the classroom. However, increasingly their job security is tied to their ability to ensure that students achieve objectives specified through standardized tests.

Under MBO, workers (whether in industry or in education) are given a degree of freedom in determining how they will accomplish the goals as long as those workers do not violate standing policies, practices, and procedures that management has set. But MBO is still a form of "boss management": Managers control what workers do and how they do it. Administrators hold the power to reward employees for compliance and punish them for not doing what they were told. Bosses set tasks and standards, often without consulting workers; employees adjust to management demands and decisions. Managers judge the quality of the finished work, leading workers to respond to external motivations, rather than encouraging them to think in terms of self-imposed standards of quality.

Although too many educational institutions still bear the hallmarks of MBO-style management, teachers traditionally have had a greater voice and involvement in setting goals related to their work than most corporate employees have had. Educators have shown an ability to overcome the sometimes stultifying effects of top-down management and to launch their own innovations or to collaborate with colleagues to change the processes and outcomes in their classrooms. This relatively greater degree of freedom is not due to a more benevolent form of MBO being practiced in education. It is due instead to teachers' extraordinary degree of personal commitment to their work and, especially, to their students. Their accomplishments only hint at what so many teachers could accomplish if their organizational structures worked in a cooperative, rather than in a controlling, way.

If this description of traditional educational management seems unfair or too harsh, consider the number of school systems, and even entire states, in which students' performance on standardized tests has come to determine teachers' and administrators' salary and job security.

THE "CONTINUOUS IMPROVEMENT" APPROACH

An alternative finding its way into schools and districts is an approach that first became known as total quality management, or TQM, and is now known by a variety of names: total quality education, the quality movement, or continuous improvement (CI). Under the processes of continuous improvement, teams set goals and objectives by consensus, giving all participants a chance to infuse their individual professional goals into a project's design and objectives. Each team member then exerts unique skills and expertise to achieve not only the project's jointly determined goals but also personal satisfaction.

When automobile companies instituted TQM in the 1970s and 1980s, the effectiveness of quality circles, in which rank-and-file workers meet to find ways to improve their products' quality, riveted the industry. (In some car factories, any assembly-line worker can throw a switch that stops the entire line if that employee notes a defect in cars coming down the line— a power unlike any that teachers have if they discover consistent problems in students' learning.)

In education, CI processes give teachers a greater voice in determining how they will do their jobs—from organizing professional development groups to determining how to assess their students' learning. CI is based in part on the following principles:

- No one knows more about a task than the person responsible for performing that task. Therefore, that person must be centrally involved in any attempt to improve the task's performance and outcomes.

- Interaction among qualified specialists will generally produce a better result than one specialist tackling a project alone.
- The more people contributing to a project or to a problem's solution, the better the result is likely to be.

When sincerely accepted among team members, these three principles foster a respect for the ideas of each individual within the group and for the collective wisdom of the group. Because these operating principles foster mutual respect, they encourage individuals taking part to invest their egos and professional identities in the success of the group. Motivation, especially for the project's success, becomes internal to each team member rather than an extrinsic matter of salary, résumé inflation, or empire building.

CULTURE CLASH

These two dramatically different management approaches of MBO and CI often meet, and clash, in a materials development project. The development team struggles to create a culture based on collaborative and bottom-up leadership. But host institutions—and many funders, including the National Science Foundation (NSF)—typically are more rigid and bureaucratic: Projects, and particularly their directors, are expected to meet various unyielding administrative and fiscal expectations and requirements—pressuring the project to succumb to the demands of MBO rather than nurturing the culture of CI.

Accommodating both needs depends, in large measure, on the project director's ability to be able to recognize which role—administrator or creative team member—is appropriate in a given circumstance. It is an ability that improves with practice.

SEPUP's experience suggests a technique that can help: holding separate meetings to handle creative and administrative matters. In administrative meetings, the project director (or, in larger projects, the management committee) must be free to function as a boss when circumstances warrant. In creative sessions, however, a director or manager functions as one among equals. Switching from administrative and development discussions in the same session can blur the distinctions between the two quite separate roles—and, therefore, between the two conflicting organizational cultures. Besides, if a program is large enough to employ administrative or support staffers, as is the case with the Biological Sciences Curriculum Study (BSCS) and TERC, expecting such staff members to sit through discussions of development issues wastes their time (and drains a project's budget).

RELINQUISHING OWNERSHIP OF—AND CRITIQUING—YOUR OWN IDEAS

Except in the smallest projects, not every team member will contribute equally to the design of every activity and each piece of material. Specific tasks will be assigned to individual team members based on their interests and expertise. But, according to the principles of CI, interaction among qualified specialists will generally produce a better result than will one specialist tackling a project alone. Therefore, the creative team must periodically reassemble as a group to critique, alter, enhance, or endorse the work begun by an individual member that now has truly become an effort of the team as a whole.

How productive those group sessions will be depends on the ways in which each team member treats the ideas that colleagues bring to the group. Because creative people invest a portion of themselves in each of their ideas, the idea, in a sense, becomes a reflection of the person who created it. There is a powerful emotional reflex in the primitive portions of our brains whispering to us that if someone questions the fruits of our creativity, that person is necessarily questioning our competence as professionals. It is a common and forgivable reaction, but it is absolutely deadly to any collaborative materials development project.

If team members come to a group session "owning" the ideas that they have created as individuals—having a sense of self invested in those ideas (and, being human, they will)—they may equate criticism of an idea to a personal attack. In such cases, they may respond by reflexively defending those ideas instead of examining the validity of the critiques. Every time that happens, damage is inflicted on the supportive, collaborative culture of trust and open exchange on which a project's success depends.

Every project member must genuinely believe not only that others' ideas are to be treated with the same balance of kindness and frankness that we would wish for our own, but also that each of us at times is prey to that whispering voice. The team should discuss its approaches to collaborative work, and especially to critiques, openly and, if needed, often in its early sessions. The team can use its success in maintaining open, yet supportive, exchange as a measure—an embedded, authentic assessment, if you will—of the project's organizational culture.

The project director can set the tenor of discussion by encouraging criticism of his or her own ideas. "I've designed this activity to communicate the principle of energy transfer," the director might say. "I'm not satisfied with this aspect of it, but I haven't been able to come up with anything better. Does anyone have any ideas for improving it?" In such cases, if the director listens to others' ideas without rancor and works those ideas into a new draft of an activity's design, other team members are likely to follow suit.

Such an inclusive, welcoming approach is especially necessary when individuals who are not team members, such as classroom teachers, are asked to sit in on development sessions. If the object is to gain the teachers' advice and insights into drafts of the materials as well as their continuing cooperation, the way in which team members treat these "outside" ideas may become a determining factor in the project's outcome. Teams must credit the creativity and commitment of individuals who suggest ideas. But once an idea is "put on the table" it becomes the property of the team—and it is the team that will decide how to use the idea to the project's best advantage.

Of course, critiques must be subject to the same scrutiny that suggested designs are. "If you give up something just because someone else doesn't like it, you might be surrendering a good idea too quickly," advises SEPUP co-director Barbara Nagle. "You need to have a discussion, and sometimes even an argument, to make sure that your activity idea is clear." For example, Nagle designed an activity to demonstrate the placebo effect as part of SEPUP's "Science and Life Issues" biology course. "I really had to explain and clarify that design in our team meetings, and even then some others had doubts. So we decided to try it in the classroom. Teachers who used it not only reported that they thought the activity was especially effective but gave us comments that helped us improve it. In team discussions, when there is disagreement about the best approach, the best thing to do is to try it in a classroom and gather the evidence about what happens." Team processes of respectful give-and-take must also allow for the fact that the minority view may be the right one after all.

POSSIBLE PROJECT STRUCTURES

There are as many ways for materials development teams to work together as there are materials development projects. However, virtually all projects fall into three organizational groups: those that work together full time in a single location; those that meet periodically (usually in summer) for collaborative writing and work sessions; and those that rarely meet physically to work together and instead collaborate through long-distance communications. There are advantages and disadvantages to each.

Working Together Full Time

Some development projects structure their budgets and allocate their resources to assemble a team that can work full time in the same office exclusively on the project and its materials. SEPUP is one such program, usually employing four to eight developers, including the program's director, at the Lawrence Hall of Science on the Berkeley campus of the University of California. The Full Option Science System (FOSS), also based at the Lawrence Hall, has a core staff of five or six developers but adds more full-time team members—usually classroom teachers and university scientists—when a new round of work is funded. In the late 1990s, when it revised and expanded its library of 27 activity modules, FOSS added more than a dozen full-time team members for several months.

Perhaps the chief advantage of a full-time development team is the ease and speed with which its developers can communicate. They can show early drafts of activities and materials to colleagues instantly, or sometimes talk through the design with others before putting anything on paper. Reactions, suggestions, and critiques come quickly; pivotal conversations about designs can and do take place at the lunch table or as team members pass each other in a hallway. Team members need not wait for mail to travel back and forth, for faxes to be read, or for distant team members to get around to answering an e-mail message before they can resolve problems in early designs and move ahead. In addition, communicating face to face is virtually always more efficient and effective than trying to communicate the subtle ideas through writing or phone conversations.

"We tried working with people part time, but it just didn't work," recalls Jacqueline Miller, director of the "Insights in Biology" high school course at the Education Development Center in a Boston suburb. "We found that when we were writing we needed people there all the time so we could pop into each other's offices to try things out. It didn't work to send things back and forth by mail or fax."

According to FOSS co-director Lawrence Malone, "The strength of this organizational model is that it's a 'total immersion' approach to development. The team functions like a family raising a child. Information exchange, brainstorming, analyzing actions and outcomes, planning, personal experiences, and everything else that contributes to good materials is most efficiently conducted continuously, face to face."

The FOSS team occasionally runs into the format's disadvantages—"inadequate space sometimes for all team members to work efficiently and so on," Malone says, adding "but these pale compared to the advantages of have continual contact among team members." Not long ago, the California-based FOSS team attempted to telecollaborate with a writing team in the eastern United States. "Never again," Malone declares. "It was laborious and frustrating because, in part, of ineffective communication imposed by distance."

But a project need not necessarily choose between expertise and maximum efficiency. By basing themselves at a major research university, SEPUP and FOSS both have ready access to a universe of world-class experts in areas ranging from microbiology to CD-ROM design and production. And, because the university is located in a major metropolitan area, the projects can easily collaborate with experienced, insightful classroom teachers working across the spectrum of socioeconomic settings and in a variety of specialties.

By choosing team members and a host institution judiciously, a small team of full-time developers can tap a full range of subject expertise without having to sacrifice swift and effective communication.

However, there is a way that projects in which team members work together full time—particularly projects whose materials have a track record—can make effective use of periodic short conferences. For example, if a team has the opportunity to revise and update its materials, it can bring the members of the project's larger, extended group together for a short session. Teachers who have used the materials in classrooms can comment from experience about how effective the current materials are and how, and at which points, they might be improved. Such comments are especially useful if those teachers now have responsibilities within their districts or states for improving science programs in their geographic areas.

Meeting for Periodic Work Sessions

This is perhaps the most common structure that development projects adopt. A project director or team identifies individuals with exceptional skills or content knowledge that can benefit the project. The individuals are brought together for a short organizational meeting, usually in the summer, at which the project plan is detailed and work is apportioned and assigned. The group may disperse after a few days or remain together for several weeks to work through initial drafts and designs of activities and materials, but team members typically complete much (if not most) of their work after they have dispersed. The structure enables a project to recruit team members with other full-time responsibilities that would bar them from taking part in the project if more time was asked of them.

The IMaST Approach. The Integrated Mathematics, Science, and Technology project (IMaST), headquartered at Illinois State University, has used the structure of periodic meetings to draw together more than a dozen specialized educators to create the project's activities and materials. IMaST's management group asked regional offices of the U.S. Department of Education to nominate outstanding middle school teachers in each of the project's three content areas. The group also scanned lists of presenters at recent education conferences and contacted some teachers directly. The project likely would not have been able to recruit from these groups if it had demanded full-time commitments.

Interested teachers were asked to submit an application that included an essay outlining their philosophy of education, writing samples, and a commitment to try the project's materials and activities in their own classrooms. IMaST leaders then invited four teachers in each of the three content areas to join the team (a cohort limited in number by budgetary constraints, not by an attitude of exclusivity on the project's part).

The project rented an apartment house near the campus and brought the teachers together for a month of close, intense work that involved designing and drafting activities and their accompanying materials. The drafts were given to three staff writers, hired by the project for their curriculum expertise and writing skills, who then created polished versions. "The design teams kept us in touch with kids in the real world," says project co-director Dr. Franzie Loepp, "and our writers elevated the drafts to a level at which they had the potential to succeed in all kinds of classrooms." IMaST tested the results in nearby schools during the following year, then brought its creative team back to the campus the next summer to revise the drafts based on teachers' comments and critiques. But, as co-director Sherry Meier notes, "Keeping the same design team of teachers over 3 years was a problem. Many teachers do not want to commit for three summers of involvement."

The BCC Approach. The materials development project Biology: A Community Context (BCC), based at Clemson University, varied the structure. Professors William Leonard and John Penick, the project's directors, scanned lists of educational award winners and well-known scientists to assemble a panel of 25 first-rate high school biology teachers, content experts, and university specialists in biology education. In a 2-day meeting, the panel developed a list of skills and knowledge that ninth- and tenth-grade biology students should master. The project's directors then brought together a cadre of about 100 teachers and scientists, including some members of the original panel, to draft the project's materials. The cadre was divided into eight groups, each tackling one content area. Each group included at least two scientists and three high school biology teachers and was chaired by a university biology educator chosen in significant part on the basis of writing skills.

Again, the project could muster such a select group only by not asking participants for full-time commitments. "Working this way gave us the pick of the best people even though we had a limited budget," Leonard points out. Among other advantages: "Having writers all over the country helped to eliminate regional bias from the materials and also provided a greater variety of examples for our environmental activities," says Penick.

Each team then met at Clemson for just 6 days. "By giving them such a short period of time, they were well motivated to write," Penick notes. "But with such a short time, we lost some of the creativity that probably would have occurred if we'd had longer." He points to another drawback of the structure: "Since each unit team was in residence during a different week, there was little opportunity for cross-fertilization among the teams." The teams continued to work together—largely by fax, e-mail, and snail mail—and tested the evolving materials in their own classrooms to revise them for a two-stage national field test.

The BSCS Approach. BSCS in Colorado Springs uses its own version of the same general approach. The group employs a full-time staff of writers and developers versed in learning theory, the effective use of activities in classrooms, cooperative learning, and other design aspects that BSCS routinely incorporates into its materials. But when a new project begins, the group invites university scientists, biology and other science teachers, and curriculum specialists to meet with its developers to offer specific ideas for the project at hand. "By combining our people with others, the meetings create a synergy that produces a greater number and variety of ideas than what we could produce by ourselves," says BSCS director Rodger Bybee.

In creating supplemental modules for health courses in various grades, project director Nancy Landes and her co-director met with scientists at the National Institutes of Health (NIH), which funded the work, to understand in greater detail what the agency wanted the modules to do. Next, the project—still working closely with NIH researchers—convened an advisory panel made up of scientists and classroom teachers. "We consider teachers to be experts in their subject area about what most students of a particular age can comprehend and what happens in the classroom," Landes notes. (A BSCS project panel might also include educational psychologists and other specialists.) The panel created a general conceptual outline of the materials and activities, which the funding agency then reviewed. Only when that outline was firm did the project convene a summer writing conference.

"We often use concept maps to create a visual picture of what a unit looks like," explains Pamela Van Scotter, also a BSCS project director for NIH-funded modules. "Then we make a different concept map to ferret out the details of each individual chapter. It helps keep everyone focused."

The GEMS Approach. The long-running Great Explorations in Mathematics and Science program (GEMS), also based at the University of California's Lawrence Hall of Science, takes a somewhat different (though no less effective) approach to the use of loose-knit teams. A principal author—typically an educator at Lawrence Hall but not a GEMS staffer—works with a GEMS team member to create an integrated suite of four to eight activities. The pair submits an outline of the activities and accompanying materials and teachers' guides for review (and, typically, extensive editing) by the full GEMS editorial team.

After the duo has produced a working draft of the activities and materials, the two present them in a nearby classroom. The principal author leads the class while the GEMS staff member sits at the back of the room and takes careful, complete notes on the teacher's and students' reactions and comments. The notes are circulated among the entire GEMS development team, and members add their comments and suggestions. The author and the GEMS staff member then revise the drafts to incorporate those suggestions and solve any procedural or conceptual problems that the trials revealed.

The improved versions are tested, this time in as many as two dozen schools, with each teacher filling out a lengthy questionnaire about the activities' and materials' strengths, weaknesses, and student reactions. After the GEMS team reviews the questionnaires and adds suggestions, the GEMS staff member who has worked with the principal author writes the final version. This "buddy system" enables a busy program with a relatively small staff to leverage its creative potential.

Drawbacks to Meeting Infrequently. As is the case with any organizational structure, using a team that meets in person only occasionally offers drawbacks as well as strengths. As Philip Gersmehl notes, because the materials development project he directs for the Association of American Geographers has contributors in 47 states and distributed production facilities, the main difficulty is "keeping everyone on the same page." Michael Smith, education director for the American Geological Institute, discovered that a day-long meeting with writing teams to explain his project's writing guidelines and chapter template was not enough. When he began to receive teams' chapter drafts, he discovered that "some teams seemed to link academic rigor with vocabulary and write for a university audience rather than grades 9 and 10," which the project targeted. "As a result, I have to address this problem through significant rewriting."

Such headaches may be worth their trouble if a project needs the special knowledge and skill of educators and scientists who are far-flung or available only for short or intermittent periods. A long-distance organizational approach also allows a project to use its budget to glean contributions from a large number of people instead of paying salaries, benefits, and overhead for a few team members who, in turn, must contribute a large number of ideas. However, the structure often cannot allow enough time for teams to fully evolve their ideas and designs: The brief conferences tend to generate ideas and outlines more than fully evolved drafts and designs of materials and activities. Also, team members who spend most of their time in other pursuits are often not available to field questions from teachers testing materials drafts in their classrooms.

Still, the advantages of recruiting adjunct participants to broaden a project's perspective are strong enough that programs relying on full-time teams often supplement themselves with consultants. In the summer of 1998, SEPUP brought to its headquarters teachers who had field-tested its year-long "Science and Sustainability" high school course to help the team craft some of the questions to be included in the project's assessment protocols.

Working Through Telecollaboration

Telecollaboration, or collaborating almost exclusively through e-mail, fax, and other means of long-distance communication, is the structure of choice for projects that must use individuals too widely dispersed to meet often or at all. The project director and team seek out individuals with the specific skills or expertise the project needs, then interact with them electronically to draft, review, and revise drafts of materials. A telecollaborative structure maximizes a project's flexibility in staffing, enabling a group to cast its net as widely as possible in recruiting team members.

GLOBE's Approach. Perhaps the most dramatic example of a telecollaborative structure is Global Learning and Observations to Benefit the Environment, or GLOBE, based in Washington, D.C. With more than a dozen teams of principal investigators, hundreds of collaborators, and thousands of participating schools in more than 80 countries, this consortium of independent projects could not be managed in any other way.

GLOBE was organized in 1995 and is funded by several federal agencies, including the National Aeronautics and Space Administration, the NSF, the Environmental Protection Agency, the National Oceanic and Atmospheric Administration, and the departments of education and state. Participating classrooms regularly collect a variety of geophysical data about their localities, including such things as precipitation, high and low temperatures, and water pH. The classrooms then use satellite global positioning systems to fix the exact location at which the information was taken. They forward the data to the GLOBE's computerized repository, where it is available to both scientists and students studying the Earth as a system.

For teachers, GLOBE's materials describe procedures for collecting individual kinds of data. Each procedure is accompanied by six or more learning activities that grow out of the data collected. (For example, participating students measure moisture in local soils. In related activities that use the techniques of guided inquiry, students collect samples of three different types of local soils and measure their porosity and permeability.)

To find the best ideas for activities to accompany each procedure, GLOBE published a request for proposals through the NSF. The project's directors then chose the proposals they judged to be most effective educationally while still being scientifically meaningful.

"Our program deals in integrated elements rather than separate pieces," says Ralph Coppola, GLOBE's assistant director for education. "So our biggest challenge is to find a synergistic way for people to work together who literally are located across the country. We're always working to find steadily more effective ways to have everyone work together." GLOBE's management team first developed a set of criteria for its teams of principal investigators to use in designing activities aligned with new national standards and recent insights from cognitive science. Drafts of the activities are then scrutinized by two teams of GLOBE staff reviewers, one team evaluating scientific content and the other the activities' educational approach. Finally, Coppola and Dickson Butler, the program's chief scientist, go over the reviewers' comments, add their own, and return the annotated drafts to the designers.

By channeling all editorial comments and changes through just two people, activities designed by far-flung individuals are shaped by a single intelligence in each of the two design areas of science content and science pedagogy. That helps the activities remain consistent with each other as well as with the program's design criteria. "If people want to react to the comments and changes, they can deal directly with the two of us instead of with one of the many people on the review teams or someone in the publishing operation," Coppola says.

Even though telecommunications technologies, and especially the Internet, make "virtual" teams possible, sustaining long-distance teamwork over the months or years of a project can pose communications difficulties that are daunting at best. Coppola estimates that he spends as much as half of his time communicating with team members.

"The processes of managing communication in a project so dispersed is a matter of continuous fine-tuning," he adds. "It will never be perfect."

To help smooth interactions, GLOBE invites its principal investigators and other participants to an annual conference to present their work, talk over procedural and other problems, and work out consensus about ways to resolve organizational and management difficulties.

Drawbacks of Telecollaboration. A project relying on telecollaboration among team members need not limit the size of its creative team. (By their design, some projects—such as GLOBE—will have few alternatives.) But telecollaboration limits the personal interaction that can spark new ideas and improvements to evolving materials. Also, telecollaborative programs are less able to alter their approach or work plans as easily as projects in which developers work elbow to elbow: The process of communicating new strategies clearly and efficiently could easily be more cumbersome than the project's leadership team could manage. The long-distance approach seems most successful when the project is creating either a textbook or materials distributed over the Internet that teachers will modify as they use them.

CHOOSING A PROJECT STRUCTURE

Based on their experiences, veteran developers often tend to favor a particular project structure. However, the form a given project takes must be dictated by the aims of the project itself, not by habit. There is no guarantee that a specific organizational model will work for a particular project.

"For the integrated materials we developed, we needed an extremely broad multidisciplinary, multifaceted design team and process," says IMaST's Sherry Meier. "Not every project needs those components."

The project's subject area or areas, the preferences and work styles of team members, available time and budget, and the strictures or preferences of the host institution work together to determine a project's shape and structure. In addition, novel combinations of these structures—or entirely new ones—may evolve as developers master emerging technologies, such as teleconferencing, that continue to appear along the ever-expanding spectrum of choice in electronic communications.

In weighing these choices, developers should recognize that bringing together a full-time staff in one place offers two specific advantages that other structures cannot.

First, bringing a project staff into common quarters for full-time work fosters informal, unplanned interchanges between individuals or among the group. Such exchanges nurture the combination of collaboration and individual creativity that will allow the group's best ideas to evolve over time instead of trying to force them to appear during short, hectic meetings driven by the calendar.

Second, a project can more easily plan and provide an element of professional development for its team members when all work together in the same place. Projects structured around telecollaboration or short, intense conferences and work sessions necessarily emphasize the efficient creation and production of materials far more than the personal and professional development of the individuals who take part. Besides, team members have other responsibilities that limit the energy and time that they can invest in the project. Educators who devote their full time and energies to a project can, and should expect to, benefit in return for their commitment.

However, such professional development should not be viewed only as a perk of full-time employment. As a specialty within education, materials development must seek to advance its repertoire of institutionalized knowledge and skills. As part of doing so, it must also build a cadre of developers formally prepared within the specialty. All projects should seek ways to devote a portion of their resources toward further educating materials developers. Full-time teams working together offer the greatest potential for adding quickly to the ranks of developers who not only have raw experience but also have had the chance to hone their specialized expertise through targeted coursework, graduate assistantships, internships, "mentorships," or other kinds of rigorous, thorough, and personalized education. (For a more detailed discussion, see Chapter 13.)

THE TEACHER'S ROLE

The teacher plays the same central role in a project regardless of its structure: to serve as the link and guide to, and the voice of, reality and practicality in the classroom. In a team's in-house design sessions or as part of a summer writing workshop, teachers guide developers at every step on questions ranging from age appropriateness to the current connotation of particular words. When a team tests early versions of activities and materials with students, teachers are the partners who open classrooms to it and give developers an initial appraisal. During national field tests, teachers provide the collective feedback that tells developers to what degree their efforts have succeeded. And, as the new materials are being implemented, it is knowledgeable teachers—especially those who have worked with the project team—who will be the most persuasive champions. Robert Chang, project director of Materials World Modules (MWM) at Northwestern University, puts it precisely: "Teachers are the most important members of a development team," he says. "They are truly indispensable."

CONCLUSION

The key to a successful project is to foster a collaborative culture. "Collaborative" in this case indicates an atmosphere in which team members feel free to criticize others' ideas in a constructive way while accepting criticism of their own ideas without feeling defensive. The leadership and tone provided by the project director have much to do with cultivating the proper team spirit.

The project must also choose a management approach that supports that culture. An approach based on the principles of continuous improvement usually meet the need effectively.

A project usually will choose its organizational structure from among three models: team members working full time in a single location, team members meeting periodically for short work sessions, and telecollaboration. Each has advantages and drawbacks. However, regardless of the structure chosen, one of the director's and team members' chief obligations is to maintain a sense of mutual respect within a climate of candor. Such an atmosphere can do much to overcome the drawbacks of long-distance collaboration.

8

Assessment and Evaluation

One had to cram all this stuff into one's mind for the examinations, whether one liked it or not. This coercion had such a deterring effect on me that, after I had passed the final examination, I found the consideration of any scientific problems distasteful to me for an entire year.

—Albert Einstein, *Ideas and Opinions*

GAUGING THE POSITIVE IMPACT of a materials development project is done in two parts. First, whether and what students learn (and how well) by using the project's materials must be *assessed*. In guided inquiry, authentic learning is best measured by assessments that are both *embedded* and *authentic*. This chapter explains both terms and details a model assessment system already in use that embodies both principles effectively.

Second, the project itself will be *evaluated*. A project team may be allowed to evaluate itself or, more likely, the project's funder will appoint an external evaluator. Evaluations examine how efficiently the project team manages itself, its work, and the funder's money. This chapter also advises project teams on how best to prepare for, and profit from, evaluations.

THE TEACHER AS ASSESSMENT LEADER

Too often as educators, we assess what is easy to measure and easy to grade—increasingly by using a machine. As a result, conventional curricula focus on facts instead of on concepts and their application. But standardized, fact-based tests do not and cannot assess the processes and skills that our newest voting citizens and workers will need to know. They also cannot assess how well students are able to use what they have learned to improve their own lives and those of their communities. Of course, standardized tests have legitimate roles. They can signal long-term trends in students' mastery of facts. Given in high school, they also can predict first-year college success because so much of freshman instruction is conducted in large groups and assessed by fact-based tests that can be scored by machines. The fit is perfect, but the shoe itself is wrong.

If we are to develop accurate, authentic means to assess inquiry-oriented, activity-based learning, we must trust the judgment of classroom teachers. If one wants to improve the condition of one's head, inside or out, one places oneself in the hands of a licensed professional—neurologist, psychiatrist, barber, or cosmetologist—and accepts the professional's judgment, seeking second opinions only from other professionals. Only in education does our society assume that the judgment of front-line professionals must be routinely validated by third parties—in this case, by the makers of batch-processed tests. Authentic learning can be assessed accurately only by the teachers who work with the students being assessed.

ASSESSMENT IN GUIDED INQUIRY

In guided inquiry, assessment should be the fraternal twin of instruction: The two should look as much alike as possible but be designed differently enough so that each fulfills its distinct purpose. These *embedded* assessments weave the tasks on which students are assessed into the learning activities, projects, and investigations that students conduct as routine elements of their learning. The activities designated as assessment tools are carefully crafted to resemble as closely as possible any other day-to-day activity. In contrast, standardized tests can interrupt learning as teachers and students "get ready" to take the test by practicing test-taking skills, drilling repeatedly on the same lists of facts, and so on.

Assessments that are more useful (as well as more valid) than conventional standardized tests are successfully being built into inquiry-based learning activities themselves, thus earning the adjective *embedded*. The National Science Education Standards explains why they should be: "Assessment practices . . . provide operational definitions of what is important . . . the methods used to collect educational data define in measurable terms what teachers should teach and what students should learn. . . . For example, the use of an extended inquiry for an assessment task signals what students are to learn, how teachers are to teach, and where resources are to be allocated" (NAS, 1996, p. 76).

We emphasize that our approach to assessment, as to development, is evolutionary rather than revolutionary. Authentic, embedded assessment is not intended to supplant fact-oriented tests. Knowledge of facts remains key to a knowledge of science or any field. The goal of these new assessment regimes is to augment the measurement of factual knowledge with measurements of students' evolving abilities to understand what those facts mean and to apply them appropriately in making real-life decisions.

THE VALUE OF EMBEDDED, AUTHENTIC ASSESSMENT

Embedding assessments in activities themselves offers three advantages. First, these assessments can measure what the national standards call the "rich and varied" outcomes of science education—not only skills in factual recall but also such accomplishments as "the ability to inquire" and "knowing and understanding scientific facts, concepts, principles, laws, and theories" (NAS, 1996, p. 76). Second, they deduct little time from learning compared to conventional tests, during which learning activities usually cease. Third, they help to eliminate conventional test-taking skills (or lack thereof) as a significant factor that too often conceals a student's actual degree of intellectual achievement.

But embedding assessment is only half the challenge of designing valid, accurate assessment protocols for guided inquiry. The other half is to make the assessments authentic. The National Science Education Standards describe authentic assessments as "exercises that require students to apply scientific knowledge and reasoning to situations similar to those they will encounter in the world outside the classroom, as well as to situations that approximate how scientists do their work" (NAS, 1996, p. 78).

EMBEDDING AUTHENTIC ASSESSMENT IN GUIDED INQUIRY

As an example, consider an assessment event in the guided-inquiry course "Science and Sustainability" for high school students. A theme of the course is energy use and its impact on issues of sustainability. Through a series of course activities, students examine the principles of energy transfer. In one investigation, students burn equal amounts of ethanol and kerosene (instead of gasoline, for safety reasons) to heat identical volumes of water. The students observe and record the change in temperature in each container of water as well as similarities and differences in how the two fuels burn. Then the students are posed a question: "Chemically, gasoline is very similar to kerosene. How could the results of these investigations affect your decision to buy fuel for your car that combines ethanol and gasoline?"

The question is an assessment item, graded against a five-point rubric, that gauges a student's ability to gather and weigh evidence and to use that evidence to make trade-offs. (For example, students learn that ethanol burns more cleanly than gasoline but yields less energy per volume of fuel used.)

This ability to weigh evidence and balance advantages and disadvantages of specific choices is not only one of five variables on which students are assessed during the course but is also a task that will confront them daily in their lives beyond school.

The course's assessment scheme has already been tested and approved by school districts. As part of the course's field test phase in Brooklyn's high school district, the New York State Education Department approved a special Regents exam for the course. To qualify as a Regents exam, the test had to include sections of short-answer, fact-oriented questions. Because such questions are of value to teachers, the course included "item banks" of them. But as part of the specially designed Regents exam, students also answer embedded, authentic questions similar to those used in the course. Equally important, for the exam students are given copies of the scoring rubric that will be used to score their responses, showing them how to coordinate information and interpretation to improve their scores. Enabling students to refer to the scoring rubric during the test communicates to them that what is being tested is not memorization but the ability to gather and use evidence—an additional sign that new, more useful approaches to assessment are beginning to displace the old.

By replacing conventional assessment techniques with embedded, authentic tools and methods, educators can begin to achieve the National Science Education Standards' new assessment criteria, listed in Figure 8.1.

But the shift toward authentic, embedded assessment that guided inquiry calls for does not just suggest new kinds of tests (although such instruments are essential). It also carries two additional powerful implications.

First, it embodies a key aspect of the mechanisms of continuous improvement that has proven effective in other fields and, increasingly, within education as well: giving ultimate decision-making power to front-line employees. In education, those employees are teachers.

Although standardized tests purportedly are to be used only to compare student groups, they are routinely used (or misused) as ad hoc ways to judge the competence of local educators. An analogy: In business, if publicly traded corporations do not show increased earnings each quarter, decision-making executives often run the risk of being ousted by stockholders—a threat that leaves those executives reluctant to invest for the long term. Instead, they concentrate on making a quick buck for their companies and spend considerably less time planning for long-term success. These executives are not given the authority that accompanies their responsibilities; instead, they are held to standards enforced by outsiders with financial clout but without detailed knowledge of the industries in which the executives work. A similar situation exists in education. Teachers, collaborating with other professional educators, are in the best position to

Figure 8.1. The National Science Education Standards assessment guidelines.
Source: National Academy of Science (1996), p. 100.

Less emphasis on	*More emphasis on*
Assessing what is easily measured	Assessing what is most highly valued
Assessing discrete knowledge	Assessing rich, well-structured knowledge
Assessing scientific knowledge	Assessing scientific understanding and reasoning
Assessing to learn what students do not know	Assessing to learn what students do understand
Assessing only achievement	Assessing achievement and opportunity to learn
End-of-term assessment by teachers	Students engaged in ongoing assessment of their work and that of others
Development of external assessments by measurement experts alone	Teachers involved in the development of external assessments

decide what and how to teach in order to achieve the best long-term results for their students. They also are best able to determine how to measure those outcomes in the most valid ways.

Most often, standardized tests—and the form of education that they measure—are not teachers' or, in most cases, administrators' first choice as frameworks for the assessment of learning. As a sign Albert Einstein hung in his Princeton office noted, "Not everything that counts can be counted and not everything that can be counted counts."

But if scores on standardized tests do not rise steadily, regulators, parents, and public officials begin to doubt teachers' professional competence as well as the school's or district's academic program. As a result of those doubts, school board members and district or state administrators may bend to public pressure to "do something" and begin to micromanage classroom policies and practices or decide not to renew teachers' contracts. By using such a weak measure as standardized tests to evaluate teachers' accomplishments, the public and its chosen administrators weaken not only teachers' performance (because they "teach to the test") but also their credentials and credibility in the public eye as professionals.

In contrast, only competent professionals—not machines—can interpret the results of more complex assessments that gauge students' growth in an array of intellectual skills. As a result, embedded, authentic assessment methods can return to educators the ultimate authority and responsibility for gauging students' full range of achievement. These new approaches to the measurement of students' learning enable teachers to strengthen their claim to public recognition and respect as professionals to be entrusted with greater authority in guiding educational progress and change. Embedded, authentic assessment delivers more accurate information about students' achievements; therefore, these kinds of assessments make better criteria for gauging schools' and teachers' performances.

In addition, these new forms of assessment can do as good a job of comparing student achievement across geographic and socioeconomic ranges as the dreaded standardized tests that warp and constrict instructional patterns. As the National Science Education Standards point out, "the information resulting from new modes of assessment applied locally can have common meaning and value . . . despite the use of different assessment procedures and instruments in different locales. This contrasts with the traditional view of educational measurement that allows for comparisons only when they are based on parallel forms of the same test" (NAS, 1996, p. 78). As radical as the idea may seem, it is already being applied in SEPUP, the Full Option Science System (FOSS), and several other development programs funded by the National Science Foundation (NSF) for materials focused on inquiry.

The second implication of the shift toward authentic, embedded assessment is that these novel assessment structures have the power to reconfigure the culture of professional development within education. They employ a more effective structure of in-service education and technical support; and experience shows that they also create a forum in which teachers feel comfortable talking openly together about what they do, reflecting on their work and their choices, and relying on one another's help and advice to set new goals and directions of personal and collective improvement.

STANDARDIZED TESTS: WHAT GETS TESTED GETS TAUGHT

The National Science Education Standards endorse embedded assessments "that sample an assortment of [student skills] using diverse data-collection methods, rather than the more traditional sampling of one [skill] by a single method." The standards also acknowledge that "assessment and learning are so closely related that if all the outcomes are not assessed, teachers and students likely will redefine their expectations for learning science only to the outcomes that are assessed" (NAS, 1996, pp. 76, 82). It is an elegant way of affirming teachers' long-standing maxim—an operational definition in itself—that "what gets tested gets taught."

In other words, assessment schemes that limit themselves to conventional quick-answer tests of factual recall fail to measure the diverse kinds of learning that a student integrates when mastering a concept or skill. In addition, they also send the wrong messages to students, teachers, parents, and administrators about what learning and education are, and should be, about.

Since the mid-1980s, more and more educators have been experimenting in earnest with portfolios, rubrics, student performances, and similar attempts at embedded, authentic assessment protocols designed to reflect not only a student's intellectual product but also how he or she crafted it.

However, educators' efforts to cultivate and master new, more meaningful assessment tools are colliding with a contrary trend: More and more state education agencies are mandating—and the U.S. government is urging—the expanded use of standardized, machine-scored tests as the primary means to measure how well and how quickly students and schools are improving. (In most cases, the tests sample fact-based language and mathematical skills in grades 3 or 4, again in grades 8 to 10, and in the senior year of high school.)

A lot rides on the outcome of these measurements. Increasingly, the results are being used as the basis to determine a student's qualification for high school graduation, to justify or reduce school budgets, to attract and retain students, to determine teachers' assignments and administrators' job security, and, ultimately in some places, to decide on the continued existence of the school itself.

But using standardized tests to prod schools to improve students' skills is inherently ironic, if not self-defeating: Nothing could lead schools farther away from the National Science Education Standards' recommendation to use multiple approaches to assess multiple variables. Indeed, remembering that "what gets tested gets taught," few initiatives could do less to help educators and students embrace guided inquiry's approach to learning that our emerging society and workplace demand. Increasingly, educators' choice of assessment protocols is being restricted by economic and political considerations—often reinforced by traditions and unquestioned assumptions—beyond their control. These considerations, and the forms of assessment they fix in place, are foes of genuine learning in science and, at least to the same extent, in mathematics and other subjects as well.

STANDARDIZED TESTING AND SCIENCE EDUCATION

Because assessment shapes instruction, the new pressure for standardized testing would marginalize science education in elementary schools even more than it is now. Teachers at that level spend more time than ever drilling students on the mechanics of the two subjects—language and mathematics—that dominate the standardized elementary-grade tests on which so much rides. Too often, science sessions are fit into whatever time is left over after reading and arithmetic have been "covered." Test scores indicate that students using science materials from SEPUP and FOSS perform better on standardized reading tests, but integrating the two subjects for the benefit of both remains an alien concept in most classrooms (Scott, 1999).

In too many elementary schools, science is studied only when a circuit-riding "science specialist" teacher visits a classroom. In short, more pressure for standardized tests means even less time to cultivate in students the inquiry-oriented skills that comprise science. In states or districts in which science is included in standard exams, the subject—and students' attitude toward it—tend to fare no better. We recently heard a 10-year-old declare that she hates science. When asked what her fifth-grade class had done that day with the school's science specialist, she reported that "first, we watched the teacher dissect something. Then we had a sheet showing all the muscles on the back and front of the human body. There are lines coming from each one and we have to memorize the names of the muscles for the test." No wonder she hates science. Assessment processes that refuse to acknowledge that science is about the process of discovery and decision making lie at the root of such travesties.

In higher grades, science is granted standing as a distinct subject worthy of being studied regularly. But, again, standardized as well as classroom science tests tend to be keyed to quick-answer questions that emphasize factual recall. As the National Science Education Standards point out, the abilities that students master in designing investigations, collecting and evaluating evidence, and drawing conclusions from their evidence are best assessed through multiple measures—not through measuring the single ability to recall facts, on which standardized tests are almost always based. But because of the dominant role that standardized tests play, rote learning takes precedence over inquiry and discovery in higher, as well as elementary, grades. As one ninth-grade science teacher from New York told us, "I'd love to use guided inquiry in my classes, but I don't have time. My kids have to pass the Regents exam at the end of the year. They have to know the facts."

The reliance on quick-answer exams is partly based on economics. Tests in which students blacken spaces to indicate their answers can be machine-scored, making it practical to assess hundreds of thousands of students quickly and, therefore, cheaply. It is also partly a matter of assumption: Regulators and administrators assume that students' performances can be accurately compared only if the students all take the same test. The problem is that, while efficient, such tests are almost meaningless when it comes to measuring the kind of learning that our emerging 21st-century economy and society are demanding—the kind of learning that grows through guided inquiry.

Embedded, authentic assessment redresses that flaw while it also expands the purposes and uses of assessment itself. Conventional tests neither diagnose the needs of individual learners as they are learning nor help teachers identify more effective learning experiences for their students. Typically, teachers conduct their most comprehensive tests at the *end* of a unit or a year. By the time the results are known, students have moved on to a different "unit" or class and, in the case of many standardized year-end tests, individual students' scores are not reported to the student but only as part of a class average. Testing students after they have completed a "unit" or textbook or subject area might show how well those particular students remembered what was presented to them. But that limited approach to assessment does little to guide teachers and developers in improving *how* facts and concepts were presented to that group of students—or can be to other students in the future. If some students had trouble mastering the material, or if all did because the instructional approach was inadequately designed, discovering those sad facts through post-testing does nothing to help those students.

Assessment processes embedded within authentic activities can help teachers identify misconceptions that students are developing (and even problems in the design of the instructional materials) in time to correct those problems *before* those same students are done with the course. This approach to assessment enables teachers and developers to modify their materials or techniques so that students' experiences and achievement continuously improve in quality as they study, and it helps to shape new models for assessment now being developed.

NEW OPTIONS: PORTFOLIOS AND RUBRICS

Clearly, reconfiguring the dominant modes of assessment to make them compatible with inquiry-oriented learning requires a tectonic shift within the culture of education if not within that of our society in general. To help foster that transition, materials developers are collaborating with assessment specialists to evolve new, objective measurement techniques that can be built into inquiry-oriented materials. At the beginning of the 21st century, thousands of schools and tens of thousands of teachers are deep in experiments with two in particular: portfolio assessment and scoring rubrics.

In portfolio assessments, teachers make judgments about a student's progress not by looking only at test scores but also by reviewing collections of the student's actual work. A mathematics teacher might review all of a student's work on a particular topic—polynomial equations, for example—to track the growth of the student's skills and also to spot problem areas in which the student might need special attention. Typically, a student's best work in a subject (with examples often picked by the student) becomes part of a permanent portfolio that accompanies the student from grade to grade, documenting growth in skills through the years.

Scoring rubrics give teachers a numerical framework within which to assess students' mastery of intellectual processes that are more complex than factual recall. A typical rubric (from an old French word for *procedure*) distinguishes five levels of skill, each one assigned a numerical score value from, say, zero to four. Each level is defined by a set of criteria that a sample of student work must meet to achieve that level. A student's performance in a particular task is judged against the criteria for each level, is assigned one specific level, and thus achieves a numerical score that can be translated into a grade. For example, the criterion for the first level might be that a completed assignment reveals that the student is off-task or shows no understanding of the concept being assessed, which earns the student no points, while a student whose assignment is complete and correct fulfills the third level's criteria and earns three points. (For an example of a SEPUP scoring rubric, see Figure 8.2.)

THE PRESSURES OF TRADITION

However, as eager as many teachers are to try new materials, they just as often balk at embracing new assessment methods. Indeed, perhaps the largest single concern teachers voice when tempted to adopt materials for guided inquiry is, "How would this change the way I assess and the way I'm evaluated?" They know that old-fashioned quick-answer tests will not necessarily measure students' growth in a range of intellectual processes. But they also know that new assessment protocols still face powerful opposition from education's cultural, political, and professional infrastructure.

Some of those opposing pressures are practical. Teachers know that personalized assessments will demand more of their time than do machine-scored tests—time most teachers already do not have to spare, especially as budgetary pressures threaten to increase class sizes in many districts. Also, many educational managers rely on the ease and reliability with which results from standardized tests can be tabulated and compared. In the 1930s, a surge of interest among educators in assessing students through portfolios—then called "profiles"—succumbed to those two forces. "They proved to be too time-consuming for teachers; also, statisticians opposed profiles because they could not be interpreted statistically," notes science educator Paul Hurd (1999, p. 23).

Many parents and conservative education activists implicitly believe that facts are the stuff of learning and, therefore, that exams that test facts are still the most valid forms of assessment. Standardized tests are beginning to find ways to probe higher-order thinking skills (Wilson & Daviss, 1996), but progress is slow compared to the speed with which government agencies are mandating machine-scorable tests. Compounding the problem: Relatively few educators have extensive, positive experience with any of the new assessment alternatives. Indeed, virtually none of those alternatives have yet been developed and used thoroughly enough so that significant numbers of teachers can use them easily and quickly with skill and confidence.

In addition, when evaluating any new assessment system, educators confront an array of issues related to the integrity of their profession and performance. How can teachers know that a new method is any more valid than quick-answer tests? How objectively and accurately does a new assessment scheme measure the mastery of processes? Will a new system demand huge amounts of teachers' time? How do teachers translate results from more free-form assessment methods such as portfolios into the letter grades that colleges, school districts, and states still require?

These concerns are fundamental to materials design, to improving what happens in classrooms, and, increasingly, to teachers' compensation and, in some cases, their job security. The concerns also are warranted: Several issues raised by the new methods have yet to be resolved.

For example, most teachers using portfolios to gauge students' learning still must translate their subjective judgments of student progress into the letter grades required by districts and states. Teachers evaluating portfolios report that they argue constantly about the fairest and most accurate ways to systematize and quantify their judgments of quality. At the same time, they still struggle to avoid the kinds of standardization that portfolios are designed to avoid (Wilson & Daviss, 1996). The grading standards derived from scoring rubrics can be made less vague and more uniform through ongoing discussions in which groups of teachers pore over examples of students' work and haggle their way to agreement about where each example falls within the rubric's hierarchy of performance levels. But that process, like portfolio assessment, threatens to cost teachers more time than they currently have available to invest in it.

Now materials developers and assessment specialists are collaborating to find new answers to educators' long-standing concerns about far-reaching assessment protocols. Developers are embedding new assessment methods within materials themselves to measure authentic learning—the kind of learning that grows from guided inquiry—in ways that teachers can understand, respect, and manage.

A PROTOTYPE OF AN EMBEDDED, AUTHENTIC ASSESSMENT FOR GUIDED INQUIRY

Since 1992, SEPUP's development team has been collaborating with assessment specialists in the Berkeley Evaluation and Assessment Research group (BEAR) at the University of California under grants from the NSF. The partnership's goal has been to design, test, and implement an assessment system for guided inquiry that would be embedded, authentic, practical, and valid. In addition to embracing new theories and methods in assessment, the system also provides teachers with data that they can use to redirect or otherwise improve classroom sessions not only after students have completed a course of study but also while that course is still in progress.

A prototype of the assessment structure was designed as an integral part of "Issues, Evidence, and You," or IEY, SEPUP's year-long science course for eighth or ninth grade, and field-tested nationally as part of the course during the 1994–1995 school year. By the year 2000, other development programs such as FOSS and Hands-On Universe were investigating or experimenting with similar systems.

The method is still a work in progress; its developers and users are aware of its drawbacks. Among them: Developing and tailoring an authentic, embedded assessment system for a set of new materials can add as much as 20 percent to a project's development costs. The new assessment scheme also initially makes new demands on teachers' time as they tackle the always controversial issue of converting assigned numerical ratings to grades.

"It looks easier than it is," cautions Richard Duquin, a middle school science teacher in Kenmore, New York, who helped SEPUP develop the system. "People need to be taught to use it; then they need to practice it a while before they feel comfortable with it." Lori Gillam, a science teacher at the Steller Secondary Alternative School in Anchorage, Alaska, says, "I've been using the system for 5 years. It took me about a year to get comfortable with it, but it's worth it. It gives me a clearer picture of what my students really know and can do. It also helps me decide what to do in future class sessions to strengthen weak areas."

Two years after SEPUP first tested its new system, the NSF's 1997 review of widely used middle school science curriculum materials cited IEY's assessment program as an outstanding example of embedded assessment at the middle-school level (NSF, 1997). One teacher using the system put it more bluntly. "This isn't the kind of assessment system where a kid can screw around all year and then do fine on a test just because he's smart. This is the kind of process where a kid needs to progressively improve specific skills in order to do well on the assessment."

The assessment system is based on the use of rubrics or scoring guides. Teachers use one rubric to gauge and chart student progress in each of five intellectual skills: understanding scientific concepts, communicating scientific information, designing and conducting investigations, gathering and evaluating evidence and using that evidence to weigh options and make choices (see Figure 8.2), and group interaction. A student's performance in each area is assigned a value ranging from zero, meaning that the student was off-task, to four, indicating that the student has exceeded the standards of being merely complete and correct in an answer and displayed some exceptional effort or additional insight.

This pioneering scoring system delivers a wealth of detail about the progress of individual students and classes as well as the effectiveness of the learning materials themselves. But it still requires teachers to maintain for each student a separate map for each skill the course sets out to teach—an investment of time that many teachers are unwilling to make.

To solve the problem, assessment specialists are working under an NSF grant to design a computer program to make the maps for teachers as student scores are recorded. According to Karen Draney, an educational psychologist and member of the BEAR team, "The software, which doubles as a gradebook, should allow teachers to handle the record-keeping aspect of the assessment system in not much more time than they need to keep up a traditional grading system" (K. Draney, personal communication, 1999). (As this is written, the computer software needed to make it practical and effective in the classroom is being tested to see if it is ready for widespread use.)

MODERATION'S MULTIPLE ROLES

The process known as "social moderation" is key to establishing and maintaining the validity of this new assessment approach. In a moderation session, a group of six to ten teachers in a school, department, or district come together approximately once a month to discuss and interpret examples of students' work against the scoring guide. Through those discussions they hone the system's assessment standards and criteria as well as their own skills in making assessment judgments.

Figure 8.2. Sample assessment rubric: Scoring guide for evidence and trade-offs (ET) variable.

Score	*Using Evidence* *Response uses objective reason(s) based on relevant evidence to argue for or against a choice.*	*Using Evidence to Make Trade-Offs* *Response recognizes multiple perspectives of issue and explains each perspective using objective reasons, supported by evidence, in order to make a choice.*
4	Accomplishes level 3 AND goes beyond in some significant way, e.g., questioning or justifying the source, validity, and/or quantity of the evidence.	Accomplishes level 3 AND goes beyond in some significant way, e.g., suggesting additional evidence beyond the activity that would influence choices in specific ways OR questioning the source, validity, and/or quantity of the evidence and explaining how it influences choice.
3	Provides major objective reasons AND supports each with relevant and accurate evidence.	Uses relevant and accurate evidence to weight the advantages and disadvantages of multiple options and makes a choice supported by the evidence.
2	Provides some objective reasons AND some supporting evidence, BUT at least one reason is missing and/or part of the evidence is incomplete	States at least two options AND provides some objective reasons using some relevant evidence, BUT reasons or choices are incomplete and/or part of the evidence is missing OR only one complete and accurate perspective has been provided.
1	Provides only subjective reasons (opinions) for choice; uses unsupported statements; OR uses inaccurate or irrelevant evidence from the activity.	States at least one perspective BUT provides only subjective reasons and/or uses inaccurate or irrelevant evidence.
0	Missing, illegible, or offers no reasons AND no evidence to support choice made.	Missing, illegible, or completely lacks reasons and evidence.
x	Students had no opportunity to respond.	

Moderation enables teachers to arrive, by consensus *at the local level*, at a common set of standards for student performance. By debating and finally settling on shared views, the teachers can fix uniform approaches and grading criteria throughout a department, school, or district with a consistency approaching that of the machine-scored tests that measure only a limited aspect of what students have learned.

Moderation meetings can be intense and frequent at first as teachers struggle to fashion common criteria for assessing students' performances, then less frequent—though regular—as teachers become more adept at applying the commonly developed criteria to individual students' work. Indeed, in later sessions teachers may bring only student work that presents problems calling for tricky or unusual assessment judgments. Working through difficult cases becomes an exercise that enables all teachers involved to further sharpen their own abilities to make judgments.

In addition to simply helping teachers score students' work, moderation sessions also fulfill three additional, equally important purposes.

First, *moderation can play a significant role in guiding teachers as they plan future class sessions as well as in evaluating and improving materials.* In moderation sessions, teachers may discover common or consistent mistakes in the work of a number of students. In those cases, the teachers might decide that there is a need to revisit those ideas in class, reviewing the concepts or skills that moderated assessment highlights as weak areas. The assessment system shows students what they have not yet mastered; moderation sessions show teachers what they need to focus on and how to adjust learning plans to help their students correct weaknesses.

"The assessment system has an effect on instruction because it gives teachers a quick way to self-assess," explains Dr. Lily Roberts, former co-director of the BEAR project.

But those weaknesses can also signal flaws in the activities themselves or in their accompanying materials. When teachers recognize a distinctive pattern of errors in the work of many students, they should review their classroom presentations, approaches, and methods (or ask a colleague to do so) to determine if the problem lies in those areas. At the same time, they should alert the activities' development team. Because developers are intimately familiar with their own materials, they can often suggest a slight change in classroom technique that can solve the problem.

If instead the flaw is inherent in the activities or materials, the development team will often hear of it from several sources and can use the various comments and views to more effectively pinpoint the source of the design defect. Developers then can correct problems in subsequent revisions or supplemental information provided to teachers using the program.

Used in this way, embedded, authentic assessment becomes a key tool in the constant process of design and redesign so necessary if learning materials are to evolve to become as effective as possible.

Moderation also can affect instruction in another, perhaps surprising way. Some teachers distribute the scoring guides and ask students to rate their own and one another's work in classroom moderation sessions. A number are finding that such self-assessment gives students new motivation. "Getting a 2 or 3 on a specific task seems to mean more to them than getting 75 or 85 percent on a general test," Roberts notes. "One girl told us that science had never been her best subject but now she's getting an A because she can see clearly what is expected of her and what she needs to do to improve her work."

Moderating their own work seems to routinely lead students to revisit their weak areas and struggle to improve their performances, taking greater responsibility for their own learning—exactly the kind of self-directed process of ongoing learning called for in the National Science Education Standards. Some teachers report that self-moderation inspires even the best students to polish their work further.

As a second purpose, *moderation can serve as an exemplar of the criteria that a number of researchers and observers deem necessary for effective, long-term professional development*: It is research-based, designed by specialists, and guided by teachers themselves; it also provides technical assistance when teachers feel the need for it. Any seasoned educator will acknowledge that the usual quick, "in-and-out" workshops and other short-term, closed-end approaches that typify in-service teacher education fail to help teachers grow and change over time. To be truly effective, teacher enhancement must be long-term and reach deeply into their professional experiences.

Because the process of moderation is open-ended, teachers can explore issues of assessment over time, sharpening their skills and growing in expertise at their own pace. Teachers determine that pace because they guide and control the discussion and direction of the moderation sessions. Administrators report that the release time given teachers to take part in moderation sessions is more than repaid in the teachers' expanded abilities to accurately assess a wider range of student learning. Just as important, teachers' increased ability to detect students' weaknesses—and to correct them swiftly and effectively before the student moves on to another course or to graduation—can only improve the public's image of teaching as a legitimate profession.

In their role as a vehicle for professional development, moderation sessions provide a forum for teachers to talk together about their work in a way that does not require them to judge one another or evaluate one another's classroom practices. As trust and comfort grow among the group's members, the give-and-take of the debates over how to rate students' work has a way of expanding to include other areas of classroom practice.

That slowly growing openness and collegiality begins to break down teachers' isolation and the barriers between teachers that mark the traditional culture of education and have so often prevented them from sharing ideas. When those barriers begin to crumble, effective professional development can begin. As Michael Fullan (1991), dean of the University of Toronto's education faculty, notes, "Other teachers are often the preferred source of [innovative] ideas. . . . The more teachers interact concerning their own practices, the more they will be able to bring about improvements that they themselves identify as necessary" (p. 13).

Third, because moderation cultivates that supportive interaction so effectively, *it has the power to foster far-reaching forms of collaboration and, therefore, positive and permanent educational change.* Experience shows that the sessions establish a culture of their own in which teachers gradually become more reflective about their classroom practices. As they talk together, they begin to discover two things: that it is safe to talk about their work and their concerns about it, and that there is power in sharing, or even pooling, their ideas and experiences.

"One teacher told us that the moderation sessions were difficult at first," Roberts says, "but as the teachers worked together over time they jelled as a group. Now, in between moderation sessions, the teachers call each other for help and advice on other things and to try out ideas on each other." In a few cases, principals have developed enough interest in the new assessment system to teach classes in the schools they administer and bring their own students' work to the moderation session.

When teachers and administrators meet together regularly to work as colleagues in an ongoing process, their working relationship changes from one of distance, and often distrust, to one of collaboration and synergy. When that happens, the transformation of entire departments or even schools becomes possible as they move toward the long-held ideal of a cooperating and collaborating group of professionals.

STRUCTURING SUCCESSFUL COLLABORATIONS BETWEEN DEVELOPERS AND ASSESSMENT SPECIALISTS

As developers create new kinds of materials to teach students new kinds of skills, they are obligated to help to create new ways to effectively assess students' mastery of those new skills. To fulfill that obligation, they must work in close collaboration with assessment specialists to design the most effective ways to assess student achievements resulting from the use of specific innovative materials.

Such collaborations are increasingly common but are not always successful. In designing the new assessment system described above, SEPUP developers and BEAR assessment specialists evolved four suggestions that can smooth collaborations between developers and assessment experts:

1. To make embedded, authentic assessment an integral component of a project's materials, the project team must include assessment specialists from the very beginning of the design process.
2. Professionally, developers and assessment specialists wrestle with different issues and pursue different purposes and goals. The goal of the partnerships is not to transform developers into assessors or vice versa. Instead, it is to enable members of both specialties to help each other achieve their unique professional objectives by working together to ensure the success of both the development and assessment components of the project.
3. For the partnership to succeed, developers must understand the dictates and implications of the research base that underlies the assessment system they adopt for their project. Similarly, assessment specialists must grasp the practical goals and expected learning outcomes of the materials being developed. Therefore, when the partnership begins each group must devote time specifically to teaching, and learning from, the other about their specific goals, methods, and concerns.
4. Developers and assessment specialists can smooth and strengthen their working partnership by investing time early in the project to work together to design one, or even a few, activities. This initial collaboration can not only show each group how the other thinks and works but also fashion a common understanding of the elements that make an activity a good candidate for assessment as well as an effective learning experience.

As developers learn to view each aspect of each new activity as a potential assessment item, they can show assessment specialists which components within activities they regard as most important to use as assessment tools. The assessment specialists can analyze those components as well as their context among others in the materials being developed. Developers and assessment specialists then can work together to refine the choices and designs of assessment items. During and after field tests of the materials and their assessment system, the team will collaborate again to review teachers' comments and use the results of classroom experience to refine and improve assessment items and techniques again.

EVALUATING PROJECTS AND THE MATERIALS THEY CREATE

An evaluation has twin objectives. The first is to determine whether the project has worked efficiently and effectively to meet its goals and obligations. This is known as *project evaluation*. The second objective is *materials evaluation*, also known as *program evaluation*. (The materials a project develops are sometimes referred to as "programs.") The new materials are evaluated to determine their effectiveness as a platform for the interactions between students and teachers that become the curriculum. In other words, materials evaluations gather evidence of whether students learn more using the new materials than they do using ones already available.

In this context, the term *evaluation* applies to the collection of evidence for these two purposes. It does not refer directly to assessing student learning. Evidence gathered from student assessments may be used in preparing an evaluation, but that is not the primary reason for collecting it.

For three reasons (if not more), project and materials evaluations are becoming essential components of publicly funded instructional material development projects.

First, public funding agencies such as the NSF increasingly require various kinds of evaluations. A project supported by public money is obligated to show the public how those funds were spent and what the public has gained as a result.

Second, schools considering adopting all or part of the output of a materials development effort require data before making a decision. Did the project conduct classroom trials? Were the trials conducted in classrooms with students like ours? Did the students learn more using these new materials than they would have using the ones we have been using? Evaluations gather the data that schools require, and projects need to supply, before making a decision to adopt and implement new materials.

Third, a good evaluation can show a project team weaknesses in its efforts so that the group can address and solve them before they get out of hand. But even if projects are not obligated to undergo evaluations, they should: A good evaluation will show a project team its strengths and weaknesses and enable the group to learn from the experience and therefore further improve the final version of the project's materials.

Project Evaluation

Project evaluations provide funders, a project's home institution, and team members and their professional community with information about whether and how well the project has accomplished its goals.

Some aspects of project evaluation are internal. These include simple checks, such as whether the team is meeting the milestones along its timeline, whether it has developed a complete plan for implementation, and whether it has recruited a diverse enough group of sites for its national field test. Evaluation should be an ongoing, integral part of all project activities, ranging from evaluating team members' job performance to purchasing project materials at the lowest possible prices.

In addition to this internal component of project evaluation, many funders—especially if the projects they fund are especially expensive, lengthy, unusual, or elaborate—will expect the project team to appoint an external evaluator. (The funder also will expect the right to approve the choice or may even appoint its own evaluator for a project.) Before finalizing the terms of a grant, a project director or team must fully understand the funder's terms and expectations regarding outside evaluators; accepting the grant will obligate the project to those terms and conditions.

Usually, an external evaluator will visit the project's headquarters periodically to collect evidence regarding the project's operations and accomplishment of its goals. For example, the evaluator may compare the project's timeline with the work it has actually completed. The evaluator might also check whether drafts of materials were adequately developed to enable the project's national field test to begin on time. The evaluator also might interview representatives of the producer-distributor to see whether the project and its commercial partner face unresolved difficulties that might delay the materials' implementation.

Frequently, project evaluations are done in two parts.

The first is called a *formative* evaluation. This aspect includes evaluation activities that take place as the materials are being developed and field-tested. In multiyear projects, funders usually rely on the results of formative evaluations to decide whether to release funds for subsequent years.

Formative evaluations usually require both a financial and a descriptive or qualitative report at least yearly, if not more often. A project must understand, and the written agreement between the funder and project must specify, a funder's benchmarks for a successful formative evaluation before a project team accepts a grant.

When a project's funding ends, the funder (and team members' professional community) will expect a *summative* evaluation of the project. A summative evaluation may be as short as a single page, summarizing the project's products and accomplishments to date. However, the project team's responsibility to its members, its host institution, its funder, and the profession requires that a more substantive report be prepared. The detailed version should include both quantitative and qualitative evidence of whether (and how well) the project operated as an organization and whether (and how thoroughly) it achieved its development and educational goals and objectives.

A summative evaluation benefits the project team as well as its funder and the larger community of educators. This report helps team members to reflect on what they have accomplished, what problems they have encountered, how they have addressed and overcome those problems, and (too often left out of such reports) which aspects have worked particularly well. For example, perhaps the project devised a more efficient way for far-flung team members to communicate or a particularly innovative agreement with its producer-distributor. Details of those examples can help team members and other developers plan more successful future projects.

Designing with Materials Evaluation in Mind

As noted above, evaluating materials is a process of determining whether a project's materials enable students to learn concepts, information, and skills more or less effectively than other materials do. That is a simple statement describing a particularly intricate process.

All developers of materials for guided inquiry face the same challenge: The more innovative their materials are, the harder it is to find well-established assessment and evaluation methods that accurately gauge the materials' range of impacts on learning in all its richness. That makes it difficult for a project to provide the kinds of evidence that education's various constituencies need to be convinced of the innovation's value. At the same time, educators face growing political demands for accountability: Their pay and job security are increasingly linked to their students' performances on standardized tests. Therefore, a project's ability to provide detailed evaluation results showing its power to improve learning of both facts and processes becomes crucial if science education based on guided inquiry is to grow and flourish.

To meet this challenge, developers can design their materials to fulfill comprehensive new standards while still meeting educators' needs for acceptable scores on standardized tests.

The National Science Education Standards set content standards that can provide a useful frame of reference for developers facing that task in creating science materials for guided inquiry. More and more, these standards are determining the content of courses in biology, chemistry, earth science, and physics. The standards, developed by a committee whose members were drawn from each of the disciplines, are not revolutionary. Indeed, their specific content guidelines form the universe of topics from which questions on standardized tests are drawn.

Developers can use that conjunction of new standards and conventional testing forms to create materials able to meet evaluation criteria in both areas. To do so, they can do two things.

First, they must specify which of the content standards their materials embody and at which grade level or levels. This means something other than which content areas their materials "cover." It is too easy to make up lists of standards that materials "cover" (too often defined by wallpapering materials with lists and definitions of technical terms). This approach contributes to the public perception that science education in U.S. public schools is a mile wide and an inch deep.

Developers will find it far more useful to compare a project's goals with the specific content standards at the grade level or levels on which the project has focused. Team members can then identify ways in which the materials and student experiences they are creating will enable students to apply the skills and knowledge specified in each standard in their own lives, as the goals of the science standards demand.

Second, after a project team has taken that step, it can develop and try out banks of short-answer questions similar to the ones that appear on classroom quizzes and standardized tests. At the same time, the team can develop embedded, authentic assessments that help the teacher measure students' mastery of the higher-order skills, mandated by the standards, that the materials have been designed to address.

To accomplish the first part of this step, developers can analyze the sample questions that publishers of the most widely used standardized tests release publicly. Through that analysis, the developers can better ensure that their materials target the ideas and understandings that are both expressed in the content standards and addressed in standardized tests for the grade level or levels on which the project has focused. This needs to be done in addition to making sure that authentic, embedded assessment of students' real learning takes place.

The emphasis a team gives to this kind of review and analysis, and the degree to which the materials developed reflect that analysis, will result from an ongoing conversation among the project team, its funder, and its producer-distributor. The project decides on its educational goals, designs materials to meet them, and establishes its own system for assessing student learning. A competent commercial partner knows the market. A good producer-distributor will use that insight to help team members shape materials that meet market demands without violating the team's own objectives. For example, a team's proposed assessment may accomplish its goals for measuring its materials' educational effectiveness. But a commercial partner can tell the team that the system is so complex that teachers are unlikely to use it and that the system therefore must be adjusted.

A constant conversation among the three constituents will ensure that each understands the demands the others face in carrying out their parts of the project. Working together, the three can create materials that meet the team's goals, help the funder achieve its objectives, and give a producer-distributor materials that address practical realities of the marketplace. This can all be accomplished while using embedded, authentic assessments to track students' real accomplishments.

THE TEACHER'S ROLE IN ASSESSMENT AND EVALUATION

The most effective embedded, authentic assessments are able to help students learn in the act of "taking a test" and also guide teachers in planning the direction and content of future class sessions. Developing such useful assessment methods is not possible without the leadership, commitment, and participation of teachers. Indeed, this approach gives responsibility for conducting assessment back to the teacher—always the educational leader essential to the success of any program.

Teachers are also essential to the success of every aspect of project and materials evaluation. Teachers working with their students in everyday classrooms are among the best sources of evidence about how well a project team is doing its job and whether and how effectively its materials are achieving their educational objectives.

Partly for that reason, project and materials evaluations are among the most persuasive tools a project has to convince educators to adopt and implement its materials. Selling materials to a school does not guarantee that the materials will be used, especially as long as classrooms have doors and teachers can close them. The more that leading teachers take part in a project's evaluations and the development of its assessment protocols, the more likely it becomes that other teachers will want to use the project's materials to create curricula in their classrooms.

CONCLUSION

Developers must prepare for two distinctly different measurements of their success. First, their materials must include *assessment* systems that accurately reflect what students have learned as a result of using the materials developers have created. Second, projects and their resulting materials are *evaluated* to see whether and how well they have achieved their objectives and goals.

Meaningful assessment for guided inquiry goes beyond the kinds of learning measured by conventional means. In guided inquiry, assessment is *authentic*, meaning that it measures processes as well as the ability to recall facts, and it is *embedded*, meaning that tests are integrated into students' learning activities.

In the model assessment system described in this chapter, teachers— not automated scoring machines—are given the leading role in determining what their students have learned. To do so, the system includes "moderation sessions." In these sessions, teachers work together to formulate common assessment standards and spot weaknesses in lessons in time to correct them before their current crop of students move on to other grades or subjects. But the sessions have also shown themselves to be powerful tools for professional development, helping teachers to reflect on what they do. The sessions can also lay the foundations of collaboration on which other improvement efforts in a school or department can be based.

Developers themselves also must take exams. The first is an evaluation of the materials (sometimes known as the "program") they have created. This is done by measuring whether students learn more or better using the new materials than similar students do using materials that are already on the market.

The second test is a project evaluation. Although projects can evaluate themselves, funders often appoint external evaluators.

A project evaluation is a kind of audit. An evaluator will check to see how efficiently a project was managed operationally and financially as well as whether the project team did what it was funded to do in the way the team had promised to do it. The result becomes part of the final report that the team will make available to the larger educational community after its grant period ends.

9

Drafting and Testing Initial Versions

The whole of science is nothing more than a refinement of everyday thinking.
—Albert Einstein, *Ideas and Opinions*

ONCE THE PROJECT TEAM has been assembled, it faces its first major creative challenge: igniting and sustaining a collaborative process that will elicit the most imaginative ideas from every member and keep comments and critiques flowing freely among the team—and yet will allow the project to meet its deadlines, goals, and the other obligations. Every project finds its own balance between creative space for individuals on the one hand and organizational procedures and structure on the other.

Regardless of the details of that process, project teams typically work through four stages in drafting and testing initial versions of materials:

- Individual drafting
- Creative interplay among team members
- Testing early drafts in classrooms
- Conducting local field trials

Each of the four steps is detailed below.

MAKING A ROUGH OUTLINE

The process begins when team members come together in formal meetings, complemented by informal office and lunchtime conversations, to translate the goals, objectives, and general content outline from the project's proposal into a more detailed plan of specific activities, experiences, and supporting materials for classroom use. Some of the activities and experiences to be included will be obvious, such as any "signature" activities or approaches that were used in the funding proposal to illustrate the project's goals and methods. But likely this rough outline will also contain a number of vague "placeholder" descriptions for activities that team members have not thought through yet.

Once the rough outline has been completed, a project team chooses a way to proceed that accommodates the creative styles of its members. Smaller projects evolve their own individual approaches to creative collaboration, while project teams based within larger, ongoing development programs may follow more well-established procedures.

For example, project teams at the Education Development Center (EDC) in Newton, Massachusetts, organize their creative work around a structural template that shapes each new curricular unit the program publishes. The material's introduction gives students a preview of the concepts and information to be covered, including its relation to what the students have studied previously. The introduction also helps teachers to discover what students already know (or think they know) about the content they will explore. An investigation or project follows, then a discussion or presentation. Finally, students demonstrate the knowledge and skills gained through the experience.

"Each individual on the team knows that they have this structure within which to develop certain concepts according to the flow of ideas that we designed together," explains Jacqueline Miller, project director of EDC's "Insights in Biology" high school course.

When SEPUP began development of its year-long "Science and Life Issues" course, the team spent a good deal of time identifying themes—drawn from the National Science Education Standards, Benchmarks for Science Literacy, and similar sources—that would recur throughout the activities. They then discussed which concepts needed to be introduced before others to ensure that the fabric of students' understanding would knit together smoothly. "At this stage, we sketch a sequence of activities and come to some initial decisions about a number of the individual activities to be included," says SEPUP co-director Barbara Nagle. "It may change a lot, but we sketch out a structure, no matter how tentative."

In addition, the outline will help team members identify and begin to talk about any activities or ideas about which they disagree. Rather than settling those disagreements, the project's first outline flags them as areas for ongoing creative discussions.

GOING TO YOUR CAVE

With a working outline in hand, team members can begin to apportion among themselves the specific activities that each will begin to create. In some programs, such as SEPUP, team members begin to work by themselves; in programs such as the Full Option Science System (FOSS) the team divides into two-person pairs, each pair responsible for fashioning the initial drafts of specific activities or curricular units. Activities are parceled out according to team members' expertise and personal interests. After tasks have been assigned, each developer or subgroup retreats to work alone—"going to your cave," as SEPUP refers to it. A project's materials will ultimately evolve out of the freewheeling interactions of team members, but the birth of an idea that will grow to become an effective activity is often the result of an individual's reflection and imagination.

"I like to go off by myself and first think about the purpose of the activity—what it is that we want someone to learn from it—and how that relates to the purpose of the project as a whole," says Nagle. "Then I work from there: Here's this idea we'd really like a student to know; what's the best way to get at it? Sometimes it's easy to see how; other times, it can be a struggle. We can't re-create in a classroom what a scientist does in the lab, but how close can we come and still communicate to that student at that grade level?"

After imagining a rough design for an activity, a developer begins researching. Typically, the developer surveys similar activities used in classrooms to judge their strengths and weaknesses. A developer scans the Internet and also talks with other staff members, classroom teachers, and subject specialists to gather their ideas. At FOSS, after shaping the initial concept for an activity, a two-person subteam asks the project director for comments; in a less vertically structured program such as SEPUP, drafts circulate among all team members.

"One person sitting at a computer screen isn't going to be as creative without a group's input," says Pamela Van Scotter, a project director with the Biological Sciences Curriculum Study (BSCS). "You need open-ended time to shop ideas around and get reactions." According to Nagle, "Sometimes we might write a page or two—very short, rough drafts—and then round up whoever we can to get feedback." EDC's Jacqueline Miller recalls, "I'd write something and run into a teammate's office next door and ask her, 'What do you think about this?' We'd sit and talk for 10 minutes, then I'd run back and pound away at the keyboard again." The Internet has opened this process of creative interchange even to members of widely dispersed teams. At Vanderbilt University's Learning Technology Center, project directors post drafts on a web page where co-workers can post critiques and pose questions.

At this stage, developers are not attempting to finalize a design; instead, they are inviting colleagues to probe an idea critically to find its weak spots as well as its strengths. By circulating rough, early drafts of an activity, the developer hopes (and needs) to provoke a variety of ideas and approaches to strengthening it. (A developer may also circulate early drafts of an idea in order to invite colleagues' expertise in areas in which he or she has less, such as the design of a piece of specialized equipment or the integration of Internet-based materials into an activity.)

In their critiques, some team members might focus on the details of the activity itself, while others might question its effectiveness in eliciting a key concept or its relevance to other activities under development. "Each of us on the team has different strengths," Nagle says. "It's the interaction among team members, each with their own strengths, that determines a project's effectiveness." If the fundamental concept of the activity has survived, the developer then also contacts the project's equipment manufacturer or supplier to discuss the feasibility and cost of any special supplies needed. If the supplier judges that the equipment or supplies are safe for school use and that they can be produced at a reasonable cost, the developer continues to circulate drafts and assimilate colleagues' comments into the activity's design.

"As an individual, you can become so involved in creating the details of an activity that you can lose sight of its larger goals or purposes," says Manisha Hariani, a SEPUP team member. "That's a very big reason why collaboration is necessary in development. Others can remind you of the reasons why you're designing the activity in the first place."

APPROACHES TO CREATIVE INTERPLAY

A major activity that SEPUP published in 1999 offers an example of the creative interplay between an individual designer or subteam and the project team as a group. Developer Laura Baumgartner hit on the idea of ending the year-long "Science and Sustainability" high school course with a role-playing game integrating issues of energy, population, natural resources, and other facets of sustainability. In the game, a classroom of students would divide into eight groups, each taking on the role of a segment of the worldwide food industry: One group would act as farmers, another as transporters, another as regulators, and so on. The groups would then discuss ways to improve the global food system.

After roughing out the idea, Baumgartner discussed it with colleague Daniel Seaver. "We realized that we would have a hard time defining the groups without forcing the discussion in particular directions," Baumgartner says. "Instead, we wanted something open-ended that could go in a lot of different directions depending on the way students used evidence to make choices." Through their conversations, Baumgartner and Seaver gradually abandoned the idea of role-playing in favor of a board game. The game board has 12 squares, each representing a month of the year. A player represents a nation and moves around the board one square at a time. Landing on a square, the player takes a card that requires the player to undergo an event or make a decision that alters the player's point totals in different categories of value, such as population size, money, and air quality. "If players decide to make all the money they can, they see the results in their air, water, and natural resources," Baumgartner says. "If they try to maximize environmental preservation, they have more value in natural resources but they might not have much money. The object is not to win or lose but to connect the decisions you make to their consequences."

After having four other team members play a rough version of the game, Baumgartner and Seaver found that the game left players feeling hopeless—that no matter how hard they tried to protect their environments, natural resources dwindled relentlessly and populations declined. Baumgartner and Seaver adjusted the game's dimensions, rules, and objectives again.

"Eventually, we evolved a version that helps students understand that trade-offs have to be made and that strategic decisions have long-term consequences," Baumgartner says. "But the game also shows them that there is hope—that people can use evidence to decide to behave in ways that make a positive difference."

Van Scotter's BSCS project to create additional health education modules for the National Institutes of Health (see Chapter 7) institutionalized these informal interchanges by organizing a series of afternoon teas. The purpose of the get-togethers was to test initial versions of activities. In one activity, developers collected various tools to simulate the shapes of bird beaks that students would use to pick up seeds and other bird food. After discussing and trying the activity at a tea, the group hit on the idea of grouping different implements at stations and letting students move among the stations as a time-efficient way to share the experience among a class. "We also came up with a much wider range of bird food and imitation beaks—a staple remover for one, a straw to simulate a hummingbird beak," Van Scotter says.

This freeform process may seem haphazard, but "chatting back and forth seems to work better for sparking ideas than having long meetings," Nagle says. Adds Hariani, "There's no linear progression for development. It's not a case of, 'here are the six steps we go through and now we've developed an activity.'"

Some programs and projects favor a more collective process of design, with team members tossing out ideas and reacting to them in group meetings until the design of each activity begins to take shape. But those projects risk homogenizing the creative process: People who collaborate that closely over long periods often begin to think alike. That reality can eliminate misunderstandings and smooth communication, but it can also narrow the landscape along which people allow their imaginations to wander.

By giving individuals creative control, as SEPUP does, a project cultivates—rather than risks narrowing—the variety of approaches and ideas that will nourish it.

Still, this creative ferment takes place within a structure. The project director (or, in large programs, a team member serving as development coordinator for a specific course or group of materials) can convene the team in regular meetings (no less frequently than every other week) to review progress in individual activities, talk about them in the context of the project outline, and adjust either as needed. The director, or management group in a multiproject program, regularly compares creative progress against the project's timelines, checks budgets and expenses, and takes any additional steps necessary to ensure that the project meets its commitments to funders and other partners.

Well-managed projects encourage individuals or informal teams to engage in freewheeling interchanges to spark and explore a variety of ideas until a deadline is reached. At that point, preliminary drafts must be finalized. When that deadline arrives, team members are expected to deliver a finalized working draft of any activity for which they are responsible. The draft specifies the activity's learning goals and objectives, the details of the activity itself, and possible questions to pose to students to prompt thought and discussion.

With these drafts in hand, team members meet more formally to finalize each activity's initial design and to determine whether the order of the activities, laid out in the initial outline, needs to be changed. These meetings may be held between a subteam and a project's director or directors. Often, however, projects bring together all team members to focus their collective insight on each activity as a link in the thematic chains that unify the project. In these sessions, a team also fixes the best order for the activities to ensure that students are introduced to new ideas only when they have an adequate background to understand them. By working on the conceptual outline and draft activities together, the team will often spot ways to improve both.

EXPLORATORY TEACHING: TESTING DRAFTS WITH TEACHERS AND STUDENTS

Testing other team members' reactions to the draft of an activity and even trying the activity with individual students are always useful ways to garner initial opinions. But nothing replaces the reaction of students and teachers in working classrooms. If curriculum is the interactions among students and teachers sparked and guided by activities and materials, then the classroom is the only place where developers will discover whether the materials they have created shape a more effective curriculum. Consequently, as soon as a developer or team completes the first rough draft of an activity, the next stop on the development path is the classroom for a session of "exploratory teaching"—leading a class through the activity to uncover its strengths, weaknesses, and possibilities.

A project cannot afford to underestimate the value of exploratory teaching sessions. Only in a classroom can developers discover how long an activity really takes. They can learn how easily and efficiently teachers and students can conduct and manage the activity. They can investigate the responses of students of varying abilities. Perhaps most important, they will be able to see whether the activity fosters the interest and discussion between student and teacher, and among students themselves, that is essential to the mastery of higher intellectual skills.

In addition, the sessions enable developers to try out the pedagogical approach and techniques that they believe teachers should use to present the new activities and materials most effectively. Even the most experienced developers occasionally design experiences for students that seem brilliant on the drawing board but fail in the classroom. It is crucial to spot those flaws *before* the resources of the project, teachers, students, and school districts are invested in materials that have not faced the test of actual use.

For example, while developing the year-long "Science and Life Issues" course for middle school students, developer Manisha Hariani devised an activity to communicate to students the nature of viruses. "All the developers at SEPUP thought it was fine," she recalls. "It turns out that it will never be used." In classroom trials, Hariani found that the activity too easily communicated misconceptions about how viruses replicate and transmit their genetic material. The activity also created confusion among students between bacteria, which are alive, and viruses, which may or may not be.

The SEPUP team counts these "failures" during classroom trials as successes: weaknesses were spotted and corrected *before* the materials were published and distributed, not afterward. Too often, materials or activities created by publishers or subject experts alone do not confront these details until thousands of copies of the material have been printed and distributed. Collaborating with students and teachers early in the development process spotlights such basic flaws before a project team invests even more time in them.

EQUIPMENT IS AS IMPORTANT AS PRINTED MATERIALS

A project also uses exploratory teaching sessions to thoroughly test new equipment that will become part of the project's materials. It might be tempting to assume that if equipment works well enough in the team's office, it will be good enough for a classroom. That is often not the case.

When it began in 1983, SEPUP set out to design issue-oriented investigations for middle school students into the everyday uses of chemicals. That emphasis required participating schools to have the needed equipment and facilities for students to conduct simple chemical reactions and make basic quantitative measurements. But SEPUP's developers found that many middle schools at the time had no such equipment. It was clear that the program had to provide the gear that students would need to do real science in rooms that often lacked even a sink and running water.

The development team began to talk with science teachers about the kind of equipment that would meet the need—inexpensive, safe, reusable, and easy to set up, take down, clean, and store. Guided by comments and critiques from teachers, the team decided to replace the separate beakers and test tubes then common in science classes with a one-piece multipurpose tray. The tray was designed with five small, built-in basins that replaced beakers and nine small cups to replace test tubes. It was packaged with 30-milliliter squeeze bottles containing just the amounts of chemicals called for in specific SEPUP activities.

Such an equipment kit depended on designing chemical reactions that would work with a few drops of chemicals rather than the amounts traditionally used in science classes. If it could be made and sold inexpensively enough, the equipment package built around the one-piece tray would be safer, less expensive, less wasteful, and easier to clean up after than the usual array of solutions and glassware.

In trying early versions of the tray in exploratory teaching sessions, the chemical reactions worked well enough, but students became confused. The activities' written instructions did not always indicate clearly which basins or cups in the tray were which; students often put droplets of chemicals in the wrong places. The project team saw that it could easily correct the problem by designating the basins referred to in the printed materials as "wells" A through E and the cups as 1 through 9. Those designations were then molded into each tray.

Exploratory teaching sessions raised another concern as well: The plastic trays were prone to scratches and stains. It was not an easy problem to solve; plastics that resist staining tend to scratch easily, while scratch-resistant plastics tend to stain easily. The latter also typically are brittle and break readily. Prodded by teachers' complaints, SEPUP worked with its equipment manufacturer, Lab-Aids, to find a blend of plastics that maximized both qualities that teachers called for. After years of tests and refinements, the current one-piece SEPUP lab tray emerged—combining, in effect, five minibeakers and nine tiny test tubes. The tray became the item for which the project first gained recognition and on which many of its subsequent activities were based.

In addition to making laboratory-based science possible in many middle school classrooms, the SEPUP tray and related items also helped emphasize the project's commitment to safety and to preventing environmental problems: It enabled students to conduct scientific investigations using drops rather than ounces of reagents.

The equipment package that the project created in collaboration with teachers made possible a more rigorous and more quantitative approach to a wide variety of classroom activities at a reasonable cost. For example, this simple set of materials made it possible for SEPUP to develop an activity in which students successively dilute solutions of food coloring in water to experience the concepts of parts per million and parts per billion—two often-used measurements common in discussions of environmental issues but not well understood by most people.

Without close, continuing collaborations with teachers willing to host exploratory teaching sessions, SEPUP's equipment could not have evolved to become so useful in so many classrooms.

EARLY SCIENTIFIC REVIEW

The first check of new materials' content accuracy is done day to day by the developers themselves and by classroom teachers hosting exploratory teaching sessions. But as drafts and activities evolve, a project's science advisory panel for the specific project should review them periodically for accuracy.

These reviews should not be a casual process. Panel members are usually volunteers and have limited time to work with the team; so rather than posing vague or general questions to them, it is more useful to frame specific queries arising from activities or materials already being tried. For example, team members would not ask an immunologist how the project can help students understand the transmission of disease. Instead, they would find it more productive to describe an activity in which students use simulated saliva (a basic chemical solution) to mimic the process of contagion and then explain the concepts they hope students will learn as a result. Panel members (including, one hopes, an immunologist) could then reflect on and react to specific wording and procedures and their implications and connotations for students. Contacts with panel members should be prepared as thoroughly as an exploratory teaching session, even though the contacts themselves can often be handled with a phone call or exchange of e-mails.

LAYING THE FOUNDATIONS FOR CLASSROOM TRIALS

Exploratory teaching sessions, in which team members lead a class of students through an activity still being developed, are held in classrooms near the office of the project or of the developer designing the activity. In addition to using students of the age or grade level for whom the activities and materials being designed are intended, a project team should select its classroom laboratories primarily on the basis of three factors:

1. *Proximity.* Classrooms used in exploratory teaching sessions should be as close to the project's office as possible so developers can minimize time lost in travel.
2. *Diversity.* A project's classroom laboratories can be as few in number as two, but they should be selected in large measure on the basis of their intellectual and social diversity. A key objective during exploratory teaching is to test the materials' ability to communicate to students across the spectrum of learning abilities as well as ethnic and socioeconomic backgrounds; the ideal test class sports a rich mix of such students. For often unforeseeable reasons, materials or activities that work well in one social or cultural context do not work equally well in all. Before materials can be finalized for commercial distribution, those differences need to be identified, their causes revealed, and the materials revised to increase the likelihood that the materials will be effective among a wide variety of learners. If possible, the chosen classrooms should include at least one urban and one nonurban setting.

   Occasionally, one teacher's participation in exploratory sessions will persuade others to open their doors to the development team. A project should capitalize on such opportunities to broaden the diversity of its test populations.
3. *Classroom culture.* Trials will be most efficient and productive in classes in which teachers have a genuine rapport with students and in which the teachers and students have already demonstrated a clear commitment to the study of science. Periodically interrupting a class's regular curricular program to test new materials is necessarily disruptive. If, in addition, the classroom attitude toward learning is casual, the teacher

and students may not be able to move smoothly back and forth between trial sessions and their usual course of study. Also, if a teacher is more concerned with classroom control than with helping students learn—or if students cannot focus, do not participate in class activities, or routinely misbehave—developers will be unable to elicit the detailed responses they need to assess their efforts.

Ideally, that classroom culture will lead not only to an openness but also to an eagerness among students to comment on activities and materials. Developers will find that the best insights and suggestions for improving materials often come from interviews and conversations with students. If such talks are not possible, survey forms or questionnaires can be left with the students to fill out after the developers leave.

More developed versions of the materials should be tested during national field tests for their effectiveness with a variety of teachers and a broad range of learners, including those who face particular challenges in learning. But, for now, testing how effectively the materials communicate basic concepts is best done among students and teachers already well disposed to learning.

BENEFITS FOR TEACHERS AND STUDENTS

Finding classrooms in which developers can learn these lessons is not difficult: A promising innovation will always attract good teachers ready to try it. Nor do administrators usually object to teachers taking part. Participating in trials confers a certain prestige on their schools, can boost teachers' morale, and—if the innovation proves effective—gives a school at least one knowledgeable teacher ready to implement it.

Equally important, perceptive teachers agree to take part in exploratory teaching sessions because they understand that participating in trials is not necessarily a curricular interruption for students, but rather can become part of the curriculum itself. When developers are invited to work in a classroom, they deputize the students as "co-investigators" in the materials development process. Students respond eagerly when given real responsibility to evaluate and improve the materials being tested, and they take their role seriously. (Again, a developer's most incisive critiques often come from students.)

At the same time, students often report that they learn as much from activity trials as from their regular lessons—or, at least, that the trials helped them gain a better understanding of concepts and facts presented in their regular studies. In one eighth-grade classroom, a SEPUP team was testing an activity that simulated a process using cement and sodium silicate to neutralize liquid heavy metal waste. For reasons that were not clear to the team, the activity did not work well enough to clearly illustrate the process and underlying chemical principles to students. The team explained to the class that the design of the activity was somehow flawed and asked for their suggestions about improving it. After four tries—and a good deal of help from the students—the team crafted a successful approach to the activity that clearly showed its underlying concepts. The classroom teacher later told the team that testing and refining the activity had been the best experience he had ever seen for helping students to understand, rather than just memorize, the steps of the scientific method. Other teachers have made similar comments, noting that the students are not "guinea pigs" but rather become active partners in a process that mirrors the realities of science.

Still, developers must be careful not to abuse the hospitality of those who open their doors. Therefore, projects need to be creative in balancing their needs with those of their hosts. BSCS has developed a network of more than 100 classrooms in and around its Colorado Springs headquarters, enabling it to work intensively in classrooms without calling on the same ones more than once or twice a semester. The Learning Technology Center has persuaded two Nashville schools to reserve one regular class period a day as a time for teachers and students to try novel curricular approaches and materials.

WORKING IN THE EXPLORATORY CLASSROOM

Leading a classroom trial leaves a developer no time to note in detail the comments, questions, and reactions from the teacher or individual students (or, often, to remember how they themselves responded). Recording all those results in written notes or, if possible, on videotape is the task of one or more additional members of the development team who take part in the trials. (In BSCS and SEPUP projects, usually one developer conducts the class and a second observes; FOSS has fielded as many as four developers to observe a class while a fifth conducts an activity trial.)

While the first team member—preferably the one who has led the team in creating the specific activity and the materials that accompany it—conducts the class, the others sit unobtrusively in the room and record every reaction from the students: the words the developer leading the class uses to describe and explain the materials and activity, what questions students ask, points that students do not understand or misinterpret, any improvisations by the developer that clarify or improve the activities or materials, and which aspects of the activity go as planned and which run into unanticipated problems or complications. The details preserved in these notes will guide any revisions that the trial reveals are needed.

Clearly, classroom trials call for developers with strong egos who can not only withstand critical comments from colleagues, teachers, and students but actually welcome them—especially because exploratory classroom sessions may need to be repeated as drafts of activities and materials evolve.

Although the developers who have created the activity being tested should lead the class, the students' regular teacher should be present as well. The teacher's presence reminds students that the session is not "substitute's time," which so often leads to disruptive behavior. The teacher also serves as an expert analyst of students' reactions. For that reason, the teacher is also the best analyst of materials' ability to shape an effective curriculum based on the interactions of teacher and students.

For example, a development team may think an activity being tried has failed to engage students because the classroom is too quiet. But the teacher might tell them that she has never seen the group work so quietly for so long—clearly indicating that the students *are* engaged. Because teachers know their students so well, they can often suggest alterations to materials that would enable them to communicate more effectively with specific students in their classes who have unusual learning styles or needs. The developers could then generalize that insight and redraft portions of the activity or material—or entire alternative versions—to be retested.

Developers also should not overlook the opportunity to collect reactions from students themselves. Team members may ask specific questions of students following an activity, ask them to fill out a questionnaire, or both. "Students are not shy about letting you know if they think something is cool or dumb," says BSCS's Van Scotter. Also, while an activity trial is underway in an exploratory classroom, Van Scotter and her team stroll the aisles and listen. "You learn a lot as you listen to kids talk during an activity," she notes. "Especially when they're talking to each other, they're very forthcoming."

OVERCOMING LIMITATIONS OF TIME AND COST

Initial classroom trials might appear to be one of the easier aspects of materials development. Team members lavish care and imagination on the creation of materials, then simply take them into a classroom and try them out. But, to be as useful as possible, each classroom trial has to be planned as meticulously as an experiment aboard the Space Shuttle.

Classroom trials are expensive. Each session in a class requires at least an hour's time in planning, an hour of class time, another hour (at least) in analyzing results in discussions among the project staff, and an hour's time or more commuting to and from the classroom serving as a lab. Therefore, because a classroom trial can be done effectively only by a pair of developers (if not more), a 10-session trial spread over 5 weeks demands at least 80 person-hours to complete, or 2 full weeks of work. That does not include the time spent revising materials to correct the flaws that the classroom trials reveal. Responsible use of the project's scarce resources of time and money demand detailed planning.

Consequently, testing every activity thoroughly, or sometimes at all, in diverse classrooms is not possible. The development team must make choices: Which activities will team members test in classrooms and which need not be?

Some choices will be obvious. If a new activity calls for students to use a microscope, competent science teachers know how to show students how to do so and the team need not draft and test its own set of instructions. Activities or materials that are relatively simple in concept and execution, or adaptations of ones previously used in classrooms or by other projects, can usually be subjected to less scrutiny than activities or materials that are significantly new in their approach or in the concepts they convey.

In other cases, classroom teachers can guide the team's decisions. Working teachers who are part of the development team typically will have the best sense of which innovations should be tested in schools. If, as suggested earlier, a project has contracted with a school district for a portion of a teacher's time during the academic year, that teacher can test the project's materials in his or her own classroom and might even recruit other teachers in the building to try them. Such arrangements not only bring teachers' practical wisdom into a project's development process but also leverage the project's budget for classroom tests.

LOCAL FIELD TESTS OF ACTIVITY DRAFTS

After exploratory teaching sessions have been completed and working drafts of activities and materials finalized, the versions are ready to be tested in classrooms more removed from the project team. In this second phase of trials, known as "local field testing," the materials and activities are not presented by the developers who created them but by the classes' regular teachers as the developers sit and watch. Again, developers need to choose these teachers and students for their diversity: Working only with the gifted might make materials seem easier to use or more communicative than they are, just as Yehudi Menuhin could make an inferior violin sound good (Chapter 1).

Local field tests are as important as exploratory teaching sessions, but in a different way. Developers know the materials they have created intimately. They can elaborate and improvise on them as classroom dynamics demand. But once a developer relinquishes personal classroom control of the activities and materials, everything the team knows about them must be communicated otherwise, usually in print. Developers may know exactly the meaning and nuance of what they have written, but that does not mean that they have communicated the full range and detail of those subtleties in their drafts. The only way to determine how well the materials communicate the developer's intent is to give them to teachers unfamiliar with them. This is the point at which the materials' creators will discover exactly what the written materials do and do not communicate.

THE LIMITATIONS OF PRINT

Every project devotes a significant portion of its resources to drafting and refining these "final rough drafts." The materials should be presented in a single, consistent voice and visual style so that teachers using them are not required to relearn them from one page to the next or guess at interpretations.

But the editorial care called for in these early drafts stems from a more fundamental imperative. As long as a developer can communicate personally with all the teachers and students using the materials the developer designs, the only limitations on the materials' effectiveness are the pooled skills and imagination of everyone involved. As soon as the materials are to be used in classrooms where the developer has no personal contact, the developer must communicate with those distant students and teachers primarily through the written word—a limited medium on which to have to rely to convey abstract ideas.

Print lacks the human interaction—the tone of voice, the gesture, the slight rewording of an explanation, an impromptu drawing—that so often leads a person to an insight. To feel the limitations of print that developers face, recall a pleasant time you have spent with someone, such as a young child, during which you helped that person learn something. Perhaps you were walking in the park and the child discovered the variety of shades of green among the plants; perhaps you helped the child learn about the world of shadows. After recalling the event, try to write a guide that someone else can follow to replicate the same experience. The limitations of written communications instantly become dramatically clear—especially when remembering that a developer is attempting to replicate the same experience among as many as 30 or more individuals at once, each with different abilities, learning styles, and background knowledge.

Developers can overcome some of print's limitations by including tutorials on videotape and digital disks with the materials, showing teachers how to present activities or use equipment. However, as every good educator knows, visual aids cannot be allowed to become a crutch to prop up poorly crafted materials. If developers hope to foster a more effective curriculum in more than a few classrooms, they have no alternative among currently affordable technologies—including computers and video—other than to rely chiefly on the printed word. For that reason, a development project must invest sizeable amounts of its time and budget in designing, testing, and refining the printed materials it will distribute.

THE TEACHER'S ROLE IN THE CREATIVE PROCESS

Especially in the early stages of designing and creating new materials, the guidance of imaginative, skilled teachers can be invaluable to a project team. Similarly, teachers themselves can find their work with a project useful. Whether by opening their classrooms to developers for exploratory teaching, taking part in a local field test, or just by serving as informal partners who chat by phone or exchange e-mails with team members, teachers can keep in touch with the growth of their profession through involvement with development projects.

Participation also enables them to take a direct hand in shaping better curriculum materials, to have early access to those materials for their students, and perhaps ultimately to join a development project as a team member. As noted, one of the most useful and efficient ways for teachers to do so is to divide their worktime between a project and the classroom. The teachers can expand their professional skills and knowledge while protecting their seniority in their districts, and participating projects gain not only the insights of able teachers but also easy access to classrooms to test new drafts.

CONCLUSION

As developers evolve early versions of materials and activities, they must be able to test their effectiveness on real students in real classrooms. The experience of many projects indicates that these "exploratory teaching" sessions and local field tests yield the most useful information when they follow these six guidelines.

First, one member of the project team should hold final authority and responsibility for preparing drafts of a specific activity to be tested and for its subsequent revisions. There is wisdom in the warning that "a camel is a racehorse designed by a committee."

Second, before trials begin, developers must make the closest possible match between the materials and activities they want to test and the teachers and classes that will test them. For obvious reasons, materials intended for, say, ninth-grade biology students should be tested in ninth-grade biology classes. More specifically, if the developer is creating an activity that will communicate ideas about the nature of blood, for example, the trial should coincide with the course's study of the circulatory system. By allowing teachers to select, when possible, which activities they wish to participate in and when, developers can help to ensure that the trials enrich the regular curriculum instead of disrupting it.

Third, when introducing themselves to a class, developers who have come to observe and record the use of the materials should make their purpose clear to the students and the teacher: that the team has come to ask their help in testing, evaluating, and improving new materials, not to judge, rate, or assess the performance of students or teachers.

Fourth, developers should try to schedule their class sessions at the end of the schoolday or just before a host teacher's free period. The development team will need time to interview the teacher to garner reactions, insights, and advice while the session is fresh in his or her mind. If the teacher has another class in 5 minutes, developers lose a precious opportunity.

Fifth, developers must limit their time in class. Every developer would like to test new ideas at least three or four days a week in real classrooms. But that is not necessarily in the best interests of the students and teachers who invite them in. Also, developers need time to reflect on what they learn in each trial session and to adjust their materials or redesign their activities accordingly.

Developers report that scheduling classroom trials about twice a week at most in a single classroom meets their needs without compromising those of the students, teachers, and their schools.

Sixth, building relationships that result in effective classroom partnerships must begin long before the trials do. In fact, building those relationships begins with the developer's affiliation with a host institution. Teachers and administrators are leery of taking part in a development project housed in an institution with a reputation for using local schools as test sites without contributing value (or even sharing research results) in return.

When a new development project is being organized, a wise project director invites the best local classroom teachers to join the project as consultants and advisers. Also, the project should be explained to parents and the materials made available to them—a requirement if the development project is funded by the NSF. The more partners a project has, the more people there will be contributing toward its ultimate goal of widespread effectiveness.

A final guideline: Under no circumstance should developers voice judgments to people at a school hosting trials about the school's science program in general, the quality of instruction, school administration, or any other aspect of the place. Stray comments can destroy the trust on which these relationships (often already delicate) are built. If a host school asks a developer for help or advice in improving some aspect of its program, the developer has a responsibility to respond. But any such discussions must be clearly separated from conversations about the results of the classroom trials. If the developer is perceived in any way as being there to evaluate teachers, assess students, or force uninvited change, the development team could lose a valued partner.

10

Preparing for Publication:
National Field Tests and Final Revisions

One should guard against preaching to young people success in the customary form as the main aim in life.

—Albert Einstein, *Ideas and Opinions*

EVEN AFTER A PROJECT TEAM completes its exploratory teaching sessions, the new materials still are not ready for commercial distribution or widespread classroom use. They first must undergo a national field test, which usually lasts for at least one complete schoolyear. For courses that run a full academic year or more in length, 2-year field tests are recommended.

The field test includes nine steps, each detailed in this chapter:

- Recruiting and selecting field test sites
- Organizing the sites chosen
- Preparing teachers and administrators who will participate
- Finalizing materials for testing
- Incorporating assessment
- Processing teachers' and students' responses
- Evaluating student assessment results
- Finalizing commercial versions of the materials
- Preparing test sites to serve as implementation centers

The first year tests the effectiveness of presentation, the flow of ideas from unit to unit, the performance of equipment, and the effectiveness of the items in the assessment protocols. In the second year, changes from the first year's test are implemented and evaluated. Also, the materials' full assessment system is tested, both to see how well it works as a whole and to gather data on how well students learn as a result of using the new materials.

In a national field test, revised versions of materials that emerge from exploratory and other local teaching sessions are distributed to a number of classrooms in different geographic and socioeconomic settings around the country. During the test, the project team works closely and continuously with participating teachers. The team helps teachers to use the materials effectively, answers educators' questions, and collects responses and critiques of the materials from the teachers and their students.

PURPOSES OF THE FIELD TEST

The national field test, perhaps the most demanding phase of a materials development project, serves three purposes:

1. It enables the project team to gather results of, and responses to, the new materials from students and teachers from a variety of social, economic, and educational backgrounds. Perhaps most important, the data are gathered from classrooms in which the project's developers can neither personally conduct classes nor continuously interact with or coach teachers; the materials stand or fall on their own. The resulting responses will guide the team in improving the materials further to create the materials' initial commercial version.
2. The field test, particularly in its second year, enables the team to use the materials' assessment instruments and methods to gather data on outcomes for students using the new materials.
3. The national field test helps to set an infrastructure in place for the materials' commercial distribution and implementation.

These three purposes are united by a broader, underlying reason to conduct national field tests. As noted earlier, exploratory teaching sessions are conducted by the same group—often the same person—that created the materials being tested. Developers know their materials, as well as their own aims and intentions, intimately. Therefore, when they use the materials in classrooms, developers can often overcome weaknesses in the materials by explaining additional details out of their own knowledge. They can spontaneously reword explanations if the printed version proves inadequate, and they can otherwise improvise during classroom trials to help students accomplish the results the materials are intended to bring about.

But, also as noted earlier, when developers send newly created materials into a classroom over which they have no personal control or supervision, every detail and nuance of an activity must be conveyed primarily through written words and their accompanying graphics. The same set of words and pictures must be able to communicate precisely the same concepts and processes to teachers and students from rural Appalachia to urban Chicago and from wealthy suburbs to the blighted neighborhoods of the inner city. It is unlikely that the classrooms that hosted exploratory teaching sessions near the project team's headquarters offered that full range of diversity. The only way to ensure that materials communicate with full and equal effectiveness among those diverse groups is to test those materials among a representative sample.

"A national field test provides the critical link in the materials development process," notes Robert Horvat, professor emeritus of science education at Buffalo State University and former SEPUP field test center coordinator. "A good field test can tell you what works, what doesn't, and—perhaps—why."

RECRUITING FIELD TEST SITES

In effect, the process of recruiting field test sites begins when a project is funded. The team's announcements of its work and goals, made in professional journals and at conferences, can pique the interest of educators who later might participate in field tests. Through similar venues, as well as its own newsletters and website, a project can keep alive those teachers' interest and curiosity by posting progress reports and perhaps even an example of an activity or two.

If the project's communication with potential users of its materials has been effective, more than enough teachers in diverse settings around the country will be eager to try the materials when national trials are ready to begin. Of course, team members also can approach teachers, schools, and districts they know personally that they think possess the vision, venturesomeness, standards, and sense of professional responsibility that would make for good field test sites.

To give everyone enough time to prepare, a project needs to recruit, collect applications from, and select field test sites during the academic year before the one in which the field test will begin. Consequently, at least a year before it is scheduled to begin, the test should be announced through the project's usual venues—professional journals and conferences as well as its own newsletter, website, and team members' personal contacts. In advertising for participants, a project should offer as many details as possible: the test's time period, what the project will provide to test sites and participating educators, and what will be expected from them in return. The more detail included in the announcements, the better qualified will be the schools and districts that apply.

BENEFITS FOR FIELD TEST SITES

It might seem that schools and districts that participate are doing a project a favor—setting aside their usual curricular programs to risk trying out untested materials. In fact, a national field test is a partnership from which participating educators and districts, as well as the project, benefit. The schools and teachers receive a library of new materials and, sometimes, cash honoraria. As they learn to use the new materials and assess their effectiveness, teachers grow professionally. In addition, they are recognized by their peers as innovators.

Because each partner in the field test benefits, each must contribute materially to the success of the partnership. Obviously, the project must provide each participating teacher, at no charge, with full sets of the materials and equipment to be tested (usually done with the help of the project's publisher-producer). But the project team also introduces participating educators to its philosophy, approach, and pedagogy, making them aware of concepts that might lead them to try new ideas or approaches in their classroom work beyond the field test.

Developers show teachers how to use the new materials; they provide continuing coaching, education, and technical support throughout the test; and they also furnish the operating funds to run the field test center. In a typical field test of a year-long course, a project might typically provide as much as $7,500 in operating funds for each center. The centers choose how to allot the funds, but the project suggests specific uses for much of the money. Those uses may include expenses of field test educators visiting the project's headquarters for orientation and follow-up sessions, clerical and other operational costs of the center, teachers' expenses as they attend local meetings to evaluate the project's materials, and perhaps an honorarium for the center's director or teachers. (Because of district-to-district differences in policy and teachers' contracts, whether to pay field test teachers and center leaders for participating in the tests should remain a local decision.)

SELECTING FIELD TEST SITES

Because of its considerable investment in each field test site, a project should ask each organization interested in becoming a field test site to submit a detailed application.

In its application, a school or district should detail the resources it is prepared to commit to the test. Such resources include the following:

- The potential site's willingness to release teachers from their classes to attend meetings and workshops related to the field test, usually monthly
- The applicant's willingness to pay for substitutes to cover teachers' classes on meeting days
- In some cases, clerical help

"Make sure you get commitments for release time not only from a district's central administration but also from the most important local decision maker—the building principal," Horvat counsels. "Without that person's support, it can be difficult to get a teacher out of a classroom."

In addition to an applicant's financial and logistical commitments, the project must also weigh (even more critically this time) the same factors of educational culture that it looked for in the classes in which it conducted its exploratory teaching. Those factors include demographic diversity, a range of abilities and approaches among teachers and students, and the applicant's demonstrated, ongoing commitment to first-rate science and mathematics education.

To determine those qualities, the developers of the Integrated Mathematics, Science, and Technology (IMaST) materials at Illinois State University asked each school that applied to send a 10-minute videotape. The project team specified certain scenes that were to be included: a general look at the building, a panoramic view of the science labs and facilities, the lunchroom in peak use, and the halls as classes change. "We weren't interested in how well the video was produced," explains project director Dr. Franzie Loepp. "We wanted to get a sense of the school and its culture."

In addition, teachers and principals who would participate in the field test each made a 1-minute statement or presentation on the tape detailing their reasons for wanting to take part. "The videos were tremendously helpful," Loepp recalls. "You get a much more immediate sense of the place, its people, and their enthusiasm and commitment than you can from only a written application."

At the project office, each team member involved in the field test reviews the applications and prioritizes them. The team members then meet to compare and contrast their choices and reach a consensus on the final candidates.

The pool of applicants should be large enough to let a project sample a full range of geographic, ethnic, and socioeconomic diversity as well as a range of student achievement levels and variations in teachers' competence. A tip: To recruit teachers of differing abilities, a project can try to work with teams of teachers in a single school. Such teams can provide moral support, help maintain individual teachers' commitment to the field test, and prompt teachers to deliver feedback according to the test's schedule. Whenever a project recruits a specific teacher, it can always ask the teacher to suggest colleagues who might want to take part.

To balance the factors, between 25 and 50 teachers distributed among five to ten national field test centers should offer adequate results. However, the number of sites and teachers can vary with the scope, funding, and ambition of the project; in testing its year-long "Issues, Evidence, and You" middle school course, SEPUP operated 15 test sites at once.

However, a project team must balance the need for a diverse sample against the number of people and places around the country that the team can effectively deal with. At some point, adding more participants means the team will be able to work less effectively with each. "Our experience indicates that an optimal pool is 35 to 60 teachers in 7 to 12 centers," Horvat says. Ideally, each center would house at least 5 teachers in an urban or suburban center and no fewer than 3 in less-populated areas.

In choosing field test sites, a project team will find that large school districts, especially urban ones, usually offer the greatest range of diversity among students and teachers in the smallest number of classrooms. Participating teachers in the district can work together to compare the ways that different groups react to the materials and activities and thus can help a project more quickly target portions of the materials that need improvement. However, a field test also must include districts with fewer students so that materials can be tested in rural settings and in districts that often provide little central-office leadership in science education.

ORGANIZING FIELD TEST SITES

Preparing sites to participate in a national field test is chiefly a matter of patterning the flow of information between each site and the project team in a way that makes communication between them—and, if feasible, among sites themselves—as easy and as rich as possible. Communication between the team and the sites is the project's umbilical cord, the lifeline that enables materials to evolve and develop until the team releases them into the wider world. Without that abundant flow of comment and feedback, a national field test is pointless.

Field test centers can be organized in any number of ways, but two are most common. A center is usually housed in a school district with several schools and teachers taking part. Alternatively, it is distributed among several districts, with their participation coordinated through one of the districts or the education department at a nearby college or university. The structure does not materially affect the results or validity of the field test, and it is most often chosen based on the networks, partnerships, and collaborations already established among sites selected to participate in the test.

Each field test center is administered by a director chosen from among the local educators involved in the field test. In most cases, the director will be an obvious choice—a curriculum supervisor, department head, senior teacher, or university professor. In other cases, the teachers at a field test center may choose one of their own to lead the effort. (If the choice is a teacher, the person must have explicit support from administrators as well as their clear commitment to the field test. Without it, the director might lack the time or power to administer the center effectively.)

The person chosen should possess some administrative experience; much of the director's job entails translating requests and ideas from the project team into actions among participating teachers. But, more important than management experience, a center's director also must have the trust and respect of administrators and teachers alike. If a district's administration seems to be ignoring or rethinking its commitment to the test, the director must command enough moral authority among those administrators to hold them to their promises. Similarly, a center director often will have to bring to bear a certain weight of authority on participating teachers. "If you stand in front of a group of field test teachers and ask if anyone has questions or comments about the materials or procedures, and if no one says anything, you might be tempted to assume that everyone agrees with everything," says Dr. Stan Hill, science curriculum coordinator for the Winston-Salem and Forsyth County schools in North Carolina and a veteran SEPUP field test center director. "But just because people are silent doesn't mean that they're in agreement. The only way to be sure that they are is to ask each person directly what they have to say. Very often people will declare that something can't work even before they try it. So I ask my teachers, 'Will you conduct this procedure just as it's written and just the way we talked about doing it?' Then they have to say yes or no. If the answer is no, then I ask what we have to do to reach agreement."

Each test-site director is responsible for ensuring that participating teachers are presenting the materials as they are written, often visiting classrooms and talking with the teachers to make sure they are trying the project's version of the materials first before improvising on them. The center director is also available to teachers who have questions or need help in understanding how to present certain activities or materials. In addition, the director organizes and chairs regular meetings in which participating teachers gather to discuss and analyze the activities they have conducted. The director ensures that teachers complete and submit their feedback reports in a timely way and serves as the administrative contact between a test site and the project team.

PREPARING FIELD TEST TEACHERS AND ADMINISTRATORS

Once chosen, participating teachers will need to learn how to conduct the activities and use the materials. To make the most efficient use of teachers' time and project resources, a project can use a "train-the-trainer" approach.

Selected teachers from each field test center can be brought together at the project office in a group session the summer before the test begins. For example, SEPUP invites a "leadership team" from each participating district (usually the person serving as the test center's director and two teacher-leaders from each field test center) to its Berkeley campus office for a week. The week-long conference has the following aims:

- To immerse the participants in the philosophy, goals, and objectives of the project, in its materials, and particularly in the specific materials and activities participants will test
- To help participating educators analyze the approach, methods, and learning objectives of those activities and gives them direct, supervised experience in conducting them
- To prepare educators to introduce the activities and materials to colleagues participating in the field test in their districts
- To detail the kinds and quality of analysis and feedback the project expects from field test teachers as well as a timetable for recording and forwarding their responses
- To help test-site teams plan the organization and operation of their field test centers, including modes of communications among the centers themselves—particularly Internet-based venues such as websites and chat rooms if teachers have access to them

After the conference, each participating leadership team returns to its district and conducts sessions much like the one the team has just attended to introduce the project and its materials to colleagues taking part in the field test.

PREPARING MATERIALS FOR FIELD-TESTING

Even though the versions of project materials have been revised—sometimes extensively—through exploratory teaching sessions, the materials undoubtedly will be subject to substantial additional changes as a result of the national field test. Therefore, it is not worth the effort and expense to polish the materials a great deal in preparation for a national field test. On the other hand, the materials must be edited and designed with enough finesse to be both engaging and clear to a variety of teachers and students across a range of settings and conditions.

There is no formula to tell a developer exactly how much effort to invest in editorial refinements before sending materials to field test sites; the judgment is subjective. If too much of a project's already-scarce money or time is invested in refining field test versions of materials, too little of either (or both) might remain to invest in producing the best possible commercial editions. But if not enough resources are invested in the field test versions, teachers and students might not be able to penetrate the materials' prose or graphics well enough to conduct the activities as the developers expect them to. If they cannot, then they will not be able to give the kind of feedback the developers need to make necessary improvements before producing a commercial version of the materials. The considerable investment in the field test will be squandered if too many teachers say "This sentence isn't clear" or "How am I supposed to interpret this drawing?"

Usually the most effective way to determine whether materials have crossed the threshold of clarity is to achieve a consensus among the project team—with special attention paid to comments from its working classroom teachers. If a project team has developed good working relationships with local teachers, the developers also can ask those teachers to review specific materials for ease of understanding. A project's commercial partner should be not only willing but also contractually obligated to help fund and conduct such preparation of materials for national trials.

In addition to design considerations for field test materials, there also are considerations of accuracy. In readying field test versions, the project team should give the materials' informational and pedagogical content one final review, taking into account what has been learned through exploratory teaching and local trials. Assuming that the project has followed the procedures suggested for identifying and developing the project staff, the first level of scientific review of the project materials takes place day by day among the project team and the educators with which it works. Later, as it prepares the commercial version of the materials, the team will solicit a thorough scientific review from outside content specialists.

TIPS ON CONDUCTING EFFECTIVE FIELD TESTS

Coordinating and keeping tabs on the work of several dozen individuals spread around the country is a daunting enterprise at best, made all the more so when those individuals are doing things unfamiliar to them. Field tests can be made smoother if project teams follow some advice hard-won through others' experience:

1. To be efficiently coordinated, *a field test should be administered by a single member of the project team.* Assigning the task to one team member ensures that the project's administration speaks in one voice to all test centers; that the route for requests, information, and decisions is clear to all centers and team members; and that the project has a single, informed source of information about which centers are delivering their responses on time and which are not.

2. If possible, *a project team should include at least one nearby school or district* in its national field test. Team members can personally visit those classrooms to develop a direct impression of how the materials are playing, offer personal support or guidance to teachers conducting the test, and perhaps conduct exploratory trials of materials that have been revised to reflect comments received from test centers farther away. Ideally, the project can employ a key teacher in the local field test center as a consultant (or buy all or part of the teacher's contract for the test period) so that the teacher can serve as an ongoing liaison between the project and the local center.

3. Because the essence of a successful field test is communication, *a project needs to make that communication as easy as possible.* While administrative matters should be dealt with between the project's test coordinator and test-site directors, teachers should have complete and ready access to project team members when they have questions or need help.

    Test participants should be given a complete list of phone and fax numbers as well as e-mail and web addresses for team members that the project has designated to provide technical support to field test teachers. Also, the project may consider establishing regular Internet-based chat sessions in which test teachers interact with team members and each other. Some projects, such as the National Education Association's Mastery in Learning project, set up electronic networks enabling participating teachers to establish ongoing conversations among themselves. "Communication shouldn't just flow between teachers and developers," Horvat notes. "Teachers should be encouraged to develop the synergy that comes when they're in touch with each other."

4. *At least once during each field test year, at least one member of the project team should visit each field test center.* The team members can gather feedback firsthand, answer teachers' questions, ask about the effectiveness of specific activities or materials of particular concern to the project team, and offer additional coaching or technical support to participating educators.

5. *When field-testing a full-year course, the project should schedule a midyear conference at its headquarters in January or February of each field test year.* At these interim sessions, participating teachers can talk with one an-

other as well as with the project team about problems and issues they have noted individually during the trial. Team members also can interview participants in detail about points of specific concern.

By concentrating and focusing participants' range of experiences and insights, the conferences yield an additional dimension of information and feedback that a team cannot collect by visiting or corresponding with individual teachers or sites. In addition, the conference can speed the project team's collection of responses by creating a synergy of insight and reaction among participants who are fresh to each other. Midyear meetings also can be used to introduce teachers to the materials to be used in the second portion of a year-long course. A project should encourage test centers to send to this midyear conference those educators participating in the project who did not attend the summer session.

INCORPORATING ASSESSMENT INTO
THE FIELD TEST

A second year of testing is also the most effective way in which to evaluate the assessment system that has been designed for a full-year or longer course. Testing the assessment system will also enable developers to collect initial data about the educational effectiveness of their materials.

Indeed, an assessment system for a new course cannot be properly implemented until a national field test's second year because a project team will not be able to finalize the materials' assessment tools and methods until the end of the first year of field-testing. Developers must have some indication of how the assessment system works in classrooms not directly under the project team's personal guidance. Therefore, teachers' responses gathered during the field test's first year provide the information that is essential to modify and improve the materials' complete assessment scheme. Just as important, the first time that a teacher uses new materials is a learning experience for the teacher as much as for students. If the materials are truly innovative, dealing with new instructional approaches and content while also trying to master an unfamiliar system of embedded, authentic assessment often involves more novelty than even the best teachers can handle in a single year.

Field-testing an authentic, embedded assessment system for a year-long course also requires a full year to provide evidence of student growth and development as a result of the course. That explains the need for a second year of field testing: The gradual, continuous unfolding of evidence often demands closer and more careful attention and analysis from the project team, including longer or additional site visits, than other aspects of the national field test.

To ease that additional burden of time and resources, the team can designate a subgroup of test sites for that kind of special attention to assessment during the test's second year—perhaps half of the sites, chosen for their diversity as carefully as was the original group of test sites. By collecting opinions and data about the assessment plan from all sites but concentrating extra attention on a few, the team will be able to learn as much as possible about the protocol's strengths and weaknesses without robbing other tasks of necessary time and funds.

GATHERING AND PROCESSING RESPONSES FROM THE FIELD TEST

"If life were ideal," says SEPUP co-director Barbara Nagle, "a project would have a good 6 months after the final year of field-testing so every member of the development team could go through each teacher's responses." But projects do not inhabit an ideal world. Districts have materials adoption cycles; teachers who have invested time and effort learning to use new materials typically are reluctant to revert to their old ones afterward. Consequently, a project must usually have a commercial version of its materials ready by autumn after completing a field test the spring before.

This urgency mandates that, before the field test begins, a project design a detailed plan not only to launch the field test but also to analyze teachers' resulting comments as they arrive and to revise materials accordingly while other materials are still being tested in the field. The plan must highlight the major goals the project seeks to achieve through the field test and allot the team's resources to ensure that those priorities are met first.

Drafting the plan forces a project team to set a timeline for processing responses. Team members can then review (and perhaps again adjust) their overall timeline, realistically gauge the person-hours and other resources available to manage the job, and allocate those resources adroitly for best results. Because the team's goal is to keep the work flowing smoothly and without interruption from field test to commercial production, a project must finalize the first third of its materials and send them on for pre-publication work while the second third is being tested and the final third is still being prepared for field-testing. Alternatively, in the 2-year field test typically needed to evaluate materials and activities for a year-long course, a project might submit the first section of a course for production based on revisions resulting from the first year and a half of field-testing. The following autumn, commercial users would be able to use a temporary form of the first portion of materials while the complete versions were being produced.

Staging testing, revision, and production in this manner gives a project additional time to complete testing and revisions while still making the program available commercially at the beginning of the schoolyear following the final year of field-testing. (Obviously, carrying out such an intricate process requires full involvement of a project's producer-distributor from planning through completion.)

As part of the field test plan, a few team members—led by the field test coordinator—should be appointed to process and collate teachers' responses, make the collated responses available for review by all team members, and develop a plan to revise the activities and materials in response. The plan must include exact dates by which all team members will have reviewed teachers' comments. It must also specify dates by which team members will be prepared to make explicit suggestions about changes to particular activities and materials.

COMPLICATIONS IN FIELD-TESTING

In carrying out the plan, however, the team will have to be prepared to improvise as the group juggles a variety of complications. Time constraints will make it impossible to review every comment from every participant about every activity. Often, it will not be possible to plan which materials or activities to review closely until participants' comments begin to arrive and highlight problem areas. Also, it may not be possible to evaluate the effectiveness of one portion of the material until well *after* it has been tried in classes. (If an early activity introduces the laws of thermodynamics, a project team might not know how effective the materials were until several activities later when students are asked to apply the laws again in a different context.)

Complicating matters further, not all field test centers will conduct the activities, gather comments and results, and send them to the project team at the same pace. A project team may be facing a deadline and still not have collected an adequate number of responses to a particular activity or from sites in a particular geographic or socioeconomic setting. Ultimately, the team must balance the ideals of its plan against the realities of the field test and make decisions as the calendar dictates.

Also, the promulgation of new standards and new assessment demands are changing educators' expectations for learning materials. Those changing expectations make it necessary for the project team to be ready to deal with the unexpected.

As an example, consider the sudden challenges that SEPUP faced as it field-tested its year-long course "Issues, Evidence, and You."

The project, funded in 1992, was formed in part to create an activity-based, inquiry-oriented middle school course in physical science intended for use in the eighth grade. During the second year of field testing in the 1994–1995 schoolyear, while the project team was concentrating on evaluating the course's assessment system, some districts around the country began using the course in ninth grade as an introductory high school science course.

At the same time, the National Research Council published the second draft of its National Science Education Standards. (In fact, the final version of the standards and the course's materials both were published in 1996.) So, while the project team was focused on the demanding task of integrating embedded, authentic assessment into the course—a major factor in its being funded—external events were pressing the team to give more and more attention to necessities it had not been able to predict: adapting the materials for ninth-grade use and articulating the course's relationship to the newly emerging national standards.

Obviously, SEPUP's four developers could not attend to all demands at once, even though the team considered them to be equally important. The group decided to concentrate on completing the field test and preparing the materials for commercial release while using what resources it could muster to help ninth-grade educators adapt the course materials to their specific needs. Because SEPUP's materials had long been activities-based and inquiry-oriented, the team recognized an overall "fit" between the course and the national standards; so it decided to wait to see if the course was widely adopted before addressing that connection specifically. Currently the project team is more closely correlating the course materials to the final national standards in preparation for the planned second edition of IEY.

Clearly, a project team must use every available resource to evaluate field test results. Much of the evidence of activities' and materials' effectiveness or weaknesses will arrive as comments, critiques, and analysis from participating teachers. But team members can often gain equally valuable information by noting participants' informal comments and even the tone of those comments. Team members can also analyze used classroom equipment packages to determine how easy the materials are to assemble and use and how well they hold up under the rigors of classroom use. (It was by visiting participating classrooms and inspecting used equipment that the SEPUP team found that its plastic trays were subject to excessive staining and scratching, as discussed in Chapter 9.) Each avenue of information contributes in unique ways to the team's impressions and insights about the qualities of the new materials across a wide spectrum of students and teachers.

EVALUATING STUDENT WORK

The team must also examine samples of students' work and their performances on assessments. In evaluating students' work, SEPUP has found it useful to ask each participating field test teacher to select six students—two high achievers, two low achievers, and two from the middle of the performance curve—and submit samples of those students' work from different phases of the materials. It is neither necessary nor productive to collect and examine every bit of every student's work. The project team can specify samples from particular activities or projects—saving the teachers and team members the burden of managing every bit of written work from as many as 300 students (if a team actually does collect six students' work from each of 50 teachers). Although the steady stream of samples from so many students can potentially drown a team in the tasks of analysis, rarely will all teachers submit the full number of student samples on each activity. Therefore, it is necessary to ask for enough samples to drown in to ensure that the project will not "go thirsty" for enough material from which to make a comprehensive analysis.

METHODS OF DATA COLLECTION

The process of gleaning all possible insights from such an array of sources begins with the design of a detailed questionnaire (see Figure 10.1) and assessment form (see Figure 10.2) for each participating teacher to complete for each activity the teacher tests. The form asks teachers' reactions to a range of elements: the length of time an activity actually takes to conduct, its strengths, its problem areas, and students' subjective responses as well as those of the teacher. The form's questions may be as general as "Did you like teaching the activity?" and as detailed as "Were students confused by the wording on Discussion Question 6?" SEPUP's version has been designed to require as little of teachers' time as possible and still elicit the essential information the project team needs about an activity's performance and effectiveness.

An effective response form also includes optional, open-ended questions that encourage teachers to provide more detail about the materials and their own and students' reactions to them. A project will receive a richer array of responses if, in addition to distributing forms, it also encourages

Figure 10.1. SEPUP teacher questionnaire.

THANK YOU for your involvement with the development of *Science and Life Issues.* To aid you in writing your feedback, we suggest addressing the following areas. However, please feel free to include other types of input.

Activity Number ____

I taught this activity for ____ (number of periods) to ____ (number of students).

Science and Life Issues **Teacher's Guide**

1. Was the actual class time required to teach the activity:

   equal to   more than (by how much: ____)   less than (by how much: ____)

   the time stated in the Teacher's Guide?

2. Was the background information adequate for teaching the course material?

                 Yes   No

   If not, what additional information was required?

   _____
   _____

3. **General comments** on the content and "teachability" of the material in the Teacher's Guide, including suggested additions, deletions, or changes:

   _____
   _____
   _____
   _____
   _____

4. General comments on laboratory materials included or not provided in the kit:

   _____
   _____

Science and Life Issues **Student Book**

5. **General comments** on the laboratory investigations, readings, supporting materials, etc. Identify strengths and weaknesses of the activity or parts of the activity as well as

(*Continued*)

Figure 10.1. (*Cont.*)

specific additions, deletions, or changes you made or would have liked to have made to the activities, materials, student pages, homework, content, etc. *Please provide a copy or a description of any materials you added.*

_____

_____

_____

_____

_____

Student Response and Classroom Effectiveness

6. General reactions from different segments of your classroom population to each activity. What was the most or least effective? Why?

_____

_____

7. *Suggestions:* How could student learning and understanding of these concepts have been improved?

_____

_____

8. What is your overall recommendation for this activity? Please consider its relationship to the preceding activities and the course as well as your experience with the activity itself.

1	2	3	4
OK as it is	Minor revisions	Major revisions	Start over

participating teachers and administrators to send audio- or videotapes, send e-mails, make collect phone calls, or communicate with the developers in whatever way the teachers wish.

TEST-SITE MEETINGS

Teachers bring their completed forms to regular meetings at each field test center. In the sessions (typically day-long and held monthly or bimonthly), the teachers dissect each activity, discuss their reactions and responses and

Figure 10.2. SEPUP teacher assessment form.

THANK YOU for your involvement with the development of *Science and Life Issues.* To aid you in writing your feedback, we suggest addressing the following areas. However, please feel free to include other types of input.

Activity Number ____

1. What did you see as the major science concepts and processes in this activity?

   _____
   _____
   _____

2. How did you assess this activity?

Elements

DCI:	Designing Investigation	Selecting & Recording Procedures
	Organizing Data	Analyzing & Interpreting Data
ET:	Using Evidence	Evidence and Trade-offs
UC:	Recognizing Relevant Content	Applying Relevant Content
CM:	Organization	Technical Aspects
GI:	Time Management	Role Performance/Participation
		Shared Opportunity

3. What suggestions/changes do you have for improving student assessment in this activity?

   _____
   _____
   _____
   _____
   _____

4. Other general feedback comments:

   _____
   _____
   _____

those of their students, pinpoint the elements of each activity that warrant attention, and suggest changes to be made. (Some centers make audiotapes of the meeting and send them back to project headquarters so developers can get a more intimate sense of teachers' feelings about the materials than written words can provide.)

In addition, some centers make assessment "moderation sessions," described in Chapter 8, a part of these meetings. Their inclusion not only adds an extra dimension of professional development to the meetings but also often sharpens teachers' insights into the effectiveness of the activities and materials themselves as well as the project's assessment system. "Teachers talking to each other, sharing ideas, suggesting modifications, and so on will create a powerful synergy far beyond what would result if individual teachers just filled out forms and mailed them in," Robert Horvat says.

At the meetings, teachers also turn in their comment forms. A center director then can collate all comments related to one activity and group those comments according to the activity's separate phases or sections. As a result, for each activity a field test center then can submit a single roster of comments rather than a stack of forms or hastily scribbled notes from individual teachers. "You've got to organize the responses somehow," says Stan Hill. "It's one thing for a developer to get a piece of paper from a teacher saying that something doesn't work, but I cannot imagine how complex it would be to be deluged with questionnaires and comments from dozens of individual teachers, each with a distinct opinion."

KEEPING THE PROCESS RUNNING

To keep the process running smoothly, the project team member who coordinates it must keep steadily in touch with each field test center's director throughout the test period. Regular contact not only lets each center's participants know that the project is interested in what they have to say but also provides a gentle (or, when warranted, firm) reminder that responses are eagerly awaited by the project team and, therefore, are to be submitted according to schedule.

Reminders will be necessary; not all field test teachers or centers will be timely in reporting back. In those cases, the project can delay sending subsequent portions of the materials to be tested until the tardy responses are received. The tactic gives the project team and test-site director additional leverage to "encourage" laggards to fulfill their responsibilities as test participants. It also gives the project a way to keep from investing additional resources in individual teachers who have lost the interest or ability to continue participating in the test.

At the project's office, the team member coordinating the field test matches the responses from all field test sites and teachers to each activity, section by section. (The responses can be kept in a designated place in the office, giving all team members access to them and saving the trouble and expense of making copies for each team member.) According to the schedule it has planned, the development team then meets regularly—at least as often as the field test teachers. At these sessions, team members can solve the problems the tests have uncovered, revise the materials accordingly, and prepare improved versions that perhaps can be retested in other classrooms if time permits.

DESIGNING FINAL VERSIONS

As materials undergo final revisions, they will be edited and designed for commercial production. But this will be only the final step in design and editorial processes that have been an integral part of the creation of materials and activities from the beginning of the project. Every version of an activity or material used in an exploratory teaching session and field test is an opportunity to try out wording, graphics, and other presentation elements and to refine the materials further.

Obviously, a project's commercial partner will want to participate in design choices: The first visual impressions a set of materials makes will be crucial in persuading educators to adopt it. But final authority over the internal design and consistency of a project's printed materials must rest with the project team. The reason: In this context, "design" means much more than how materials look. It also denotes the ways in which wording, layout, pictures, and other elements work together to help students and teachers to use the materials effectively, to quickly and easily develop accurate concepts, and to be able to draw valid conclusions from investigations. Given the ethnic, cultural, and socioeconomic diversity of U.S. students, printed materials must also ease the teacher's burden in dealing with individual differences among students. Materials designed and edited with those differences in mind can engage a greater range of students, from those with limited English proficiency to gifted students well able to work beyond the grade levels for which the materials are intended.

Graphic design is a fundamental element in fostering students' understanding. Therefore a project team should include at least one design specialist who assumes chief responsibility for the physical appearance of all of the project's printed materials. (It is particularly helpful if a project's commercial producer shares the cost of adding a design expert to the team.)

Including a design specialist as a team member enables the group to experiment continuously with alternative presentations of the same material and to reach consensus on the most effective presentation of each activity. In addition, the series of questions a good designer poses to developers will help the team clarify its educational objectives and intentions for each activity—and perhaps also help team members improve their own senses of design and presentation.

The option of continuously exploring and refining design choices is made possible by the technologies of computer-based publishing. A separate design, layout, and paste-up department is no longer required; all design tasks can now be accomplished with a computer keyboard and a few clicks of a mouse. Consequently, alternative ideas for graphics, materials designs, and page layouts can be tested continuously—beginning in initial exploratory teaching sessions and continuing on until commercial publication. This new ease and flexibility enables the entire project team, staff, field test participants, and external reviewers to take part in designing the materials' commercial version. (Of course, it also can lead to a case of too many cooks spoiling the broth, as well as delaying production and wasting the project's scarce resources. This opportunity must be closely managed so that it does not transform itself into a liability.)

EDITING FINAL VERSIONS

Editing also needs to be part of materials' creation and testing from a project's beginnings. Consistency and clarity of language are no less vital to students' and teachers' understanding than are graphic images.

With any development project, some team members will be more adept at, and committed to, editorial detail than others will be. If a project can afford to appoint one or more team members as full-time editors, so much the better. However, even with in-house editors, a project should engage the services of an external editor during final production, if not before. The external editor can review, critique, and offer suggestions regarding content, organization, consistency, and clarity of the materials as a single unit—including the correlation between teachers' and students' materials. Team members who are expert editors may be no less competent than an independent reviewer. But working with the same text for an extended period can make one "too familiar" with it: Inconsistencies or other shortcomings that would be apparent to a fresh reader can escape those who have already worked with the materials for long hours. As with design, the costs of editing—as well as the choice of editor—should be shared between the project and its producer-distributor. Ideally, the latter will bear the full cost of final editing.

FINAL CONTENT REVIEW

Before the commercial version of materials is produced in quantity, the accuracy of its academic content must be scrutinized from beginning to end—ideally by a single content expert, or small group of experts, in the field that the materials target. Filtering the entire suite of materials through a single, expert's intelligence is often the most productive way to glean a unified analysis of the whole. Such an analysis will reveal, for example, that the wording of a statement in Activity 5 might create conflict or confusion with a related concept or statement in Activity 14.

Using a single expert is not always possible, however, especially in the case of multidisciplinary materials. When more than one person reviews materials' content, the outcome will be most effective if the experts work together and talk through issues that any one of them raises. The resulting synergy draws greater insight from each participant and can also yield a single, consensual, and thus consistent approach to the treatment of the materials' content.

Content review means just that: The content expert or group focuses on the accuracy of the materials' academic content rather than on the materials' pedagogical approach. Therefore reviewers should be practicing scientists and engineers who have an interest in science education but do not consider themselves science educators. The current popularity of early retirement plans and the availability of highly qualified retired individuals interested in challenging short-term projects is an opportunity projects should consider when seeking scientific reviewers.

CREDITS AND COPYRIGHTS

A project team has a professional and moral responsibility to publicly acknowledge the contributions that individual team members, participating teachers, advisers, consultants, and reviewers have made to the project. Teachers who hosted exploratory teaching sessions and participated in field tests, content experts, and pedagogical reviewers can be noted on a page or two in students' and teachers' books or classroom materials, usually listed alphabetically within their categories of contribution.

Denoting specific contributions of individual team members is more difficult to do in print. If the team has been genuinely collaborative, each member has not only relinquished ownership of ideas that he or she has created but also has had a hand in improving the ideas of others. Consequently, credit for the project's finished products must be shared as equally as was the work of creation. However, individual team members must still be able to specify their unique contributions to the project in résumés and academic vitae.

Ensuring that team members receive equal yet individual credit involves two steps. First, all team members can be listed alphabetically (not hierarchically by title or position) on an authors' page included in the completed materials. Second, the project's director or leadership team can write a letter or participation summary for each team member, detailing the person's unique strengths, skills, and contributions to the project. To be most accurate as well as most effective, the summaries should be written as part of closing the project—not delayed until some future time when the team member asks for written particulars and memories might be less vivid. Over time, a series of letters can document an individual's specific value to projects as well as his or her growth in knowledge and skill. However, this two-part method of apportioning credit is far from perfect: People hiring academic personnel or members for new development teams still focus too often on more overt signs of professional achievement, such as job titles, credits as a senior author, and so on. Development projects are always searching for more effective ways to recognize individual contributions without eroding the collaboration and pooling of ideas that is essential to a project's success—a persistent problem not easily resolved.

Among its list of credits, the project team also has a moral and, almost always, legal responsibility to acknowledge any use of previously published materials included in its creations. Usually the team's editorial specialist or the team member wanting to include text or graphics already in print becomes responsible for determining whether the material is under active copyright. If it is, the project must secure permission to use it. (In many cases, brief excerpts may be used without permission if the source is cited.) An attorney with the project's host institution is best equipped to make the judgment. If permission is required, gaining it might require a fee for use; and if the project must pay more than a token honorarium for permission (as may be the case with corporate logos or product images), the project may choose to reconsider using the copyrighted material at all. Many school systems discourage or ban the use of corporate logos or brand names in educational materials they are considering for adoption.

Gaining permission to use copyrighted material can be a lengthy process; making necessary arrangements should begin as soon as the team decides to include the copyrighted items in its materials so that any anticipated reprint fees may be included in the project's budget.

TURNING FIELD TEST SITES INTO IMPLEMENTATION CENTERS

In addition to exploratory teaching sessions and presentations made at professional meetings, national field tests are among the most effective ways to introduce a project's materials to potential users. In addition to being a test site, each national field test site also can serve as a local or regional demonstration center where other educators can learn about the project and, more important, see its materials in use in real classrooms.

With that goal in mind, during the field test's second year the project—especially its commercial distributor—usually begins to encourage additional schools and districts to join the test. The invitation can expand the pool of teachers and students offering reactions to the materials while also introducing more potential users to the project's products.

However, before swelling the ranks of its field test centers, a project must be confident that it can accommodate the needs, demands, and responses from more centers than it is dealing with already. The additional comments, questions, requests for help, and accompanying paperwork could overwhelm a project's ability to react to and process interactions not only with the new centers but also with those already taking part in the test. If a team gathers reactions from a test center but is too busy to offer satisfactory replies to the site's educators, test participants could develop the impression that the project is not interested in those responses—an opposite message from the one a project hopes to communicate. Therefore, when field test centers are added as a step toward implementation, the kinds and amounts of information that a project expects from each center, and what the center can expect in return, must be made clear.

To gain maximum exposure for its materials, a project can encourage field test educators to make presentations about the project and its activities to other teachers at local, regional, or national professional gatherings or in less formal visits between nearby schools. Often, the teachers do not need a great deal of encouragement; sometimes they are paid for their work by the project or the producer-distributor, but often they do it solely for the opportunity of professional participation and recognition. To help make the most of these exchanges, the team can provide each center with literature about the project and its materials. In addition, the project's producer-distributor often can be persuaded to provide samples of the materials for teachers attending the sessions to try in their own classes.

If a project's materials are educationally successful, after the field test many (and ideally all) participating teachers and districts will want to use the materials as part of their curricula. That becomes a powerful endorsement that may influence other educators to adopt the materials. To make that an easier decision for test participants, and as an additional incentive and reward to field test teachers and their school districts, a project can agree to donate commercial versions of its materials to them to replace the field test versions. The costs of the donations can be built into the project's funding proposal or negotiated as part of the agreement between a project and its producer-distributor.

THE TEACHER'S ROLE IN NATIONAL FIELD TESTS

In national field tests of new materials, teachers again provide an indispensable link between a development project and its chief clientele—educators. Teachers are every school's curricular co-creators, leaders, and managers. Therefore project teams depend on an array of working educators from diverse geographic and socioeconomic areas to let them know whether the materials are easy and efficient to use, whether they engage the teachers, whether the teachers can use the materials effectively to engage students and create a curriculum, and so on. In this way, every participating teacher becomes part of the development project's creative team. Without detailed, thorough, and honest responses from teachers who agree to take part in a project's national field test, the project's success is in jeopardy.

But a field test does not benefit only materials developers. Teachers who join in a field test often gain stature in their districts as innovators to be looked to for leadership generally, especially in new curricular areas. In addition, teachers who take part in field tests learn to use the new materials, giving their districts an advantage in adopting the materials (and their students an advantage in using them) should the new materials prove successful.

Finally, being part of a field test has proven to be a powerful tool in teachers' ongoing professional development. Participating teachers work with colleagues and experienced developers locally and from around the country to implement and assess new ideas, often gaining new insights into subject content, classroom practice, and other areas of educational management and leadership.

CONCLUSION

Conducting a successful national field test involves an intricately coordinated series of steps, including recruiting and selecting field test sites, organizing the sites chosen, preparing the teachers and administrators who will participate, finalizing materials for testing, incorporating assessment, processing teachers' and students' responses, evaluating student assessment results, finalizing commercial versions of the materials, and preparing test sites to serve as implementation centers. As in every stage of materials development, success here depends on a collaborative spirit. But this spirit now must extend from the project team to a national network of educators and administrators. By cultivating such a spirit among its members, a team can naturally extend that spirit to external collaborators and partners—a crucial element in a project's overall success.

11

Implementation, Dissemination, and the Role of the Teacher

Precious things are conveyed to the younger generation . . . not, in the main, through textbooks.

—Albert Einstein, *Ideas and Opinions*

THE FINAL PHASE of a project, a phase that the team hopes will not end, is the implementation of the materials the group has struggled so long and hard to create. Implementation means more than commercialization. It also involves all the dissemination, professional development, and other activities the project undertakes—independently as well as in cooperation with its producer-distributor—to encourage teachers, schools, and districts to adopt and use the materials.

The elements of implementation, discussed in this chapter, include the following:

- Converting field test centers to implementation centers
- Developing local leadership for implementation, especially among teachers
- Accommodating special requests from test sites and potential adopters
- Working effectively with the project's producer-distributor
- Making use of professional publications and the Internet

LAYING FOUNDATIONS

It should be clear by now that implementation is not separate from a project's earlier activities. If the project has been designed and conducted effectively, it has laid the foundations for implementation from its earliest days. It has consulted teachers about the need for the proposed materials and has continued to work with educators during design and testing. It also has kept the larger educational community informed of the project's aims, approach, and progress through publications and presentations at professional meetings. Each of these ongoing activities improves the project and its resulting materials while stirring anticipation and enthusiasm among educators for a project's products.

CONVERTING FIELD TEST CENTERS INTO IMPLEMENTATION CENTERS

It is a truism that educators are most comfortable adopting innovations that they have seen colleagues use successfully. As a result, the most effective way for a project to disseminate its materials is to establish demonstration sites—what might be called "implementation centers"—as widely as possible.

At a school or district serving as an implementation center, area teachers can see new materials in use and question the teachers using them. They can gather advice and support as they decide whether to adopt the materials. If they do adopt them, they then can turn to these same knowledgeable colleagues for advice and support in learning to use the materials properly. The most efficient way to build a network of implementation centers is to enlist field test sites to continue in this new role after the test has been completed. Consequently, the choice of national field test centers should be made with the project's plan for implementation in mind.

Many of the characteristics that lead a project to choose a district as a field test center—including the interest and availability of skilled teachers, the district's commitment to innovation, and strong local leadership—are equally important in an implementation center. Just as vital, but more difficult to assess, is a test center's commitment to adopting the project's materials when the field test ends. (Some districts and administrators see participation in field tests as a way to gain prestige or to appease innovative teachers by taking part even though they have no interest in adopting the materials they help to test.) The commitment of a district's senior administrators to the field test is not only essential to a field test site's effectiveness but also goes a long way toward ensuring later adoption of the materials being tested.

However, more immediate and practical concerns often hold sway: The end of a field test may not coincide with a science department's turn in its district's materials adoption cycle, or the district might simply not have enough money to buy the materials. Such budgetary constraints sometimes can be skirted if the project's producer-distributor is willing to negotiate prices and flexible terms with an eager district. A project's team needs to be similarly flexible: the degree to which it is willing to meet the needs of schools and districts expressing special desires—wanting to adopt only portions of the material or asking for customized versions, for example—can significantly expand the materials' adoption.

The strongest, most effective advocates for a project's materials will be educators who have used them successfully to improve the quality of teaching and learning in their classrooms. Therefore, during and after field-testing, the project team should identify and encourage informed, effective teachers to serve as local spokespersons and demonstrators for the project's materials. However, genuine enthusiasm and commitment among teachers for implementing the materials are not enough. The school's and district's administrative leadership must also demonstrate a commitment to serving as an implementation center if a genuinely cooperative relationship between the center and project is to flourish. Without firm administrative support, teachers will not be granted the release time and other resources that they will need to fulfill their roles as local implementation leaders.

As part of its effort to cultivate field test sites as implementation centers, the project team must use the field test period to help participating teachers, schools, and districts connect the materials to their long-term goals for teaching and learning. A project team's attitude and approach in working with centers will be its initial demonstration of that commitment. If a center's educators (especially its teachers) are given reason to believe that the team's primary interest is in picking teachers' brains for outcome data, their interest in continuing as an implementation center will evaporate. A center's educators need to see the project team as a partner in improving teaching and learning in their classrooms. If the project team is ready and willing to help those educators understand how the materials will help them meet state and local goals, their interest in continuing to work with the project is likely to grow exponentially.

DEVELOPING TEACHER-LEADERS FOR IMPLEMENTATION

The conferences a project sponsors to introduce participating field test teachers to its materials can become a demonstration of that commitment by the project. To make it so, the project team must ensure that the events are more than just "training sessions" about the mechanics of conducting classroom activities. The conferences need to include leadership education and seminars that help participants to develop a thorough understanding of the project, its philosophy, and its goals.

As part of leadership education, participants at each center need to do more than plan the specific use of the project's materials and program in their individual schools. They also need to meet with their counterparts from other centers to discuss common challenges.

Often, problems that one center faces can be resolved by advice or anecdotes from others. For example, in elementary and early middle school, science may be taught either by circuit-riding science specialists or by a class's regular teacher. Participating teachers need to know that the difference can significantly alter the ways in which a project's materials can be used. A circuit rider with a thorough knowledge of science makes it unnecessary for all teachers to know the subject in depth. Using a science specialist can also make possible cost-efficiencies when materials travel with the specialist instead of being provided to every classroom. However, the circuit-rider approach makes it difficult to conduct long-term activities and investigations over successive days. It also works against the integration of science learning experiences with the other subjects and activities that make up a class's overall academic program. Similarly, block scheduling and other novel approaches to structuring time in high schools raise new questions. How should a teacher structure a "double period" when two successive steps in a science investigation require the passage of 24 hours between them?

Educators at different field test centers that face similar problems— such as dealing with large populations of students with limited English proficiency or with the distinctive problems facing urban schools—should have opportunities to compare and discuss their plans for dealing with these challenges and, later, to compare outcomes. Often, the discussions lead centers to modify their plans and approaches in ways that make not only the national field test but also later implementation smoother and more useful for the project team, teachers, and students alike.

HANDLING SPECIAL REQUESTS

To sustain that enthusiasm and commitment, the project team must be sensitive and responsive to special requests from teacher-leaders and other participating educators, schools, and districts. That means providing individual help and meeting special requests to the extent that the project's time and budget permit.

A school district field-testing a project's materials might be revising its curriculum or embarking on its materials adoption process. If the district asks for special help learning to work with the materials, the team should take pains to provide it. Fulfilling special needs and requests can win the project local champions for its implementation phase, but it also can quickly add new complications to an already complex field test. (For example, some districts might decide they want to use the project's materials in a different way than the project intended—to use just three parts of a year-long course instead of all four, perhaps.)

The project team and its producer-distributor must develop policies before implementation begins to define how they will handle such requests. If, as is probable, the team or its publisher is printing directly from computer files, customizing printed materials is usually only a minor inconvenience. However, extra costs are incurred in preparing and producing special editions of both printed materials and equipment kits. Districts making the request should be informed of the costs and be expected to bear at least a portion of them. For the project, and especially for its commercial partner, the extra costs of extensively customizing materials often will not be affordable unless the district or organization requesting the special editions plans to purchase a sizable number of the materials. (Defining *sizable* in these cases is more of a marketing consideration than a policy decision.)

The more flexible a project and its producer-distributor can be in responding to such requests, the more positively they will be perceived by the larger marketplace—even though the number of districts that will actually want to customize the program is usually small.

The time and effort invested during a national field test to meet the special needs of secondary schools can pay hefty dividends during implementation. Because secondary schools need to meet the specific expectations of other agencies and institutions, their special needs often arise from questions of assessment; for instance, whether colleges or state regulators will judge the new materials to be as effective as older ones in meeting academic standards for high school graduation and university admission.

An example: the Brooklyn, New York, High School District took part in the field test for SEPUP's year-long "Science and Sustainability" course. The district's policy states that any science course it offers should be what the state calls a "Regents-level" course—earning credits leading to a Regents diploma when graduating from high school, traditionally the most academically prestigious diploma and soon to be the only one offered in the state. (It has also been the diploma that most of the state's colleges and universities have required for admission.) The only way a student can earn Regents credit is to pass an approved Regents examination based on a course's content. When Brooklyn's field test center was established, the district's participating educators asked for and received authorization from the New York City Board of Education and the state education department to prepare a special Regents exam for "Science and Sustainability." Veronica Peterson, a district science specialist, and her colleagues worked with SEPUP's project team to create a Regents exam that, with a few modifications, the state education department approved. Students who participated in the field test then had the opportunity to earn Regents credit.

As a result, by the time the course was commercially available, any school district in New York state was more easily able to apply for and receive Regents credit for the course because of Brooklyn's precedent. The approval gave SEPUP a significant advantage in implementing the course in New York State and helped other educational jurisdictions concerned about assessing and validating new learning materials

In responding to special requests, a project team must understand that the final decision about how a project's materials are used is made by the districts adopting them. Inevitably—and usually without asking the project team's advice—at least a few schools or districts will adopt a project's materials at what team members believe to be an inappropriate grade level. Then they will ask the team's help in making the materials work. When that happens, the team faces a decision. It can simply refuse (and sometimes time and other logistical considerations make that necessary). It is more useful for the project team to work as closely as it can with the school or district leaders who made the decision—and especially with the teachers who will implement the materials. Together, they can find the best possible fit between the materials and the way the adopters have chosen to use them.

Such extra trouble can sometimes open new markets for the project's materials. Brooklyn's high school district wanted to use parts of SEPUP's "Issues, Evidence, and You" in a summer program designed for eighth-graders expected not to do well in a ninth-grade biology course beginning the following September. The project team and its producer-distributor adapted, then separately produced, a selected group of the activities and materials to meet this special request. With guidance from the project team, district educators then modified the selected materials' uses, added some activities of their own, and integrated the new materials into the summer course. The modified materials were so effective that the district decided to replace the locally designed summer enrichment course with a specially produced partial version of "Issues, Evidence, and You." The project continues to succeed with SEPUP's help, an outcome that has led to an expanded, ongoing relationship between the program and the district.

As another example, in SEPUP's early days an elementary school asked for the team's help in using middle and secondary school modules as part of a program for gifted third-graders. For several sound educational reasons, the team declined to become involved.

Experiences during the design, field-testing, and currently the implementation of "Science and Sustainability"—the new SEPUP high school course—have clearly demonstrated that at the high school level the independence in how materials are used intensifies. To put it succinctly, at the high school level projects develop courses; districts, schools, and teachers adopt resources. That is, they adopt a course because they think it is the closest approximation to what they want to use, but they expect to augment and supplement it with their own and other materials. This may be because early in the commercial life of the project we are still dealing with "early innovators" who tend to be more independent and creative in their use of materials. Considering the diversity and complexity of American high school students, this independence can be a positive trend. Projects and their distributors need to develop more effective ways to meet and encourage it.

While these unplanned uses can expand a project's adoption and impact, a project team must be judicious in accommodating them. The team's decision to adapt its materials for unplanned applications must be consistently guided primarily by the project's larger goal of effective and appropriate use of its materials—not by marketing considerations.

DEVELOPING LOCAL LEADERSHIP FOR IMPLEMENTATION

The purpose of materials development is to contribute an essential element—more effective learning materials—to the continuing redesign and improvement of education. An equally essential element is a teacher able to use the materials to fashion the interactions between teacher and student that we call *curriculum*. If a project team acknowledges the equal importance of both elements, it will understand that its work will be largely ineffective unless a true partnership links the team with local educators. As noted earlier, a wise project team will begin to forge those links during (if not before) the preparation of its proposal and, later, with a larger number of educators as the team prepares for and implements a project's materials nationally.

In planning its materials' implementation, a project team must foster the materials' use among a nationally representative diversity of school districts, teachers, students, expectations, and various kinds and levels of support available to educators around the country. One goal of the national field test is to recruit test sites that will exemplify that diversity should the sites later adopt the materials.

Teachers and administrators—particularly lead teachers and curriculum administrators—who think in serious and sustained ways about the future of teaching and learning in their field, or even just within their own districts, can be especially helpful to a project team. First, these local leaders can help a project director or team assess the practical need for the materials they propose to develop. Second, when the project is funded, local leaders can bring team members together with other teachers willing to serve as formal or informal advisers to the project. Teachers involved so intimately with a project will often become local or area leaders in implementing its materials later. Also, understanding teachers' needs and views will help team members answer (and even anticipate) similar concerns among other educators evaluating the materials—and thus earn greater confidence among them.

COMPLEMENTARY ROLES OF THE PROJECT TEAM AND PRODUCER-DISTRIBUTOR

As a project's products are commercialized and adopted, the project team and the producer-distributor have complementary roles. It is the role of the producer-distributor, not the project team, to sell materials; team members should not become salespersons. Instead, team members serve as professional experts with two roles. First, they help teachers, schools, and districts understand the role the project's materials can play in improving teaching and learning. Second, they help adopters use the materials properly and well.

To oversimplify the difference, the producer-distributor is primarily interested making a sale; the project team is primarily interested in what happens before and after the sale.

At times, the complementary purposes can lead to conflict between a project team and its producer-distributor. For example, there will be times when a school or district wants to adopt the materials to use at an inappropriate grade level. Salespeople might encourage the prospective buyer to rethink the decision, but usually they will not work hard to discourage a sale. In contrast, the project team has a responsibility (if asked for advice) to offer the buyer the best information and counsel it can even if it jeopardizes the sale.

USING PROFESSIONAL PRESENTATIONS, PUBLICATIONS, AND THE INTERNET

Professional Presentations

From a project's earliest days, team members should be seeking opportunities to make presentations about the project's approach, intent, and materials at state science teacher conventions and other gatherings, such as regional and national conventions of the National Science Teachers Association, the National Association of Biology Teachers, or other subject area conventions. (Making presentations at meetings of more general organizations, such as the National Middle Schools Association and the Association for Supervision and Curriculum Development, can be useful as well if the project's time and budget permit.)

After a national field test, those presentations can become increasingly rich in data and detail. The test will have provided evidence about the effects of the project's materials on students' achievement. Also, teachers who took part in the field test, have used the materials themselves, and have seen students' reactions will often be willing to make presentations—a particularly effective stratagem to win the attention of teachers often skeptical of innovators' claims. However, in such presentations it is not the role of a project's team members or field test teachers to make sales pitches. Instead, their role is only to enlighten colleagues about the educational implications and possible values of the project's materials. Sales pitches will be made by the project's distributor, with team members' advice and counsel, at the appropriate times and places.

Publications

Publications are also an effective venue to inform educators of a project's materials and field test results. The project can use its own newsletter to detail outcomes, include comments from participating teachers, answer questions about the materials' design and use, and announce introductory workshops. The National Science Teachers Association and the American Association for the Advancement of Science are just two of several organizations that publish newsletters for educators offering information about projects and their products. Team members can ask these organizations for article guidelines, publication deadlines, and future special issues in which an article about a specific project may be particularly appropriate.

It is more difficult, but still worthwhile, to prepare articles based on the project's work for publication in professional or scholarly journals. Many such publications, particularly those that subject manuscripts to peer review, hold submissions to rigorous requirements of form, content, and documentation, so preparing the article can be arduous. (The effort is also less likely to influence educators' materials adoption decisions than articles in other publications.) However, journal articles do help a project to be recognized among university-based science and mathematics educators. Such recognition can help a developer or ongoing development program secure funding for additional projects.

Research

A project also can earn recognition in the academic community for its innovative nature by hosting or taking part in research projects conducted by master's or doctoral students who take an interest in the project's work. Within 5 years of the final publication in 1977 of the original Science Curriculum Improvement Study materials, the program and its approach had been the subject of more than 50 doctoral dissertations. The program's willingness to open itself and its research to the academic community earned it wider attention among university educators. By 1999, various aspects of SEPUP's work had been the subject of five doctoral theses. That kind of attention helps to establish a project as a source of innovation within its subject area and to make it better known among science teachers and district administrators.

The Internet

The Internet has opened vast new opportunities to spread the word about a project and its materials inexpensively. Independently or with the help of its host institution, a project can maintain its own web page to let educators worldwide know about its materials and their educational impact. On its web page, a project can include a brief description of the program and its goals, the latest issue of its newsletter, detailed descriptions of each of its materials sets and other products, and a selection of sample activities from its projects. Once the web page has been established, it requires work to maintain and update but is more than worth the effort.

However, a word of caution: Do not promise more from your website than team members can deliver without interfering with their other work. For example, it may be tempting to set up a listserv or chat room on the site. But before doing so, a team must estimate the time and energy its members can commit to responding to the questions, comments, and other demands that such a public forum invites. There is no quicker way to turn off interested educators, especially potential adopters, than to encourage them to communicate with a project that then neither answers nor acknowledges them.

A DEVELOPER'S OPPORTUNITY: SYSTEMIC INITIATIVES

The National Science Foundation (NSF) has long funded a variety of university-based teacher enhancement projects aimed at improving participants' content expertise and classroom effectiveness. But it was only briefly during the 1980s that the agency directly funded the implementation of a specific project's materials. The reason: The NSF is a federal agency and educational decisions, including choices of learning materials, are a state and local function. Until the 1990s, the agency had come no closer to endorsing or commercializing materials than to expect the teacher enhancement projects it funded to introduce participants to materials from a variety of projects—those funded by the NSF as well as others—in the course of their programs. (We use the word *expect* because the NSF technically did not explicitly require projects to do this, although we know of none that were funded without promising to do so.)

Then, in the late 1980s the NSF began funding "systemic initiatives" aimed at helping state and local educators fundamentally change the way that science or mathematics or both are taught within their educational jurisdictions. As part of the initiatives, the NSF has expected educators to select new learning materials. These materials are expected to be inquiry-oriented, materials-centered (especially at the elementary level), and used to refashion the science and mathematics programs in the adopting schools.

Since the National Science Education Standards were published in 1996, the NSF has pressed the systemic initiatives even more forcefully to choose materials specifically designed to align with and implement the new standards—particularly materials that have been created with NSF funding. That insistence necessarily points grantees toward some specific materials and away from others. As might be expected, this guidance has led educators proposing systemic initiatives to concentrate on adopting NSF-funded materials.

This conjunction of the NSF's funding of systemic initiatives and the publication of the national standards has broadened dissemination and implementation opportunities for the NSF-funded materials development projects (and others) that best embody the standards. A project can ask the NSF for a list of systemic initiative projects and send each program's leaders information about the project and its materials. In the past, SEPUP has invited participants in systemic initiatives to attend its National Fellows Conference held each summer and to become part of the project's national field-testing efforts. As a result, many systemic initiatives have adopted and implemented SEPUP's materials.

THE TEACHER'S ROLE IN ADAPTING NEW MATERIALS

Part of teachers' indispensable role in adopting new materials lies in *adapting* those materials to suit their districts' individual curricular approaches and philosophies as well as their students' unique needs. In adaptation as much as in development, teachers can contribute to improving the materials used in their own classrooms.

It has become a far too customary expectation that teachers should develop new curricular materials in their "spare time" or in short summer workshops and conferences. As the development process outlined in previous chapters has made clear, materials that engage students while also educating them cannot be developed in quick workshops. However skilled and experienced a group of teachers might be, they lack the funding, time, and breadth of specialized skills to produce effective, inquiry-based materials and assessment systems from scratch.

Instead, these briefer sessions should be reserved for groups of teachers to work together—in close collaboration with the original developers—to adapt, combine, and fine-tune materials created by others to the specific individual needs of their schools and students. As leaders and facilitators of the curriculum in their own classrooms, teachers are best able to determine how materials created for guided inquiry can be adjusted to be even more effective among their own students.

Rather than viewing these adaptation sessions as casual affairs, districts need to recognize that the sessions need full support—in funding for materials, research, and time to plan and conduct—as if they were an essential aspect of a full-scale development project. The reason is simple: These sessions *are* materials development projects at the local level. As such, when properly planned, supported, and conducted, they help teachers to grow professionally by analyzing, reflecting on, and rethinking their own evolving approaches to leadership in teaching and learning. Teachers' professional growth in skills and insight is essential in transforming effective instructional materials into a curriculum that engages students.

CONCLUSION

Successful implementation of a project's materials is neither an afterthought to development nor something that can be left to a commercial partner. The project team must regard commercialization of their materials to be an integral part of their work. It must prepare a plan to convert field test centers to implementation centers; develop local leadership for implementation, especially among teachers; accommodate special requests from test sites and potential adopters; work effectively with the project's producer-distributor; and make use of professional publications and the Internet. By approaching these steps as methodically as it does the act of creation, a project team will help to ensure that its work achieves the impact team members hope.

12

Closure and Continuity

The intuitive mind is a sacred gift and the rational mind is a faithful servant.
We have created a society that honors the servant and has forgotten the gift.
—Albert Einstein, quoted in the *New York Times*

AFTER A PROJECT'S IMPLEMENTATION phase is under way, the project team must meet a few final obligations, some short term and some possibly ongoing. The short-term obligations involve completing reports to funders and to the profession about what the project did and how its results compare with its hopes and intentions. If a project's materials succeed commercially, the team's longer-term obligations probably will include responding to adopters' ongoing needs and requests; continuing a course of professional development for adopters; and planning and conducting revisions to the materials. In addition to these topics, which are discussed below, teams face the larger question of what to do next and deciding whether the team wants to do it.

DEFINING "SUCCESS"

Earlier, we noted that the only projects a developer has to be concerned about are those that are funded. Similarly, the only projects that a developer needs to continue to be concerned about are those that succeed in the materials marketplace.

However, that statement does not mean that only development projects whose materials are commercially accepted are successful. The Chemical Bond Approach project (CBA), described in Chapter 3, was so radical in its approach to high school chemistry instruction that its textbook was not readily adopted and a second edition was never published. Most educators seeking new materials at the time chose to adopt the CHEM Study text. However, CBA succeeded in showing educators the effectiveness of organizing basic aspects of chemistry education around the concept of chemical bonds—an approach that since has become fundamental to many secondary school chemistry texts now in use. One way to think about each project's different form of success is to consider that CHEM Study accomplished "percentage implementation," being used by a large number of students, while CBA achieved "intellectual implementation," introducing new ideas that influenced the field greatly over time.

Success can also be defined by the project itself rather than the marketplace. The Global Laboratory project, developed at the private, nonprofit TERC development center in Cambridge, Massachusetts, "wasn't necessarily intended to make money," notes Joe Walters, the project's director. "Its primary purpose was to demonstrate a certain kind of integration of activity-oriented science. We're confident that it does that successfully."

A key distinction between a project that succeeds commercially and one that does not is that the former endures beyond the life of its supporting grant. Because its materials continue to be used and adopted, such a project incurs obligations to continue to work with adopting teachers, to help publishers and producers update materials, and otherwise to ensure that the effectiveness and success of the materials continue—and perhaps to extend its work into additional projects as well.

REPORTING TO FUNDERS

When its grant period ends, a project is obligated to provide its funder or funders with one or more final reports. First, funders require a full financial account of the project's expenditures. This report is usually prepared by the project's host institution, which has managed the project's money, but the project director is required to sign the report and so must review it in detail for accuracy. Second, the project submits to its funders a narrative summary of what the project had proposed to produce and what it delivered. Both reports are part of the summative evaluation described in Chapter 8.

Many government funding agencies, such as the National Science Foundation (NSF), require final narratives, which might be only a page or two in length, noting the project's accomplishments. Public funding agencies keep these reports on file and open to the public. They are useful to graduate students or other researchers investigating the nature or outcomes of specific projects, the historical path of development in a specific field, or the nature of the development process generally. (The reports can also be useful to congressional or other investigators seeking to support or attack public agencies' funding choices.) Other funding agencies, particularly private or corporate foundations, usually require more extensive reports.

Whatever the funder's reporting requirements, a project team must be scrupulous in fulfilling them. In doing so, the team should think carefully about how to present its results in the best possible light: The same team or program may wish to approach the same funder again in the future. Also, funding agencies often check with others that have funded a group in the past for a report on that group's effectiveness and reliability.

REPORTING TO COLLEAGUES

Detailing the project's accomplishments to a funder is only part of the team's reporting responsibilities. The team was singled out to explore a particular way to enhance some aspect of education. Therefore, the team is also obliged to report to colleagues and educators generally about what the group set out to do, the materials it has produced, any outcomes that those materials have yielded, and, in particular, what the team learned that could be useful to other researchers and developers. Meeting these professional obligations requires an additional final report or reports, usually more detailed than the one the team prepares for funders. A typical project report to the profession may include demographic and academic details about the schools that participated, implementation problems and how they were addressed and overcome, and more detailed evidence of student achievement. If the project included an unusual approach, such as distance learning via the Internet for teachers participating in field tests, an explanation of the approach and its results could also provide guidance to other developers. Many projects publish these comprehensive reports themselves and provide copies at cost to any interested educators and free of charge to the schools and districts that worked with the team and other individuals who collaborated with the project.

Preparing this second report is perhaps the most effective way for a team to assess its own work. It gives the group an opportunity to compare what it had intended to do with what it actually has achieved. Such close assessment often suggests topics for more detailed journal articles and other professional presentations that can be of additional use to researchers or other developers. (The presentations can also call additional attention to the project's achievements as well as enhance team members' professional stature and credentials.)

ONGOING TASKS AND RESPONSIBILITIES

A project team's work in the post-grant period will be defined by the negotiated agreements detailing the roles, rights, and responsibilities of the project team, host institution, and producer-distributor. The more successful a project's products are in the education marketplace, the more important those agreements become.

If a project's materials are widely adopted and continue to be used, the project almost certainly will have continuing obligations to the materials' users even though its grant period has ended. Even if the project has contracted production and dissemination of its materials to commercial firms, the contract's terms will usually require the host institution (and team members, if they are available) to help educators learn to use the materials well. For example, the project team or host institution must be ready, and a structure must be in place, for someone connected to the project to respond to queries from teachers.

If the project or its host institution holds copyright of the materials, that ownership also implies legal responsibility for any problems arising from the project's materials. The responsibility to resolve questions and concerns about safety, possible misunderstandings about how materials are to be used, malfunctioning parts in equipment kits, and so on should be shared contractually by the project team and the materials' producer-distributor.

Educators also will raise questions more complex than those a producer or distributor can address. They will ask how parts of a course or module might be used with a particular group of learners such as the gifted or physically handicapped, whether the materials can be adapted to other grade levels, or how the project's materials might be used in other applications or as parts of other programs. Such questions require the expertise of the project team (or teacher-leaders prepared by the team). If, as suggested, a project or its host institution has retained copyright of the materials, sales will provide royalty income that can support individuals assigned to carry out these tasks even though the project's grant period has ended. (A project director or team that has legally defined themselves as authors of the materials and thus receives royalties as individuals will usually be contractually obligated by the producer-distributor to cover such costs themselves.)

REVISING PROJECT MATERIALS

After a time—no more than 3 or 4 years if a project's materials are commercially successful—the questions of revisions or new editions will arise. There are three main reasons. First, many school systems, as well as many of the states that authorize materials for adoption in their schools, stipulate that no materials may be adopted if their copyright is more than 5 years old. Second, science knowledge is being continuously revolutionized. Consider how dated a thoughtful examination of AIDS and the HIV virus written in the 1980s would sound today. Guided-inquiry materials that couch subject content in the context of real-world issues are even more liable to become outdated quickly. Third, new standards are emerging, being tested, and then being refined. For example, in the late 1990s as schools, districts, and states reconsidered their curricular plans in the wake of the National Science Education Standards, demand surged for classroom materials embodying the new standards.

A project team hoping to create materials that will endure must plan from the beginning how it will meet the obligation to revise and improve its products after external funding has ended. In updating materials, the specific design, editorial, financial, and other rights and obligations of the project team, host institution, and producer-distributor are (or should have been) spelled out in full detail in the contract the two parties signed earlier.

If a project's materials need to be updated simply to make them more competitive in the ever-evolving marketplace of educational materials, commercial producer-distributors will be expected to fund the work. Typically, they will be willing to do so, expecting the more desirable updated materials to more than repay the cost of revisions out of increased sales revenue.

However, a commercial producer-distributor that is funding revisions will also often expect to control the materials' graphic design and, to some extent, content in order to make the product more "marketable." In addition, as part of the bargain, the commercial entity will frequently demand to own the new edition's copyright. If the producer-distributor assumes ownership of the materials' copyright, the project effectively ends. To transfer copyright, the project and its producer-distributor must negotiate a detailed agreement assigning legal rights and complete control over the materials to the commercial entity. (Any such changes to the contract between the project and its producer-distributor must be reviewed by the host institution's attorneys.)

If the project team and host institution will not control the character or quality of the final product, the agreement should reflect the team's and institution's wishes about the use of their names in the new edition of the materials. The new agreement must also specify legal protections for the project team and host against any liability arising from the new edition's production, distribution, or implementation (another reason why legal advice is necessary at this point). Although the materials are no longer in their creators' hands, the project team should realize that this agreement will include some degree of ongoing responsibility to work with the producer-distributor and with teachers and schools adopting the materials. Team members should carry out this work as individuals and be compensated for their efforts by the producer-distributor.

DECIDING WHAT COULD BE DONE NEXT
AND WHETHER YOU WANT TO DO IT

Any substantial grant to support a materials development project takes at least 9 months to secure. Consequently, a project team hoping to remain together and work on new ventures must decide what it wants to do next well before the project's current grant period comes to an end. The team should begin to consider its future options at least a full year before any current project runs out of funds.

Usually a project team has three choices:

- To try to secure funding to continue and extend the current project's design and development work
- To seek funding to continue and expand the current project's dissemination, implementation, and teacher education
- To design and propose an entirely new development project that may or may not be related to the team's present work

If the team's present project has been funded by the NSF (which it probably has), chances for receiving support for the first option are remote. One exception: if the project's materials are being widely adopted and, at the same time, a significant and unforeseen event (such as publication of new national subject or professional standards) places a new urgency on revising existing materials to align them with the new standards or other realities.

Even in those cases, the NSF will consider proposals to revise recent materials or extend development only if a project's commercial producer-distributor agrees to contribute a sizable portion of the funds needed for the effort. For example, 1996 saw the advent of the National Science Education Standards, an event coinciding with markedly greater interest and progress in new and more effective ways to evaluate the outcomes of development projects on such variables as student learning and attitudes. Spurred by those innovations, the NSF funded a few efforts to align popular materials—created before the standards and the new assessment techniques had come onto the education scene—with those new principles. However, such funding events are exceptions, not the rule.

CONTINUING PROFESSIONAL DEVELOPMENT

The team's second option—securing grants to continue to disseminate the materials and work with teachers and administrators who adopt them—is often equally difficult. As a matter of policy, the NSF does not directly mandate which specific materials schools are to use; therefore, it infrequently underwrites teacher education programs using only one project's materials. But through its various systemic initiatives, the NSF and its education office may underwrite districts' or schools' choices of innovative materials to implement. Often, as part of such purchases, producer-distributors will include on-site workshops, conducted by project team members or by suppliers' representatives trained by the project team. If teacher education is not included as part of the purchase, a district itself may ask the project team for help learning to use the materials. Usually the individuals conducting the workshops are paid under a private arrangement with the organization requesting the workshops, whether producer-distributor or school district.

Corporations offer another promising source of funds for dissemination, implementation, and teachers' professional development. (However, businesses usually fund initiatives only in geographic areas in which the corporations are located.) Arch Chemicals, Inc., in Charleston, Tennessee, pays teachers' costs to attend SEPUP's summer workshops and organizes its own regional summer sessions to introduce science teachers to activity-based materials. "Our involvement underscores our need to ensure a technically skilled future work force," says Laura Tew, Arch's director of stakeholder relations. "But we also want to ensure that, as adults, today's students will be able to think more constructively about science and technology issues, make better-informed decisions, and become more effective policy makers." The Hewlett Packard Company has invested millions to support materials development programs such as the Full Option Science System (FOSS), SEPUP, and Great Experiences in Mathematics and Science (GEMS). The company has given cash to support materials development projects and to underwrite the costs of introducing teachers to new materials.

Even if a project cannot persuade a public or corporate funding agency to support its portion of the work of ongoing implementation, the project's commercial producer-distributor can usually be counted on to help. Typically, the project's commercial partner will pay the fees and expenses of team members or teacher-leaders to travel to schools or districts to demonstrate the materials and help educators learn to use them. In such cases, the producer-distributor usually hires former team members or other qualified educators as consultants.

PROPOSING NEW PROJECTS

The team's third option is to propose an entirely new project. (Most funders, including the NSF, will regard a project as distinctly new even if a team proposes to continue the approach of its previous project but with a new category of users, such as elementary instead of high school students.) Clear evidence of the current project's success—including wide adoption, positive student outcomes, sound management, and the availability of most or all of the same team—will boost the new proposal's chances if the team can also demonstrate an appropriate degree of expertise in the proposed project's area of endeavor.

As before, letters from schools and districts expressing their commitment to participate in the new project can help persuade potential funders that the new project's chances for success are similar to those of the previous one. Often those schools and districts that have worked with a project in field tests and other aspects of its previous ventures will be the most ready source of those commitments and endorsements. A tip: Those same schools and districts can help a project team identify and shape ideas for additional projects. Proposing a project designed to meet classroom needs already being expressed by specific schools can help persuade potential funders that the proposed project is not only necessary but perhaps more urgent than others.

Whichever option a team chooses, it must bear in mind that the new venture should be demonstrably based on the team's ability—and, again, the personal goals and passions of its members—to effectively design and manage the planned project. Deciding to apply for new funding largely to keep a team together or to guarantee work for colleagues who have become friends is not only short-sighted but also potentially dangerous: The team might become obligated to carry out a project in which it has no genuine interest, a quick route to burnout, poor project outcomes, damaged professional reputations, and broken personal relationships. Yet it can be tempting to do so. Anyone who has been part of a major development project knows that forming a group of individuals into a cohesive and cooperative team is a daunting task; it is far easier to keep together a team that already knows how to function smoothly as a group. Therefore a project team will continually keep alert to new project opportunities and seek consensus among the group as to whether to pursue them.

Established teams should seek new opportunities as a group not just because the group wants to continue working together but also for the very practical reason that an established team has an advantage in seeking funds over those just forming: if an established team is proposing a project in an area in which it has already demonstrated expertise, the new project can be launched much more quickly and efficiently.

BALANCING THE NEEDS OF PROJECTS AND TEAM MEMBERS

As noted earlier, a project's success depends on the commitment, energy, and skills of its team members. In deciding whether to propose any new project, a director or project team must carefully weigh the team's strengths and interests against the skills and demands that any subsequent venture will require. Often, that can be an intricate calculation. The subject, size, and design of a new project might dictate that not every member of the previous team would have a place in the new one. A particular skill that was crucial to the past project might be irrelevant to the new one; the new project might be removed from some team members' areas of interest; and, of course, team members themselves might simply feel that it is time for them to move on.

If the previous project has been a positive experience for its team members, the team—especially, perhaps, the director—will be motivated to take some trouble to keep the previous team together or, at least, loosely associated. When most of a project's team members are tenured or otherwise secure employees of the project's host institution, concerns about their future (as part of subsequent projects or otherwise) are less immediate: Project participants not only have positions to return to but also will remain physically near enough that a new project can ask for their help and advice, if only informally. But if members of the project team are employed by the host institution only for the current project's duration, a project's leadership likely will take even greater pains to evaluate and plan those members' potential roles in future ventures.

In either case, if a project's leadership decides to seek funding for a project that will have no place for a member of the current project team, that fact must be made clear to the team member as soon as the decision is finalized. The project's leadership should make sure affected team members understand why they will not be part of the next proposed project and what the project team can and will do to help them find new positions when the currently funded project ends. (If the project team works together in a genuinely collaborative way, the entire team will contribute to designing additional projects, so team members with a reduced or no role in future ventures will see such decisions coming.)

At best, these conversations will be less than comfortable. At worst, such decisions about a team member's separation from future projects can wither the person's enthusiasm and dedication to the project already under way. There is no pat advice about how or when to broach such delicate subjects with individual team members. A project director or leadership group must judge the temperament of the individuals in question and choose their words or moments accordingly.

Unfortunately, some project leaders have trouble bringing themselves to raise the subject. Often in such cases, leaders take on a sense of personal responsibility for each team member's future. They feel the need to guarantee some sort of place in later projects for all current members.

As noted above, these personal considerations can come to dictate the kinds of projects that a team will or will not pursue and can also become the basis for a kind of professional welfare system or make-work jobs program. Projects designed around those concerns violate two basic principles noted earlier. First, they often cannot directly target a project director's or team's professional passions. Second, they also prevent a new project from recruiting as widely as it should to acquire the people best suited to carry out the demands of that new project. In either case, the quality of a project's work and resulting materials will suffer.

These delicate and potentially damaging situations can be avoided if a project's leaders take two steps.

First, the director should make it explicitly clear to every person joining the team that positions with the project last only as long as the grant supporting the project. While team members might find berths in future projects, those places depend entirely on whether a person's particular skills and experience are as closely suited to other projects as they are to the current one.

Second, every ongoing development program should work with team members to help them develop their own skills in designing projects and drafting funding proposals. Each team member then becomes a source of ideas for future projects that can be pursued either as part of, or independent of, the present group. That approach does much more than help team members feel more confident of their individual futures. By helping them develop the abilities that enable them to follow their own aspirations, the program wins additional loyalty and commitment from them. Cultivating team members' specific talents also enables them to replace any feelings of dependence on institutional tenure with job security based on personal competence—what is sometimes called "tenure between the ears." Team members' ideas and proposals can then ensure an extended life, new missions, and a broader purpose to the present team and its program, a situation in which everyone wins.

THE TEACHER'S ROLE IN ONGOING DEVELOPMENT PROJECTS AND PROGRAMS

Even after the national field test is complete and a project's materials are on the market—and even after a project's grant expires and the team disbands—there are still roles for teachers to fill in disseminating and revising the project's materials.

Commercial distributors often rely on teachers as paid consultants to conduct workshops and courses to introduce the materials to other teachers or show potential adopters how to conduct the activities involved. In many cases, these consulting teachers go on to conduct more advanced workshops for colleagues. Also, the competitive nature of the U.S. education marketplace dictates that even successful materials be revised and updated at least every 5 years. Even if key team members are still available to contribute to the needed revisions, they cannot do it effectively alone.

To improve and update materials, developers rely on experience gained from the use of the materials in the classroom. Therefore, teachers experienced in using the materials are essential. For similar reasons, teachers—especially those who already know the materials well enough to pinpoint differences between old and new versions—are just as indispensable in field-testing the revised materials. When the revisions are complete and the new editions published, experienced teachers again will be needed to help colleagues implement them effectively. These activities can not only provide teachers with some additional income but also help them develop experience in, and reputations for, curricular leadership in the project's subject areas.

The novel experiences, additional knowledge, and greater confidence teachers gain from working with development projects may also give teachers enough background to work with colleagues to initiate their own development projects. Such a move is one of the few career transitions possible within education that doesn't entirely remove teachers from the classroom.

CONCLUSION

All good endeavors, including development projects, must come to an end. When they do, a team must first meet its obligations to report on its work and outcomes to its funders and to the profession as a whole. If a project's materials succeed commercially, the team must also plan for ways to meet the ongoing needs and requests of adopting teachers as well as to fund and conduct periodic revisions of the materials.

In considering what challenge to take on next, a project team usually can choose among three options to try to secure funding to continue and extend the current project's design and development work; to seek funding to continue and expand the current project's dissemination, implementation, and teacher education; or to design and propose an entirely new development project that may or may not be related to the team's present work. Each has its advantages and drawbacks. But if a successful team can identify a project that will keep it together, it will have an advantage over many other projects seeking support.

13

Professionalizing Materials Development

Nothing truly valuable can be achieved except by the . . . cooperation of
many individuals.

                              —Albert Einstein, *Ideas and Opinions*

AS THE PREVIOUS CHAPTERS make clear, developing effective learning materials is a specialty within education. However, it has not been recognized as such. It is time to remedy that lack of recognition, thereby professionalizing materials development.

By "professionalizing," we mean that the field should be afforded the formal recognition it has earned through its work and contributions to education generally. That recognition would include the following:

- Support for formal research in the specialty
- Journals, conferences, and other means of communication through which developers can communicate, share ideas, and advance their mutual knowledge of the profession
- Formal university-level courses of preparation for materials developers, leading to advanced degrees
- The establishment of a National Center for Learning Materials Development

MATERIALS DEVELOPMENT AS A SPECIALTY

If one asks developers, from project directors to newly hired team members, what their professional field is, their responses are usually "teacher" or "professor"—descriptions of what they did before their projects began, are doing concurrently with their projects, or hope to do after their current projects end. Educators who invest significant portions of their time or careers developing materials for use in classrooms other than their own rarely realize that they are members of a professional specialty within education. They do not recognize classroom-based materials development as a professional specialty because the field of education itself does not recognize it as such. (Individuals who refer to themselves as textbook authors comprise a very different specialty from the kind of materials development that we are talking about.)

To understand what the current lack of recognition implies, one can contrast the state of materials development as a specialty with that of evaluation and assessment. The latter became a growth industry especially during the 1990s, blossoming into a recognized area of professional expertise and concentration that many universities have welcomed as a distinct specialty within their doctoral and post-doctoral programs.

More than a dozen journals are devoted to the subject. The field organizes conferences at which practitioners share their experiences, learn from one another, and debate issues of common concern. Because evaluation and assessment has been afforded recognition as a professional discipline, new and more effective methods of student assessment are springing up and more sophisticated and reliable techniques for evaluating projects and their materials are evolving.

The field of materials development lacks that kind of collective focus and momentum. Few, if any, of the institutions conferring advanced degrees in education offer a degree, or even a course of study, in classroom-based materials development.

Academic institutions could spark this much-needed and deserved recognition by structuring and accrediting formal processes of preparation through which educators could earn graduate degrees in materials development. With that imprimatur, the field would begin to evolve the standards, structures of communication, and archival knowledge that define and drive other professional specialties.

ADVANTAGES OF PROFESSIONALIZING MATERIALS DEVELOPMENT

Recognizing materials development as a separate professional specialty within education would confer at least five practical advantages on the field—and on education generally.

First, recognition would foster a greater exchange of information, ideas, and experiences among developers by enabling them to identify themselves as individual professionals instead of only as project representatives. If they define themselves only as members of a specific project, developers are too easily aware of their competitive relationship with colleagues in other projects over funding and potential adopters of their materials. Such competition can lend energy and ingenuity to individual projects, but it is not necessarily healthy for the long-term intellectual and professional growth of individual developers or for the field as a whole.

As a distinct specialty, materials development could begin to publish its own journals and organize its own conferences, as other specialties do. These avenues of communication could help developers to move beyond the parochial concerns and limitations of their individual projects. Journals would offer them venues in which to analyze what they are doing, to investigate the results and meaning of their work and their projects, and to share their findings with colleagues. At present, that information and experience remain locked in the minds of individual developers.

If materials development were recognized as a distinct specialty, developers could use the specialty's means of communication to transform raw data into shared information that could contribute to improving the entire field. As developers learned from one another, an archive of tested concepts and best practices based on project evaluations could evolve and enable developers to avoid repeating the mistakes of, or having to rediscover knowledge already learned by, their predecessors or contemporaries.

Second, formally denoting materials development as a professional specialty would encourage talented educators to enter the field. They would recognize the specialty as offering the same opportunities for recognition and advancement that other fields do: advanced degrees, recognized areas of research, technical journals, and clear career paths, including the possibility of pursuing tenured positions as instructors or professors specializing in materials development. The specialty could become a field that education schools would recognize as providing needed expertise. Such recognition would also help developers who earned their stripes in action, rather than through a formal preparation program, to better appreciate their own accomplishments. It would also enable those accomplishments to be better recognized and appreciated by colleagues.

Third, giving materials development the structures of a recognized specialty would make it easier for project directors and teams launching new projects to select the most able and qualified team members.

Currently, when a project team or director—especially a first-time project director—is putting together a team, it can be hard to define any obvious or reliable pool of candidates to draw from. Because there is no course of formal preparation for materials developers, a project must recruit candidates from among professionals who have relevant experience, such as university-based researchers or classroom teachers. Because those candidates have no formal preparation in materials development, a project team or director often must select team members based on a combination of an applicants' experience and team members' subjective instincts and hunches about the person in question.

If materials development were structured as a recognized professional specialty, potential team members could be chosen not only for their experience but also for their academic preparation, publishing history, and other credentials created and recognized by the specialty itself, much as colleges and universities select faculty members in current specialties.

Fourth, recognizing the field would offer new career options to skilled and dedicated developers. At present, every member of a development project's team remains a developer only for the duration of a project's funding. That reality prevents team members from becoming complacent, but it also places a natural limit on their personal horizons: From the day a project begins, team members begin to think about what they will do after the project ends. The only job security for developers is their ability to generate a continuing flow of new project ideas and new funding or to land berths on projects that are beginning as their current ones are ending—something that is certainly possible but uncertain at best, if not nerve-wracking.

As a recognized academic and professional specialty, materials development would be able to offer its dedicated practitioners teaching and research positions within academic institutions—a key element in cultivating a large, diverse, and increasingly knowledgeable pool of qualified developers from which projects could draw team members.

Fifth, establishing materials development as a separate field with its own body of knowledge and standards of practice would confer on the field the status and prestige of a professional specialty. As such, the field could become a distinct and independent voice in policy, funding, and programmatic discussions among post-secondary institutions, professional groups, and legislative and regulatory agencies at all levels.

Perhaps the greatest advantage of professionalizing materials development would not accrue to the field itself. Professionalization would release and direct the field's energies in ways that would make its work more and more effective and, therefore, increasingly useful to all educators.

THE ELEMENTS OF A PROFESSIONAL SPECIALTY

To be recognized as a formal specialty within education, materials development needs to implement four components:

- Formal courses of preparation
- Ongoing research

- Journals in which to publish research results
- Conferences

Fortunately, not all of these efforts need to be designed from scratch. Fore-runners of some are already in place, although in rudimentary ways.

Formal Courses of Preparation

Anyone aspiring to become a materials developer must have a practical understanding of classroom realities. Therefore the new professional specialty of materials development should be opened up as an advanced-degree option to experienced teachers wishing to pursue graduate studies.

Because development is a fluid, creative process, it cannot be learned from books or seminars alone. Indeed, trying to capture the essence of development in conventional coursework alone would rob it of the spontaneity on which its success depends. Conventional academic courses can lay a conceptual basis for a developer, just as they can for a classroom teacher. But to hone the working knowledge, imagination, and teamwork abilities an effective developer needs, candidates for the new specialty must go beyond the halls of the university.

An internship with a project, similar to a post-doctoral experience, could help candidates blend theoretical knowledge with practical experience. Of course, development projects regularly hire experienced teachers with advanced degrees as developers—positions that are, in effect, informal post-doctoral experiences. But the value of those experiences (not only to those who undergo them and to their projects but also to funding agencies and education generally) would soar if those experiences were supplemented by organized programs of study, seminars, and support embraced by projects, funders, and host institutions together.

The same kinds of experiences could be opened to teachers not pursuing degrees in the new field. Teachers seeking only professional certification or other forms of advanced standing within the profession could also take part. Their concentrated work in materials development would enable them to better understand how to analyze and evaluate materials for adoption in their classrooms, school systems, or states. Also, participating teachers could become better able to select and adapt materials to create the interactive relationship between teacher and student that we define as the curriculum.

As more school systems make sabbaticals and other forms of professional leave available to teachers, the demand for such internships may grow. The current policy of the National Science Foundation (NSF) states that all large systemic change initiatives (and many teacher enhancement projects) must be school-based. Because most such projects include materials review, evaluation, and adaptation, school systems might well decide that it is in their interests to support teachers seeking to refine their skills as materials developers. Refining their skills in an organized way could also help interested teachers meet the requirements for national board certification in their fields.

Ongoing Research

A professional specialty is defined by a unique body of knowledge. In any academic area, such knowledge is created, refreshed, and continuously expanded through ongoing research. As noted in a previous chapter, materials developers routinely conduct research as part of their work—although typically it is neither as formal nor as specialized as education's customary research projects housed within the academic departments of universities. Of course, materials development projects often work in tandem with education researchers—particularly with doctoral students, as earlier examples cited from the Science Curriculum Improvement Study and SEPUP illustrate. Such research can supply vital insights that guide and inform the work of materials developers. However, it is a specialty that is different from materials development—a difference similar to that between pure research on the one hand and application or engineering on the other, each of which demands specialized knowledge and procedures of its own.

There are examples of the kinds of tailored research the specialty might conduct, especially as part of an advanced degree program. During the 1990s, professors Joseph Schmuckler and Francis Sutman (2001) at Temple University worked with doctoral students to investigate the role of the laboratory in high school and college chemistry courses. As part of their studies, the group necessarily looked into teachers' classroom behavior. "Teachers were telling us that they were practicing inquiry-based teaching," Schmuckler says, "but we found that there were as many definitions of 'inquiry' as there are people making the definition." The investigators demonstrated inquiry-based teaching for chemistry teachers in five Philadelphia schools, then analyzed how the demonstrations changed what the teachers did in their classrooms.

From the work, Schmuckler and Sutman have evolved a precise definition of inquiry and also a "levels of inquiry matrix." In the matrix, level 1 represents teaching without inquiry, meaning that teachers do or prescribe everything; at level 5, students do everything with no guidance from the teacher. Participating classroom educators found their teaching to be most effective and satisfying at levels 3 and 4—when the teachers orient students, then turn work over to them while serving as facilitators. "Most doctoral studies in education don't deal with real problems faced in the classroom," Schmuckler notes. "We wanted our research to be useful for teachers. We find that they can use our matrix to determine what level of inquiry teaching they want to employ, then plan their work and select or create materials accordingly."

Such studies could enable advanced-degree students in materials development to unite research with classroom realities. More specifically, this kind of research conducted by developers themselves could enhance the field's ability to create, for example, materials precisely matched to specific levels of inquiry, which would be helpful not only to teachers and students but also to producer-distributors seeking a marketing niche for new materials. Again, this is only one example. There are myriad ways to benefit materials development through research that builds the field's own particular knowledge base and educates present and future generations of practitioners.

Presently, however, the constraints on time and money that shape a materials development project do not allow the luxury of such research. Nevertheless, it is a rare developer who does not reflect on the results of a project and their implications. As noted previously, developers often do (as they should) detail those outcomes, as well as what the project team learned in achieving them, in reports that they make generally available. Developers' desire to conduct formal research is not what is missing. Rather, the limiting factors are three.

First, at present, professional preparation for classroom-based educators rarely includes adequate experience or the specialized knowledge they would need to conduct rigorous research and analyze results. Second, there are few venues in which to publish research findings that focus on materials development. Third, developers share with virtually all other educators the lack of time—in this case, brought on by project deadlines and limited budgets—to conduct formal research as part of their regular work.

While education journals do publish some papers on subjects related to materials development, such papers are few. In addition, there are so many subjects competing for journals' pages that periodicals are rarely willing to explore specialized aspects of materials development in depth— even though such questions may be of vital importance to the development community as a whole.

Journals in Which to Publish Research Results

Conducting research is pointless if the findings are not made available to those who can do something useful with them. Therefore formal research in the field of materials development must be accompanied by publications serving the specific needs and interests of materials developers. As research within a given specialty multiplies and expands, journals naturally appear, like wildflowers in a spring meadow. In addition to offering researchers a way to communicate with one another and with educators generally, such journals would also provide the beginnings of an archive of professional knowledge in the field of materials development.

The publications could also accommodate the sometimes unusual needs of the field. For example, many materials development projects work with schools during national field tests, but a district's policy may forbid disclosing the kind or degree of details about internal practices that a typical journal might demand in order to accept an article for publication. Similarly, members of an individual project might not feel comfortable disclosing details of their working relationships with particular test centers to other project teams. A journal that would accept generalized articles about the relationships between projects and test sites would enable developers not only to generalize their experiences and communicate them but also to research the experiences of colleagues and generalize those as well.

Finally, publishing in the journals would serve developers' practical need to establish professional credentials, gain recognition, and earn promotions in their academic or other institutions.

Conferences

Professional gatherings are at least as important as journals to the exchange of ideas. Meetings can speed the dissemination of new ideas and information throughout a profession more rapidly than periodicals can. They offer forums in which controversies can be debated and sometimes resolved, and they enable professionals to network with colleagues. (Project ideas, formal collaborations, and even the occasional conceptual breakthrough often evolve from chance meetings at professional conferences.)

Beginning in the 1990s, the NSF has worked to initiate those kinds of exchanges among developers through its sponsorship of a series of "Gateway to Mathematics" and "ScienceGate" conferences (now merged). These weekend conferences bring together team representatives whose projects share a common direction—such as the creation of year-long secondary mathematics and science courses—to exchange ideas and problems in a range of subjects from assessment methods to relationships with publishers. These conferences are a vital early step in creating the formal structures of regular communication that any professional specialty needs in order to thrive and grow. But by themselves, these conferences can accomplish only a limited purpose. More needs to be done.

A NATIONAL CENTER FOR THE EDUCATION OF MATERIALS DEVELOPERS

It is crucial that the profession of education foster the necessary elements of a formal specialty of materials development (a step that would gain more efficiency from the more than $35 million the NSF alone spends each year to underwrite projects in precollege materials development).

To initiate that process, we propose the establishment of a National Center for Learning Materials Development, to be funded through the U.S. government and by contributions from private and corporate philanthropies to an endowment fund. (A combination of public and private money would enable the center to operate more independently, more imaginatively, and more effectively.)

This new center could be headquartered at one or (with cooperative or distributed leadership) more already-established centers for materials development such as TERC, the Education Development Center, the Biological Sciences Curriculum Study, or the Lawrence Hall of Science at the University of California at Berkeley, among others. The center, which should be connected to the education department of a major research university, would be staffed not only by materials developers but also by professors of education, experts in related specialties such as cognitive science and assessment and evaluation, and highly skilled and experienced classroom teachers.

The center would serve multiple purposes:

- To design and conduct institutes and short courses for educators beginning or continuing concentrated work in materials development
- To design and coordinate one or more year-long post-doctoral programs in materials development for individuals attached to specific materials development projects
- To advise colleges of education and other institutions in establishing courses of specialization and advanced-degree programs in materials development
- To help the profession identify and prioritize research opportunities in materials development (such research could be funded, at least in part, by the NSF through the center)

- To organize and conduct conferences, seminars, and other activities to help experienced materials developers improve their skills and guide work in the field
- To establish a journal or a monograph series to publish research, project descriptions, and other information about and accomplishments in materials development
- To conduct the other activities necessary to help establish materials development as an academic specialty

Such a center could be adequately launched with an annual budget of no more than $700,000 in direct costs—less than one-half of 1 percent of the NSF's yearly funding for all the materials development and teacher enhancement projects it underwrites. Rather than a cost, the money would become an investment that would improve the long-term return on all grants made by the NSF and other funders for materials development projects.

THE ISSUE OF DIVERSITY

The new center could also focus the profession's efforts to solve one of its most persistent problems: the lack of ethnic, gender, and cultural diversity among developers.

A guiding principle of the National Science Education Standards and virtually all other initiatives for the improvement of science education is that "science is for all students" (NAS, 1996, p. 19). In the United States, adhering to that principle means that science teachers and courses must cultivate the talents of the multi-ethnic, multicultural populations that make up so many of our schools and communities.

This is no small task: Among the different ethnic, cultural, and social groups that send their children to our public schools, there can be an equal diversity in their styles, approaches, values, and goals for education. An activity that guides some children to understanding might leave others confused or, perhaps, offend them or their parents. No less than classroom teachers, materials developers grapple daily with issues of diversity—and, it must be admitted, not always successfully.

Ideally, materials development project teams would reflect the diversity of the students in the classrooms they hope to affect. But, for two reasons, that goal is not yet feasible. First, the proportion of minority educators earning advanced degrees in science or mathematics education is far less than the proportion of those minorities in the student populations of our schools. Second, materials development has not been recognized as a distinct specialty within education. Therefore, it cannot offer the same professional recognition or a clear career trajectory—such as positions that lead to tenure—that other specialties can offer to the small number of minority science or mathematics education graduates.

Currently, careers in science education do not offer the same professional and financial rewards as careers in other university-level fields (not to mention in the technology industry). Until they do, it will be up to each project director and team to reach out to minority educators in schools and to tap their unique contributions to the design of materials able to lead *all* students to learn.

BROADER GOALS

This National Center for Learning Materials Development could serve a broader purpose within the profession as well. Ideally, materials development (especially for guided inquiry) is a process of continuing, evolutionary improvement in education. One of its essential purposes is to translate the educational needs and demands of our society into learning experiences for students. If the development process is to continue to do so effectively as our society's educational needs and demands change—as they will continue to do dramatically in the years ahead—then the ways in which materials are designed and developed must have the capacity to change with them.

The proposed national center could become the profession's locus for ongoing "development of the materials development process." By uniting the fruits of continuing research with emerging social, economic, and classroom realities, the center could lead education continually in the direction of excellence, even as our society alters those directions.

The center, with its cadre of professional developers and researchers, could also become a forum for discussion and debate about development-related policy and serve as the development profession's unified voice in policy matters.

For example, the NSF—the primary funding agency for U.S. science and mathematics development programs—changed its funding criteria in 2000. Previously, the NSF encouraged a wide variety of development proposals across a spectrum of ideas and approaches that had originated with individual scientists, educators or teams. At times, the agency sponsored initiatives that focused developers' attention on age groups or learners with special needs. But even those embraced a general set of expectations that not only tolerated, but also encouraged, creativity and innovation.

In 1999, the NSF's guidelines (NSF, 1999), along with statements and correspondence from program officers, set a different direction. The foundation adopted a policy that urges developers first to select specific content standards from the National Science Education Standards that their materials will address. Then, the guidelines say, developers should plan how to assess students' attainments of those standards and learning goals. According to the new guidelines, only after those two steps should developers begin to design relevant specific activities.

There is nothing inherently wrong with this as one approach to development. However, if developers view these criteria as prerequisites for support from the agency supplying most of the field's funding (as seems the case), the new policy could easily dampen developers' creativity and exploration of unusual ideas.

To some developers, the new NSF guidelines seem to specify what is to be developed and how. Then the agency proposes to fund "systemic change" programs to implement the materials developed according to these new criteria. Such an approach raises questions about the imposition of a federal course of study and threatens to lessen the importance of states and localities in making educational policy and choosing educational materials.

When such complex policy issues arise, the center's professionals could become advisers to the NSF and other policy-making agencies. The center could also serve as education's voice in such discussions and debates.

CONCLUSION

The process of developing materials for guided inquiry can become an engine of positive change throughout education. It is one of the few areas in which the best ideas (new or old) from the range of specialties within education are pooled and then integrated by design. Therefore, strengthening and institutionalizing the evolutionary process of materials development described in the previous chapters can become a means to speed lasting, effective change throughout education generally.

To achieve that goal, however, materials development must be accorded the status of a recognized, formal profession within education. The elements of the profession would include formal courses of preparation; ongoing research; journals in which to publish research results; and conferences, symposia, and similar professional gatherings.

To foster development of those venues, and to initiate formal recognition of materials development as a distinct profession, we propose the creation of a National Center for Learning Materials Development. Among its functions, the center would provide advanced education and internships for developers; advise colleges of education in creating advanced-degree programs in materials development; foster research in development and related issues; organize venues of communication among developers, such as journals and conferences; and provide the development community with a voice in related policy issues. Creating such a center is not only afford-able but would return its costs many times over—in improved classroom materials and the curricula that result, in greater intellectual growth and capacities of our children and future citizens, and in a positive new ap-proach to educational change.

14

Designing Your Project and Preparing Your Proposal: A Checklist

Everything should be made as simple as possible, but not simpler.
—Albert Einstein, quoted in *Reader's Digest*

THE FOLLOWING CHECKLIST CAN HELP GUIDE developers, especially those who are less experienced, as they design a project in detail and draft a funding proposal. Each item on the checklist is keyed to a previous chapter to which the reader may refer for additional details.

☐ *Demonstrating the need for the project (Chap. 2)*

Every funder expects a proposal to explain the social and educational needs that the project intends to address and how the project's materials will meet those needs. This "needs assessment" section in a proposal could be separated into two parts.

The first part might highlight the structural changes in our economy that are forcing fundamental new approaches to education and, therefore, to what schools do and how they do it. A proposal should also note new understandings about the mental processes through which people master information and skills, and students' growing demand for relevance in their coursework.

The second part might detail the ways in which a proposed project's materials will embody new understandings about learning processes, engage students by making the materials meaningful to the age groups targeted, and prepare students for the world beyond the classroom.

Of course, the developer must also place the project's methods and goals within the context of standards such as the National Science Education Standards or the Benchmarks for Scientific Literary, published by the American

Association for the Advancement of Science. The proposal must show explicitly how the project fulfills those standards and benchmarks.

By presenting the specific goals and approaches of an individual project within this larger context, a team can make a powerful case for creating materials that structure a curriculum of guided inquiry.

☐ *Defining a clear approach to the development process (Chap. 3)*

An effective proposal communicates a clear approach to the development process and the project's goals. As new standards continue to emerge and to reshape teaching and learning, those approaches and goals also change.

Increasingly, these new standards embody three elements often absent in previous generations of learning materials. The first element is interdisciplinary, inquiry-oriented experiences for students—a framework that succeeds in direct proportion to the degree of collaboration among specialists in creating instructional materials. The second is what might be called an "operational" orientation, emphasizing intellectual processes over grocery lists of factual content for students to "acquire." Third, the mounting urgency of making lasting, measurable improvements in student outcomes (as well as simple conservation of education's already scarce resources) dictates that developers identify and retain workable elements of past as well as contemporary designs. Educators are learning to recognize value in facets of previous materials as well as in other projects that perhaps did not succeed commercially but nonetheless proved the value of a certain element or technique.

Revolution leads to setbacks at least no less often than it leads to progress; but evolution—in educational materials as in biology—can grow a small improvement into a powerful and far-reaching entity.

In sum, a proposal should acknowledge that collaboration among specialists, an evolutionary rather than a revolutionary approach to development, and an operational approach to learning are becoming the organizing principles for effective development in science education. Showing potential funders how a project and its materials will address and embody these principles improves a proposal's chances for funding. That approach also helps a developer or team to structure a development process (and the project's goals and planned outcomes) more clearly and cogently. Also, by taking an evolutionary rather than revolutionary approach and accenting the accomplishments (even if limited) rather than the shortcomings of prior efforts, proposers avoid creating resentment among those reviewing the proposal who might have a personal stake in one of the prior efforts being criticized.

☐ *Passing a funder's first reading* (*Chap. 4*)

The key element in crafting a compelling proposal is to propose only projects that reflect the deeply felt passions and educational ambitions of the developers. Once that test is met, project proposers can concentrate on the tactical details of drafting an effective presentation. Those include ensuring that the proposal:

- Explains clearly how and why this particular project will help the funding agency meet its own goals and objectives
- Shows potential funders how and why the project will achieve new, more comprehensive subject-area standards such as the National Science Education Standards or the Benchmarks for Science Literacy
- Identifies key project staff members and cooperating school systems and secures their commitment, in writing, to participate if the project is funded
- Explains in detail how the project will measure what students have learned as a result of using the materials
- Does not give prospective funding agencies an administrative reason to reject the proposal, such as violating submission guidelines

A proposal is also more likely to succeed if the project team has thoroughly considered budgetary contingencies before they arise and prepared in advance a vigorous defense of its proposed cost outline. If funders propose cuts in the planned budget, successful rebuttals can often be based on a dramatic presentation of the impact the cuts would have in limiting the funding agency's ability to achieve the goals it seeks by funding the project in the first place.

☐ *Putting together a strong team* (*Chap. 5*)

The skills and experience of a project's team are its capital. A proposal needs to assure potential funders that a team is not only rich in abilities but also able to invest and manage that capital wisely.

In making those points, an effective proposal will detail the relevant, specific capabilities of individuals already committed to the project and show why those individuals are necessary to helping the project achieve its goals. An effective proposal also will lay out tasks and goals along a timeline, an exercise that also makes clear the need for particular skills. Almost certainly, points along the timeline will need to be replotted as the project evolves. Consequently, a flexible timeline is an essential tool in helping team members (and funders) know in what areas and at what points the team should be investing particular aspects of its expertise.

A proposal should also recognize and acknowledge a project's various constituencies—including classroom teachers, parents, administrators, other developers in related fields, and teacher educators—as part of a project's extended team. In doing so, the proposal should explain how the project's working group will communicate the project's goals, progress, products, and value to those constituencies.

To this end, a succinct goals statement of one or two sentences is worth the time and effort needed to draft and polish it. A well-honed statement placed on or near a proposal's cover page can serve the additional purpose of enticing those who receive the proposal to read it thoroughly.

☐ *Choosing and working with a producer-distributor (Chap. 6)*

A project's goal is not only to create materials but also to put them into the hands of teachers everywhere. To achieve that goal, a project must partner with a compatible and competent producer-distributor.

Because this aspect of a project is no less important than creating materials in the first place, a proposal should include a commitment in writing from a producer-distributor prepared to work with, and invest in, the project to make its products a commercial success.

Securing that commitment involves a planned process of contact and review. Other projects, team members' personal contacts, and even authors' agents can help.

The relationship and division of responsibilities between the project and its commercial partner must be negotiated in explicit detail and set down in a contract between the two parties. Further, a project must seek legal advice in negotiating any such agreement. (Usually the project's host institution will have staff attorneys well able to assist and advise.) The agreement between the project and its commercial partner should be detailed as fully as possible within the length limits of the proposal.

☐ *Choosing a project structure (Chap. 7)*

Structuring a development project is a balancing act. On the one hand, team members must be able to collaborate and communicate efficiently, effectively, and often. On the other, many of the best potential team members may have limited time to give to a project, while others whose skills are less well suited may be able to commit themselves fully to the work.

If a proposed project is to be housed at an established development center such as TERC or the Biological Sciences Curriculum Study, the structure will probably be largely determined before the proposal is written. If this is not the case, then the project director or team members drafting the proposal will be forced to choose a project structure. The most common structures are a full-time team working together in one place, a part-time team that gathers periodically for work sessions, or a scattered group of telecollaborators whose work is coordinated through the project director or small management team.

In practice, there may be little opportunity for choice. The amount of funding offered or the availability of key team members often gives a project its final shape. However, when there is a choice to be made, those drafting the proposal must weigh several factors together. The amount of time key team members can give the project, the budget that a potential funder is likely to provide, and the degree to which team members need to be physically in one another's company to accomplish the project's tasks and goals will all figure into the decision. An effective proposal will explain the choice of structure, how the structure will be managed, and the chosen structure's advantages in achieving the project's aims.

☐ *Assessment and evaluation (Chap. 8)*

Increasingly, a detailed plan for a valid, comprehensive assessment system is a crucial aspect of any project seeking funding. Funders are becoming acutely aware of the shortcomings of conventional testing formats: Such formats not only fail to measure key aspects of learning but also offer educators too few clues in identifying current students' difficulties in mastering the processes they are expected to internalize. To have the best chance of securing funding, a proposal must present a detailed, practical plan to embed authentic assessment into the materials the project will create. The plan should include a means by which the project will secure independent assessments of what students learn by using the new materials.

In presenting such a plan, a proposal can explain that embedding assessment within instruction gives it an authenticity that helps meet goals for valid assessment emphasized in the National Science Education Standards and other recommendations for change. The model sketched in Chapter 8 leads developers and educators toward that goal, in part by making assessment an ongoing measure of growth among teachers as well as students. The "moderation" sessions included in the model help teachers to develop a consensus around comprehensive standards of student achievement. The sessions also enable them to grow in their abilities to use assessment to guide improvements in their own work.

A proposal will stand out among its competitors if it goes beyond outlining a generic assessment approach. Instead, the proposal should explain how the project team will collaborate with measurement specialists to tailor an authentic, embedded assessment scheme for the materials being created.

Finally, developers must understand that they and their project will be evaluated by funders and, perhaps, others.

The project's financial and operational management will be reviewed in detail, usually by an external evaluator chosen either by the funder or by the project with the funder's approval.

The educational value of the project's materials will also be evaluated through comparative student assessments. To be judged effective, materials must prepare students to perform well both on standardized, fact-oriented tests as well as in embedded, authentic assessments. By following a few guidelines, developers can create materials that help students succeed in both and ensure that their project's materials will be evaluated positively.

☐ *Drafting and testing early versions (Chap. 9)*

It is not enough for a proposal to describe the materials the project team plans to create. It also must assure potential funders that the team has structured a process by which to validate the educational effectiveness of those materials in working classrooms before the materials are released commercially.

That process begins with the team itself. A proposal must explain how members will circulate and comment on evolving drafts among themselves, especially if team members are far-flung. The team must also include, either as working members or as consultants, content experts to review drafts for accuracy and learning specialists (often classroom teachers are competent for this role) to review drafts for educational effectiveness. The proposal should explain, if only briefly, how the team will handle those tasks.

A project must then decide, and its proposal explain, how nearby classrooms have been, or will be, chosen as hosts for those exploratory teaching sessions. Taken together, the classrooms chosen should show a diversity of teaching and learning styles and abilities as well as variety in students' socioeconomic backgrounds. Citing and abiding by the three criteria of proximity, diversity, and classroom culture described in Chapter 9 will strengthen this section of a proposal.

As noted earlier, every project would like to test every activity in classrooms. However, due to the constraints of money and time, that is often not practical. While a proposal can describe an ideal structure for testing early drafts, the project team should be ready to make choices among activities and materials to test when a funder offers less money than the proposal had specified.

☐ *Planning a national field test and applying its results (Chap. 10)*

One of a funder's chief concerns, if not the predominant one, is that the materials being created with its money be proven to be useful and effective in classrooms. The local trials that team members conduct are useful in demonstrating materials' effectiveness, but they are not conclusive. An effective proposal details a plan for a national field test to put the new activities and materials in the hands of a variety of teachers who work without the direct supervision of the project team.

The plan must convince funders that the team has provided for all key aspects of a comprehensive field test, such as the following:

- Diversity, by including urban and rural schools and schools from both poor and wealthy areas
- Direct and speedy ways that participating teachers can communicate with team members as questions or problems arise during the trial
- An effective system of collecting meaningful critiques and insights from participating teachers
- Equally effective methods for team members to process and respond to teachers' comments and suggestions

Outlining the project's criteria for choosing participating schools and teachers, with a timeline for the field test's operations, will strengthen the confidence of potential funders. (So will a written commitment of financial and logistical support from the proposed project's producer-distributor.)

This section of the proposal is also the place to explain how the project will organize, review, analyze, and act on teachers' and students' reactions gathered during the national field test. It should also explain how the project team will use the data to prepare production-ready versions of activities and materials. This section of the proposal should also detail provisions for a final independent, comprehensive review of the materials' subject content by working scientists.

☐ *Dissemination and implementation (Chap. 11)*

Funders do not only want to support development of better materials. They also want to see that a development project has a workable plan in place to introduce and disseminate those materials and to help teachers adopt and use them effectively. A proposal must outline that plan in specific detail.

The implementation plan should reflect an understanding that dissemination is a long, sequential process. Classrooms taking part in local trials and national field tests can become demonstration centers for the project's materials; participating teachers can become teacher-leaders or coaches for other educators in their districts or regions who are adopting the new materials. Dissemination also continues after grant funds have been spent and project teams disbanded. A proposal should explain how team members, individually or as a group, will continue to support the producer-distributor's commercial efforts for as long as needed.

An effective proposal also demonstrates a dissemination and implementation plan in which each step evolves in tandem with other aspects of the development process. A comprehensive plan includes initial publicity and teacher involvement as the creative process begins. As the project prepares for national field trials, it must conduct more widespread teacher education, prepare to provide full support for teachers participating in the trials, and secure the growing involvement of a commercial partner (both in preparing materials and in helping teachers to learn about and adopt them). The plan must also explain how the project will revise the materials based on the results of national trials and prepare them for commercial production. A proposal that is any less specific in this area than it is about the materials to be created or the team that will create them risks rejection.

☐ *Addressing ongoing responsibilities (Chap. 12)*

A strong proposal includes an explanation of how the team will handle project responsibilities that continue after grants end. (Including this information also bolsters the confidence of potential funders that a team has foresight and that the team itself is confident of success.)

It is easy for a proposal to state that the project's commercial partner will assume all responsibilities when grant funds run out. But a stronger and more responsible approach is to commit a portion of royalties earned through sales to the project's ongoing work—fielding questions and requests from teachers, revising materials, and so on. (Of course, such a commitment cannot be made without the agreement of key team members and compliance with the rules of the project's host institution.) That commitment sends proposal reviewers and funding agencies a forceful message about the team's sense of the importance and enduring qualities of its proposed products.

List of Science Projects

Active Physics
Route 1, Box 136
Gordon, WI 54838
jlharkness@aol.com
http://www.Its-About-Time.com

ARGWorld
Department of Geography
University of Minnesota
Minneapolis, MN 55455
gersmehl@tc.umn.edu
http://www.aag.org

The Astrobiology Curriculum
TERC
2067 Massachusetts Ave.
Cambridge, MA 02140
Jeff_Lockwood@terc.edu
http://astrobio.terc.edu

Biology: A Community Context BioCom
Clemson University
415 Tillman Hall
Clemson, SC 39634-0708
leonard@clemson.edu

BSCS Integrated Science, Biology and Elementary Science Programs
5415 Mark Dabling Blvd.
Colorado Springs, CO 80918
rbybee@bscs.org
http://www.bscs.org

BSCS Middle School Science & Technology
5415 Mark Dabling Blvd.
Colorado Springs, CO 80918
pvanscotter@bscs.org
http://www.bscs.org

ChemQuest
5151 W. 29 St. #107
Greeley, CO 80634
aushako@unco.edu
http://www.unco.edu/chemquest

Constructing Ideas in Physical Science (CIPS)
8020 Prospect Way
La Mesa, CA 91941
fgoldberg@sciences.sdsu.edu
http://cipsproject.sdsu.edu

DESIGNS
Harvard Smithsonian Center for Astrophysics
60 Garden Street, MS-71, D-315
Cambridge, MA 02138
philip_sadler@harvard.edu
http://cfa-www.harvard.edu/cfa/sed/projects/designs.html

EarthComm
American Geological Institute
4220 King St.
Alexandria, VA 22302
ejc@agiweb.org
http://www.agiweb.org/education

Elementary Science Study (ESS)
Education Development Center
Newton, MA 02160
(617) 969-7100
Several modules may be purchased from Delta Education; some activities are
    available on Science Helper K68.

Exploring Earth
TERC
2067 Massachusetts Ave.
Cambridge, MA 02140
Dan_Barstow@terc.edu

FACETS
American Chemical Society
1155 16 St. N.W.
Washington, DC 20036
g_belleman@acs.org
http://www.acs.org

Full Option Science System for Elementary and Middle School
University of California at Berkeley
1 Centennial Drive, Lawrence Hall of Science
Berkeley, CA 94720-5200
ldelucch@uclink4.berkeley.edu
http://www.fossweb.com

Global Lab Curriculum Project
TERC
2067 Massachusetts Ave.
Cambridge, MA 02140
harold_mcwilliams@terc.edu
http://globallab.terc.edu/

Integrated Math, Science and Technology Project
Illinois State University
207 S. Main St., MC 5960
Normal, IL 61761-5960
flloep@ilstu.edu
http://www.ilstu.edu/depts/cemast/

Issue-Oriented Life Science
University of California at Berkeley SEPUP
1 Centennial Drive, Lawrence Hall of Science
Berkeley, CA 94720-5200
bnagle@uclink4.berkeley.edu
http://www.sepuplhs.org

Living by Chemistry
University of California at Berkeley
1 Centennial Drive, Lawrence Hall of Science
Berkeley, CA 94720-1460
jclaes@uclink4.berkeley.edu
http://www.lhs.berkeley.edu:80/LBC/

Materials World Modules
Robert Chang
Northwestern University
2115 North Campus Drive
Evanston, IL 60208

Minds on Physics
Department of Physics, Box 34525
University of Massachusetts
Amherst, MA 01003-4525
wjleonard@physics.umass.edu
http://www.umperg.physics.umass.edu/projects/MindsOnPhysics/

PSSC Physics by Uri Haber-Schaim et al. (7th ed., 1991)
Kendall Hunt (publisher)
4050 Westmark Drive
Dubuque, IA 52002

Science and Technology Concepts for Elementary and Middle Schools
National Science Resources Center
Arts and Industries Building, Room 1201
Washington, DC 20560-0403
dlapp@nas.edu
http://www.si.edu/nsrc/pubs/stc/overv.htm

Science Curriculum Improvement Study SCIS3+
Delta Education
80 Northwest Blvd., P.O. Box 3000
Nashua, NH 03061-3000
mbacon@delta-edu.com

Science Education for Public Understanding (SEPUP)
University of California at Berkeley
1 Centennial Drive, Lawrence Hall of Science
Berkeley, CA 94720-5200
thier@uclink4.berkeley.edu
http://www.sepuplhs.org

Science in a Technical World
American Chemical Society
1155 16 St. N.W.
Washington, DC 20036
g_belleman@acs.org
http://www.acs.org

Voyages Through Time
SETI Institute
2035 Landings Drive
Mountain View, CA 94043
edevore@seti.org
http://www.SETI.org

Worldwatcher Curriculum Project
Northwestern University
2115 North Campus Drive
Evanston, IL 60208
d-edelson@northwestern.edu
http://www.worldwatcher.northwestern.edu

NSF-SPONSORED SCIENCE EDUCATION IMPLEMENTATION SITES

EDC's K–12 Science Curriculum Dissemination Center
Education Development Center
55 Chapel St.
Newton, MA 02458
bberns@edc.org
http://www.edc.org/cse

IMPACT
716 Columbus Ave., Suite 378
Boston, MA 02120
suecohen@mail.lesley.edu
http://www.cesame.neu.edu

LASER
National Science Resources Center
955 L'Enfant Plaza North S.W., Suite 8400
Washington, DC 20560-0952
eernst@nas.edu
http://www.si.edu/nsrc/laser/laser.htm

The SCI Center at BSCS
BSCS
5415 Mark Dabling Blvd.
Colorado Springs, CO 80918
jpowell@bscs.org
http://www.bscs.org

References

American Association for the Advancement of Science. (1990). *Science for all Americans: A project 2061 report on literacy goals in science, mathematics, and technology.* New York: Oxford University Press.

Barrow, J. B. (1999). Is nothing sacred? *New Scientist Magazine, 163*(2196), 28–32.

Bowyer, J. B., & Linn, M. C. (1978). Effectiveness of the Science Curriculum Improvement Study in teaching scientific literacy. *Journal of Research in Science Teaching, 15,* 209–219.

Chemistry: An Experimental Science (CHEM Study). (1965). San Francisco: W. H. Freeman.

Committee on Science, U.S. House of Representatives. (1998). *Unlocking our future: Toward a new national science policy.* Washington, DC: U.S. Government Printing Office.

Covey, S., Merrill, A., & Merrill, R. (1994). *First things first.* New York: Simon & Schuster, pp. 307–321.

Dewey, J. (1915). *The school and society.* Chicago: University of Chicago Press.

Diederich, M. E. (1969). Physical sciences and processes of inquiry: A critique of CHEM, CBA and PSSC. *Journal of Research in Science Teaching, 6*(4), 309–315.

Doran, R., Chan, F., & Tamir, P. (1998). *Science educator's guide to assessment.* Washington, DC: National Science Teachers Association Press.

Downie, D., Slesnick, T., & Stenmark, J. K. (1981). *Math for girls and other problem solvers.* Berkeley: University of California.

Eakin, J. R., & Karplus, R. (1976). *SCIS final report: Science Curriculum Improvement Study.* Berkeley: University of California.

Einstein, A. (1950). *Out of my later years.* New York: Philosophical Library.

Einstein, A. (1954). *Ideas and opinions* (Sonja Bargmann, Trans.). New York: Crown. (Original work published 1934)

Einstein, A., & Infeld, L. (1961). *The evolution of physics.* New York: Simon & Schuster. (Original work published 1938)

Elementary and Secondary Education Act. (1965). Available at: http://www.house.gov/ed_workforce/publications/eseacomp/esea65pdf. (Retrieved July 26, 2000)

Fullan, M. (with Stiegelbauer, S.). (1991). *The new meaning of educational change.* New York: Teachers College Press.

Gardner, H., & Laskin, E. (1995). *Leading minds: An anatomy of leadership.* New York: Basic Books.

Gardner, M., Greeno, J. G., Reif, F., Schoenfeld, A. H., diSessa, A., and Stage, E. (Eds.). (1990). *Toward a scientific practice of science education.* Hillsdale, NJ: Erlbaum.

Graneau, P., & Graneau, N. (1996). *Newtonian electrodynamics.* London: World Scientific Press.

Hurd, P. D. (1994). New Minds for a New Age: Prologue to Modernizing the Science Curriculum. *Science Education, 78*(1), 103–116.

Hurd, P. D. (1999). *Inventing science education for the new millennium.* New York: Teachers College Press.

Isles, J. (1989, October). Corporations in the classroom. *Consuming Interest: The Journal of the Australian Consumers' Association,* 7–14.

Karplus, R., & Thier, H. D. (1969). *A new look at elementary school science: Science Curriculum Improvement Study.* Chicago: Rand McNally.

Lawson, A. (1995). *Science teaching and the development of thinking.* Belmont, CA: Wadsworth.

Linn, M. C., & Hsi, S. (2000). *Computers, teachers, and peers: Science learning partners.* Hillsdale, NJ: Erlbaum.

Lorsbach, A., & Tobin, K. (1992). Constructivisim as a referent for science teaching. Available at http://www.exploratorium.edu/IFI/resources/research/constructivism.html.

Merrill, R. J., & Ridgway, D. W. (1969). *The CHEM Study story.* San Francisco: W. H. Freeman.

Monk, B. J. (1993). *Toward quality in education: The leader's odyssey.* Washington, DC: National Leadership Network Study Group on Restructuring Schools.

National Academy of Sciences (NAS)—National Resource Council. (1996). *National Science Education Standards.* Washington, DC: National Academy Press.

National Council of Teachers of Mathematics. (1995). *Assessment standards for school mathematics.* Reston, VA: Author.

National Science Foundation (NSF). (1997). *Review of instructional materials for middle school science.* Available at: http://www.nsf/gov/cgi-bin/getpub?nsf9754. (Retrieved July 26, 2000).

National Science Foundation (NSF). (1999). *Grant proposal guide* (NSF 00–2). Available at: http://www.nsf.gov/cgi-bin/getpub?gpg. (Retrieved July 26, 2000).

New, C. C., & Quick, J. A. (1998). *Grantseeker's tool kit.* New York: Wiley.

Office of Technology Assessment (OTA), U.S. Congress. (1990). *Worker training: Competing in the new international economy* (OTA-A-473). Washington, DC: U.S. Government Printing Office.

Office of Technology Assessment (OTA), U.S. Congress. (1992). *Annual report to the Congress: Fiscal year 1991* (OTA-TE-457). Washington, DC: U.S. Government Printing Office.

Olson, S., & Loucks-Horsley, S. (Eds.). (2000). *Inquiry and the* National Science Education Standards: *A guide for teaching and learning.* Washington, DC: National Academy Press.

Piaget, J., Gruber, H. E., & Vonèche, J. J. (1977). *The essential Piaget.* New York: Basic Books.

Rogers, E. M. (1995). *Diffusion of innovations* (4th ed.). New York: Free Press.

Ryand, B. (1996). *The learning pyramid.* Diagram, Western Regional Resource Center of the U.S. Dept of Education, University of Oregon, Eugene. Available at http://www.wrrc.edu.

Sarason, S. (1999). *Teaching as a performing art.* New York: Teachers College Press.

Schmuckler, J., & Sutman, F. (2001). *Levels of inquiry/discovery in laboratory centered science instruction: A practical understanding of inquiry.* Manuscript submitted for publication.

Science Education for Public Understanding Program (SEPUP). *Chemicals, health, environment, and me (CHEM 2), Enhanced.* (1997). Ronkonkoma, NY: Lab-Aids.

Scott, G. (1999). *SEPUP matters for science reform in the LAUSD.* Unpublished report, Los Angeles Systemic Initiative.

Skolnik, S. (1995). Launching interest in chemistry. *Educational Leadership, 53*(1), 34–36.

Stohr-Hunt, P. M. (1996). An analysis of frequency of hands-on experience and science achievement. *Journal of Research in Science Teaching, 33*(1), 101–109.

Strong, R., Silver, H., & Robinson, A. (1995). What do students want (and what really motivates them)? *Educational Leadership, 53*(1), 8–12.

Stubbs, H. S. (1983). Acid precipitation awareness curriculum materials in the life sciences. *American Biology Teacher, 45*(4), 217–221.

Tafoya, E., Senal, D. W., & Knecht, P. (1980). Assessing inquiry potential: A tool for curriculum decision-makers. *School Science and Mathematics, 80*, 43–48.

Thier, H. D., & Hill, T. (1988). Chemical education in schools and the community: the SEPUP project. *International Journal of Science Education, 10*(4), 421–430.

U.S. Department of Education, National Center for Research on Evaluation, Standards, and Student Testing (CRESST). (1992). *Measurement of Workforce Readiness Competencies* (Program Two, Project 2.3, CFDA Catalog # 84.117G). Washington, DC: Author.

Wasserstein, P. (1995). What middle schoolers say about their schoolwork. *Educational Leadership, 53*(1), 41–43.

Welch, W. (1981). Inquiry in school science. In N. Harms & R. Yager (Eds.), *What research says to the science teacher* (Vol. 3; pp. 53–72). Washington, DC: National Science Teachers Association.

Wilson, K., & Daviss, B. (1996). *Redesigning education.* New York: Teachers College Press.

Index

About the Authors

HERBERT D. THIER is the founder and director of the Science Education for Public Understanding Program (SEPUP) at the University of California at Berkeley. In 1963, Thier began his contribution to today's movement toward the design and development of activity-centered, issue-oriented, inquiry-based materials for primary and secondary students. More than 60,000 teachers and tens of millions of students across the United States, Europe, and Australia have learned science by using the activities and materials his programs have created.

For his work, Thier has been awarded the Distinguished Service to Science Education Award by the National Science Teachers Association and named a fellow of the American Association for the Advancement of Science. He is listed in *Who's Who in America*.

Thier's work has been and continues to be supported by the National Science Foundation, the Exxon Mobil Education Foundation, the University of California at Berkeley, and the University Roviri de Virgili in Spain.

The Science Education for Public Understanding Program, which Thier founded in 1987 and of which he remains director, now supplies investigation-oriented, activity-based science kits and instructional materials to more than 3,000 middle and high schools on three continents. Major SEPUP products include "Science and Sustainability," a full-year, activity-based, and investigation-centered high school environmental science course; "Issues, Evidence, and You," a full-year, issues-oriented, activity-based middle school general science course; "Science and Life Issues," a full-year, investigation-based middle school life science course; and "Chemicals, Health, Environment, and Me 2," a program for elementary school students that relates science concepts and principles to children's everyday experiences. Among the other development projects he has created or directed are the landmark Science Curriculum Improvement Study (SCIS), of which he was co-developer and for which he served as senior author of the revised 1998 edition (SCIS3+).

Earlier in his career, Thier worked as a classroom teacher in science, a school district science curriculum coordinator, and an assistant superintendent of schools. He earned his doctorate in education administration and curriculum development from New York University.

BENNETT DAVISS is the co-author (with Kenneth Wilson) of *Redesigning Education*, which Seymour Sarason called "the best book I have read on public education in decades." An independent journalist who has reported on and analyzed issues in education and education reform since 1989 for the IBM Corporation, the Winthrop Rockefeller Foundation, the Association for Families and Television, and other clients, Daviss has written more than 350 magazine feature articles, which have appeared in *Smithsonian*, *Discover*, *Omni*, *Money*, and more than 40 other publications on four continents. He also works with school districts as a grants researcher and proposal writer.